*Storytelling* WITH

PUPPETS

# Storytelling WITH PUPPETS

Connie Champlin

Original edition by Connie Champlin and Nancy Renfro

AMERICAN LIBRARY ASSOCIATION
Chicago and London 1998

Project Editor: Louise D. Howe

Text and cover design by Baugher Design, Inc.

Composed by the dotted i using QuarkXpress 3.32

Typefaces: Electra, Antique Olive, and Caflisch Script

Printed on 60-pound Finch Opaque, a pH-neutral stock, and
bound in 12-point coated cover stock by Edwards Brothers

The paper used in this publication meets the minimum require-
ments of American National Standard for Information Sciences—
Permanence of Paper for Printed Library Materials, ANSI
Z38.48-1992.

Library of Congress Cataloging-in-Publication Data
Champlin, Connie, 1942–
    Storytelling with puppets / Connie Champlin. — 2nd ed.
      p.   cm.
    Includes bibliographical references and index.
    ISBN 0-8389-0709-1
    1. Puppet theater in education.   I. Title.
PN1979.E4C48   1998
372.66—dc21                97-24810

02 01 00 99 98      5 4 3 2 1

**T**o Nancy Renfro
creative
artist
mentor
friend

# CONTENTS

Figures   ix

Charts   xi

Preface   xiii

**Part One   Before the Story   1**

CHAPTER 1   Using the Puppet in Storytelling   3

2   Adapting the Story for Puppets   14

**Part Two   The Puppets   23**

CHAPTER 3   General Puppet Types and Styles   25

4   Building the Puppet Collection   52

5   Developing Puppets for Storytelling   61

**Part Three   Roles of Puppets   75**

CHAPTER 6   Host Puppets   77

7   Lead Puppets   91

**Part Four   Participatory Storytelling   111**

CHAPTER 8   Anything Puppets   115

9   Sound Stories   128

10   Action Stories   140

11   Sound and Action Stories   146

**Part Five   Presentation Formats   155**

CHAPTER 12   Book Theaters   157

13   Cup and Container Theaters   162

14   Finger Stories   168

15   Open-Box Theaters   178

16   Overhead Shadow Stories   186

17   Panel Theaters   192

18   Stories-in-the-Round   197

19   Story Aprons   203

20   Story Totes   210

21   Tabletop Theaters   216

**Part Six   After the Story   223**

CHAPTER 22   The Story's Over; What's Next?   225

Appendix: Puppetry and Storytelling
Organizations   237

Bibliography of Puppetry   239

Bibliography of Storytelling   241

Index   243

# FIGURES AND CHARTS

## Figures

A flower puppet    1

The storyteller and puppet share the limelight    3

Open-box theater with stick puppets for *Amos and Boris*    23

A finger puppet and cutaway vinegar bottle for "The Old Woman in a Vinegar Bottle"    25

Large stick puppet of the giant for "Jack and the Beanstalk"    25

Cardboard stick puppets representing the Jizo Sama for *The Funny Little Woman*    26

Basic stick puppet construction    27

Variations of basic stick puppet construction    27

Variations of characters for basic finger puppet    28

Patterns for construction of finger puppets    29

Instant finger puppets    30

Five little monkey finger puppets in a decorated tree glove    30

Variations of characters for flexible-body hand puppet    31

Hand puppet pattern    33

Basic costume pattern for hand puppet    34

Wig, mustache, and beard patterns for hand puppet    35

Ear patterns for hand puppet    36

Nose and face patterns for hand puppet    37

Hat patterns for hand puppet    38

Variations of characters for talking-mouth hand puppet    39

Example of a basic hand puppet with pointed talking mouth—a wolf    39

Body pattern for hand puppet with round talking mouth    40

Mouth patterns for hand puppet with round talking and pointed talking mouth    41

Body pattern for hand puppet with pointed talking mouth    42

"Little Bo Peep" string puppets    43

A basic horizontal paper-bag string puppet    43

A basic vertical paper-bag string puppet    44

Ben Franklin bodi-puppet    45

Construction of a basic bodi-puppet    45

Construction of a basic overhead shadow puppet    46

Rod control with overhead shadow puppets    47

Construction of an animated overhead shadow puppet    47

Methods for converting stuffed toys into puppets    48

Contrasting puppet types and styles    49

A novelty puppet—a small box frog pops out of a larger-box prince    53

A squirrel hand puppet with distinctive hats    54

Character traits comparison of versions 1 and 2 of Little Red Riding Hood    63

Good and bad posture for a flexible-body hand puppet    72

Hand puppet ambulation    72

A hand puppet emphasizing degrees of expression    73

Bookworm as a host puppet    75

A host puppet can welcome children to the story hour   77

A variety of host puppets   78

Host puppet in Halloween mask   80

Paddy Bear's ensemble   81

A puppet focusing attention on the illustrations in *The Very Hungry Caterpillar*   89

Glove puppet for "The Snopp on the Sidewalk"   91

Sock puppet for *The Very Hungry Caterpillar*   92

Paper-plate puppet with detachable costume for *Dandelion*   94

A farmer and a goblin over a garden prop   100

Puppet with removable head for "The Yellow Ribbon"   102

Large paper-bag puppet with detachable paper costume for *Harlequin and the Gift of Many Colors*   103

Turnaround paper-plate stick puppet for *How Spider Saved Halloween*   104

Large paper-bag "I Know an Old Lady" swallowing puppet   106

Box swallowing puppet for *The Clay Pot Boy*   107

Tennis-sock swallowing puppet for *Gregory the Terrible Eater*   108

Cardboard puppet for *The Little Engine That Could*   111

Two types of anything puppets—round and flat   115

Three ways of holding an anything puppet   116

Children working in pairs for "Mirror, Mirror" game   117

Anything puppets converted into specific characters   125

Clothesline characters for *Fiddle-I-Fee*   132

Envelope dog puppet for "Jack and the Robbers"   134

Clothespin puppet for "The Grobbles"   136

Paper-bag tree tote for "The Grobbles"   136

Paper-plate rainbow puppet for *A Rainbow of My Own*   140

Witch bodi-puppet for *A Woggle of Witches*   143

Fox balloon puppet for *Rosie's Walk*   148

Pattern for Little Engine cardboard puppet   150

Red Hen bodi-puppet   155

Stick puppet for *The Runaway Bunny*   158

Stick puppet patterns for *The Runaway Bunny*   159

Cup theater for "Old Mother Hubbard"   162

Puppet patterns for "Old Mother Hubbard"   165

"Jack-O-Lantern" container theater   166

"Two Little Blackbirds" cup theater   166

"Mary, Mary, Quite Contrary" container theater   166

"Humpty Dumpty" container theater   166

Glove with interchangeable button scenery   168

Pond peek-through panel   169

Paper finger puppets and scenery panels for *The Teeny Tiny Woman*   170

Patterns for *The Teeny Tiny Woman*   171

Puppet construction for *The Teeny Tiny Woman*   171

Scenery panel unit for *The Teeny Tiny Woman*   172

Finger puppet patterns for "Rudolph the Red-Nosed Reindeer"   173

Basic glove pattern   174

Paper-tissue ghost puppet for *Georgie's Halloween*   176

Open-box theater for "The Big, Big Turnip"   178

Construction of a basic open-box theater   180

Stick puppet patterns for "The Big, Big Turnip"   181

Shoe-box theater for *Madeline*   182

Clothespin puppet patterns for *Madeline*    183

Group puppet for "The Gingerbread Boy"    186

Underground scene for "The Ants and the
    Grasshopper"    187

The Mountain and Stonecutter shadow puppet for *The
    Stonecutter*    188

Overhead shadow puppet construction for *The
    Stonecutter*    189

Horizontal panel theater for "The Three Billy Goats
    Gruff"    192

Vertical panel theater for "Jack and the
    Beanstalk"    193

Open-out panel theater for *Arabian Nights*    195

Picture bodi-puppet for "The Travels of a Fox"    197

Paper-bag bodi-puppet for "The Baboon's
    Umbrella"    200

A basic story apron    203

Story apron pocket components for "Shadow
    Wash"    206

Paper puppet with pleated neck for "Tight
    Hat"    207

Pail tote with fish for *Wish Again, Big Bear*    210

Madame Bodot feeds her pet boa constrictor in a scene
    from *Crictor*    212

A tabletop presentation of "The Gunniwolf"    216

Free-hanging puppet for tabletop theaters    217

Stand-up box puppets for Toby Tinker and for the ghost
    from *The Bump in the Night*    218

Tabletop theater for "Little Red Riding Hood"    219

Walking finger puppet construction for Little Red
    Riding Hood and a wolf    220

Troll puppet made from a pudding box    223

Halloween characters occupying a forest mural wall
    hanging    225

Clothesline characters for "The Night Before
    Christmas"    226

Various tote displays    227

An interest center for "Listen and Act"    231

Some instant puppets    233

## Charts

Story Analysis Chart for "The Little Red Hen"    17

Story Analysis Chart for Puppet Presentation    18

# PREFACE

THIS BOOK IS a resource for anyone who shares literature with children: children's librarian, classroom teacher, school media specialist, camp counselor, puppeteer, storyteller. The renaissance of storytelling, coupled with the added emphasis in school reading programs on developing enthusiastic readers rather than merely teaching children how to read, makes this revision timely. Research shows that successful reading programs provide an opportunity to engage in a variety of activities related to books. Retelling a story or a poem with puppets is an excellent way for children to expand their reading experience. *Information Power: Guidelines for School Media Programs* (ALA, 1988) identifies the media specialist as a partner with the classroom teacher. Accordingly, the media specialist plays an indispensable role in an effective literature-based reading program. You can adapt the ideas of this book to support the elementary reading program. Of course, you can also use these ideas outside a formal educational setting.

In this revised edition, I have recommended many multicultural titles, including Caldecott and Coretta Scott King award-winning books, along with suggestions for presenting these titles with puppets. In addition, all bibliographies and the appendix now reflect the increased interest in diverse cultures.

Along with Nancy Renfro, my coauthor for the first edition of this book, I have learned from extensive experience as a storyteller and puppeteer, working in classrooms and libraries as well as conducting national and international workshops for teachers and librarians. Our premise has been that for storytelling the physical production, such as the construction of puppets and props,

should be kept to a minimum. Instead, energies should be devoted to developing technique and application and to building interpretative skills. Our ideas will help you share stories in informal settings typical of schools and libraries. We explore all aspects of storytelling with puppets: making the puppets, creating voices and actions for puppets; models of how to present each type of story; follow-up ideas.

The organization of this book offers the reader great flexibility in trying out ideas from the simplest, such as introducing a host puppet, to theatrical techniques combining puppetry, props, scenery, and sounds. At the outset, you may prefer to concentrate on a specific idea or approach. The decision is highly personal and depends on many factors—objectives, skills, location, time, and the age level of the children. Understanding how to use different puppet types effectively with voice and movement is prerequisite to a good presentation. Before telling a story with puppets, rehearse various voice and movement activities to gain confidence.

Once you acquire basic skills and knowledge, you'll find a myriad of ideas that you can personalize as you present children's literature with puppets, whether using puppets as hosts, in participatory situations, or in formal presentations. Let your individual interests and talent guide you, choosing a presentation format appropriate to your audience, time, and purpose. Mix and match, using our ideas as a starting point. Or select a story you want to tell and adapt it to one of the formats.

The concepts presented here are appropriate for children from preschool through upper elementary grades. If a particular example does not suit the age level of your audience, make appropriate modifications.

Setting aside preconceived notions about selecting and matching puppets with story can enrich and expand your repertoire. For example, finger puppets, a universally popular form with preschool and primary grade children, are rarely used in the upper grades. Yet, finger puppets can also be used successfully with more mature material in the middle grades. For instance, the poems in *A Light in the Attic* by Shel Silverstein not only appeal to older children, but are superbly adaptable to narration with finger puppets by those children. Another example is the inclusion of host puppets. Paddy Bear, the host puppet discussed in detail in chapter 6, appeals to young children but not to fourth and fifth graders. Following the general concepts and guidelines presented in that discussion, you can select instead a host puppet that older children can relate to— perhaps a science fiction character or a rock star. Keep in mind that everyone loves puppets, even adults! Your own attitudes and feelings about the puppets will largely determine the way the children will respond to the presentation.

With practice and experimentation, you eventually will develop a keen sense of what will work and what will not in matching books with puppets. Be fearless, dare to try new ideas, and take flight!

Connie Champlin

# BEFORE THE STORY

**A flower puppet**

THE TWO CHAPTERS that constitute Part One of this book are devoted to the basic tools necessary for developing the technical aspects of story presentation with puppets. The storyteller turns words into memorable tales. The puppeteer makes inanimate objects appear to be alive. Combined, the verbal and the visual components of each enhance audience involvement and enjoyment.

Chapter 1 tells how to make the story come alive by merging the roles of storyteller and puppet in informal story presentations. The puppet as an extension of the storyteller is discussed, as are character development, audience interaction, programming options, skill areas, physical location, time constraints, and the selection of stories and puppets for children of different ages.

Chapter 2 discusses how to match stories and puppets for informal presentations. The focus is on criteria for analyzing stories to determine their suitability for puppet presentation and techniques for adapting the story to the kind of puppet the storyteller wants to use. Techniques that the beginning puppeteer will find useful are emphasized.

# Chapter 1

# USING THE PUPPET IN STORYTELLING

**W**HEN THE VISUAL world of puppetry unites with the auditory realm of the storyteller, a unique partnership evolves. The puppeteer's skill in making inanimate objects seem real becomes all the more effective when merged with the storyteller's art of turning words into memorable tales. Inherent in this relationship is an equality of art forms in which both the story and the puppet share the limelight. With this sharing, the separate art forms unite to become *more* than the sum of their parts, the result being a sense of exhilaration and excitement that only such a fusion could produce.

Both storytelling and puppetry are ancient forms of expression that came about in similar ways. When the written word was scarce or, in some cultures, nonexistent, it was the storyteller who was the preserver of knowledge, the teller of tales to a circle of intent listeners. Rarely did listeners tire of hearing the same tale again and again, since each time the story was told it took on a new ambience, special emphasis, or unexpected turn. The story passed from generation to generation and, in so doing, became a binding link between the generations. Whether it was African tribal lore, Appalachian mountain tales, or cowboy legends on the rolling prairie, the storyteller preserved what otherwise would have been lost without the written word.

Augmenting the storyteller's art, with the gift of visualization, the puppeteer took the story one step farther by adding the element of visual surprise. The cultural style of the puppeteer's society influenced this visual image and thus puppets varied from one culture to another. There are striking differences between the styles of the highly ornate Chinese shadow puppets and the pure geometric forms of the African rod puppets. Not until modern times, however, has a personal style predominated in puppet imagery; before the present, it had been neither explored nor fully accepted.

The storyteller and puppeteer often crossed paths as they wove in and out of history, depicting biblical events, political satire, or folktales of their own culture. Generally the art of puppetry was passed down through family lines whereas the storyteller's art was not. A parent taught

**A unique partnership evolves as the storyteller and puppet share the limelight. (Puppet by Nancy Renfro Studios. Photo of Jack Champlin by Michelle Owen)**

the child the fine, often difficult, skills required for manipulation of the puppets to effectively express their ideas.

Each culture had a distinct puppet form and style that was maintained in a continuing tradition. A large format characterized the Sicilian puppets, which tended to look like oversized marionettes; the English favored hand puppets, with the most famous of all being Punch and Judy; and the Japanese used four-foot-high hand-and-rod puppets, called Bunraku puppets, which were operated by three people. Most of these puppet traditions either have disappeared or are presented by only a handful of government supported performers. In their place is a new breed of puppetry, one that allows a greater degree of personal expression, wider variety, and more general mass appeal. Coupled with the changes in puppetry has been a general progression out of the exclusive domain of entertainment and theater—a largely adult world—into a broader and more general usage that includes education, therapy, communication, religion, and recreation, with a primary focus on the child.

It is difficult to talk about modern-day puppetry without reference to Jim Henson's *Sesame Street* characters, the Muppets, in particular and to the audiovisual movement in general. It is true that early television efforts featuring Howdy Doody, Lambchop, and Kukla, Fran, and Ollie had succeeded in captivating audiences and sparking an interest in puppetry in this country. Not until *Sesame Street* made its television debut, however, did the puppet gain the sensational popularity it enjoys today, fully recognized as a legitimate tool for educating and communicating with children. The puppet's comeback has been a most profound one. Almost every organization or adult who works with young children in this country has developed an awareness of or has incorporated puppets in some way into their programming effort.

The puppet's popularity has been further strengthened by its timely entrance into the audiovisual market, as experienced by schools, libraries, recreational centers, and other institutions around the country. Filmstrips, movies, flash cards, and flannel boards had already been established as part of the expanding list of visuals added to a basic media collection. Storytelling and education have taken on a profound new dimension with the addition of puppetry, one that appeals to both children and adults. Puppets, when added to this basic collection, contribute a degree of expression and flexibility not previously possible. Because of the puppet's special ability to animate, the individual has complete control over its actions as the puppet becomes an extension of its operator. Ideas and emotions may be expressed visually and audibly; the puppet may also teach a variety of concepts—speech sounds, numbers, vocabulary, sequencing. With the inevitable and rapid advance of computers onto the media scene, there will be an increased need for humanistic art forms such as puppets that can enhance individual expression and creativity.

Because of their frequent television appearances and a greater general audiovisual consciousness, the appeal of puppets has reached unprecedented heights. For the first time in history, the art of puppetry has achieved an international status as countries like England, Saudi Arabia, and Japan host, televise, and welcome Miss Piggy and Kermit, the good-will ambassadors of puppetry. With this new success firmly established, the storyteller has a particularly receptive audience, already eager for puppets. Young children are among the most eager and are therefore most receptive when puppets help introduce new areas of their learning and play environments.

## WHY USE PUPPETS?

Introducing puppets into an existing storytelling program may need rationalization for some, but for others the benefits are obvious. Of course, the greatest advantage to adding puppets is that the story comes fully and meaningfully to life. When one weaves animated puppets into the fiber of a story, the impact of the story and its characters upon the child becomes a powerful multisensory experience. Beatrix Potter's Peter Rabbit, who was loved in his two-dimensional form, becomes even more adored as a tangible, furry puppet with whom children can share secrets and cuddles. Furthermore, the rabbit serves as a reminder of the story so that the children may make stronger connections with both the story and its messages.

The storyteller, because so much of the attention is focused upon the puppet, gains a degree of anonymity not possible in ordinary storytelling circumstances. The puppet becomes a transparent shield behind which the storyteller may "disappear," freeing herself or himself to experiment with elements of the presentation. Voice, gesture, and expression become the context for change, the vehicles for experimentation in interpretation.

The puppet as an accessory provides a tangible opportunity for theatrical elements, while enlarging upon the skills a storyteller may already have. The puppet's very form may suggest a new voice or a unique mode of expression. An upturned nose may elicit a snobbish, high-pitched voice; a ponderous stomach on a character might call for heavy, lumbering movements. A puppet with a particularly evil appearance may exhibit wicked characteristics in the guise of a sly, hovering walk, a nervous tic, a scratchy voice, or a diabolical laugh. The puppet can also make ideas or idiosyncrasies larger than life because of its ability to exaggerate movement or expression. It can jump higher, bow more deeply, and flip over more dramatically than its counterpart in human form. In addition, mannerisms, by becoming more exaggerated, can also become more comical and, in so doing, can effectively illustrate a point. For example, a puppet who is told not to interrupt when others are talking may show through the use of comic gestures how utterly impossible it is for a child not to say what he or she feels absolutely has to be said, just at that

moment. Sputtering phrases, suppressed by a stern glance from the storyteller, the puppet can literally explode with the "important" news when it cannot be suppressed any longer. Moreover, children in the audience will watch the comic gestures with a knowing comprehension of how it feels to have to wait for one's turn. Thus the storyteller has a perfect vehicle for enlarging expressions and stretching them to the limit in puppet presentations.

For the child, the puppet is a welcome visitor, bringing magic and stardust to story sharing. There is an element of theater here, just a step away from reality into a world where anything can, and often does, happen! The element of surprise is what puppetry is all about. The storyteller should discover and make effective use of the elements of surprise and mystery. There are endless possibilities with which to tantalize the imaginations of children:

A turnaround paper-plate puppet that reveals a sad face on one side and a happy one on the other for use in a story such as the folktale "Lazy Jack," in which Jack's foolishness makes a princess smile.

A hand puppet with a removable head that can fall off when the puppet's neck ribbon is untied, for enacting "The Yellow Ribbon" from *Juba This and Juba That* by Virginia Tashjian.

An overhead shadow puppet with a nose that grows longer and longer as Pinocchio tells his incredible lies.

A box or apron with pockets filled with mysterious props from which a puppet pulls out surprises, such as colorful fruit gifts, to reinforce Charlotte Zolotow's charming story *Mr. Rabbit and the Lovely Present.*

It is here that the storyteller's imagination can run rampant, leaving children to wonder what will happen next.

The puppet serves as a shield for the child as well as the adult. Inhibitions and shyness are forgotten when the child, using a puppet, focuses on what the puppet is doing and saying, rather than on the immobilizing fear of his or her own sense of involvement in the process. The young child believes in the puppet, in what it says and what it does. An error committed by the puppet is attributed to the puppet rather than to the child, who is merely its conveyer. In this way, it is much easier and, psychologically, much safer for the child to express certain feelings or fears. The child who is involved in participatory storytelling with puppets quickly feels at ease and develops an understanding of language, action, emotion, and characterization which few educational or art forms are able to convey as easily or as well.

Another benefit of the puppet's inclusion in story presentation is that it increases the child's use of tactile, visual, and auditory senses. This multimedia sharing calls on all the senses to orchestrate both the enjoyment and the meaning of the story for the child. So often learning for the child is a two-dimensional experience in which few sensory impulses are brought into play. Here we have the opportunity to reach the child at deeper levels by mobilizing several of the senses at once. The child not only *hears* the words as they are read or spoken, but also *sees* them as the message is re-inforced by the puppet's actions.

Last, the puppet allows for direct interaction between the storyteller and child, which does not occur as easily without the use of puppets. The addition of puppets adds to the storytelling experience not only a verbal but a physical presence, one that results in a close bond between child and story. For example, an unhappy or insecure puppet in the story *Bearymore* by Don Freeman could ask for and receive a hug from a child in the audience as a gesture of compassion or encouragement. Or, a child may be asked to celebrate Eeyore's birthday by giving him a birthday present or assisting in pinning on his tail in an enactment of "Eeyore's Birthday Party" from *Winnie the Pooh* by A. A. Milne. Such bonding

physical gestures never cease to delight the children in the audience while enabling them to become part of the story itself. Although the actual deed may really be performed by just one child, the impact is felt by all the children watching. In a very real sense, the involvement is total, direct, and immediate.

The new approach to teaching reading stresses that if children are to know literature they need opportunities to respond to it in a variety of ways: discussion, art, music, writing, drama. Puppetry provides a wonderful chance for children to return to a story to scrutinize characters, themes, plots, and examine language while expressing personal feelings. Encourage children to:

- create a new story using the same puppet characters involved in the original story;
- work cooperatively with others to retell a story with body puppets;
- describe, with a lead puppet, how the main character felt or what it thought during the story;
- invent a new ending to a shadow puppet or box theater story;
- dramatize definitions of words or concepts for a confused host puppet;
- recreate, with anything puppets, the confrontations between characters;
- brainstorm a new list of objects for a swallowing puppet to devour;
- devise new sound effects for characters to make as a story is told;
- write new refrains and choruses of songs to present with paper puppets hanging on a clothesline;
- experience a new point of view by retelling a story from a different culture;
- savor the language of a poem presented with finger puppets.

Additional ideas are offered in the body of this book as well as in the suggested titles at the end of each chapter.

Use these suggestions as a springboard for designing your own activities to involve puppets in the reading program.

## BEGIN WHERE YOU ARE

When puppets are mentioned, people usually imagine a formal stage with window opening, drapery, and proscenium. However, this formal approach is only one storytelling option, and its requisite skills and preparation are well documented elsewhere. The puppetry concept introduced in the course of this book is based upon the storyteller as the primary vehicle in transmitting the story. Using puppets informally and in collaboration with the text of stories, the storyteller has the same kind of visibility that he or she would naturally have when telling stories in the traditional manner. Thus, puppetry becomes an extension of what the teller of tales is already able to do, without the added burden of complicated stage design or special acting abilities. With the many options available for combining puppets and stories, it is recommended that you begin where your abilities or interests already lie; then, with some positive and concrete experience behind you, progress to where you'd like to be.

### Factors Influencing Approach

Several factors will determine your choice of puppets or approach.

### Objectives

If the *physical aspects of a book*, its text and illustrations, are the primary interest in relaying a message to children, then use a method that focuses on the book. Rest the book on your lap and subtly weave a single puppet, such as a finger or hand puppet, into the text as you read. Use the puppet in a subordinate role, letting the book take precedence while the puppet is used to emphasize the text or the illustrations.

If *audience involvement* is a main ingredient in retaining the interest of young children with short attention spans, then introduce a participatory approach. The children, each with a sea life puppet in hand, will make up an enthusiastic ocean community as the characters swim and splash through their encounters with Swimmy, the lead character in Leo Lionni's book by the same name. Many ideas for audience participation are suggested in Part Four of this book.

If *practice in vocalization* is required for a child with a speech impediment, then use a puppet to motivate speech through sound activities. A hand puppet with a large talking mouth could happily encourage a child's clear diction as nursery rhymes, riddles, and tongue twisters are recited.

If *creative dramatics* is the primary focus for presenting stories, then search for ideas that maximize actions by children with puppets. Bodi-bag puppets or bodi-pictures are exciting media with which to express movements. Stories such as "Rumpelstiltskin" or "Jack and the Beanstalk" can be presented with great attention paid to the characters' actions.

If an *integrated art project* is the goal for story presentation, then choose a puppet-making activity that is challenging for the group. Young children will enjoy creating simple paper-bag or rod puppets while older children might prefer overhead shadow puppets.

### Skill Area

Your own skill and interest areas will determine to a great extent the general selection of puppet-related material to be used. The storyteller with a fine, dramatic voice will find an easy transition in using puppets to transmit diverse voices and personalities. This storyteller will undoubtedly enjoy building a cast of characters through voice exploration. A growling wolf, squeaky mouse, cackling hen, or ghoulish ogre are just a few that would be fun to try. Those who feel uncomfortable with voice experimentation may prefer, instead, to begin by adapting puppets to pantomime activities, i.e., a story told without voice. The storyteller in this case simply narrates the story while letting the puppet mimic the actions. This nonverbal presentation by the puppet can be just as intriguing and compelling, when well done, as the traditional voiced rendition.

If you have musical talents, applying them to a singing puppet character is a good way to begin. There is nothing children enjoy more than listening to songs—sweet or hearty. You might consider such unusual characters as a singing grasshopper, chanting whale, or humming bird to teach the children new songs. Or, perhaps there are other skills that you can enlarge upon through the puppet vehicle—your knack for poetry and rhyming, the ability to be expressive through the face and hands, or your power over suspense in horror themes are just a few focal points to share in the puppet's spotlight.

## Physical Location

Puppets are appropriate to introduce in almost any physical location. Activities can be adapted to the physical dimensions of whatever space is available. Both the location of the activity and actual amount of space available should be given equal consideration in determining the scope of the puppet venture. There are many possibilities:

### At home

For bedtime stories, baby-sitting, or family gatherings, intimacy is an important part of story sharing. Stories that center around family themes or sharing, such as

*More More More, Said the Baby* by Verna Williams or *Albert's Toothache* by Barbara Williams, are ideal material to consider. These gatherings are usually informal settings that suggest warm, friendly characters easily conveyed by affectionate hand puppets. As the story unfolds, interactive activities between puppets and family easily reinforce the close-knit bond that already exists.

### At the library or the school media center

Story hours and book fairs are popular dwelling places for puppets. Programming and exploring basic material for storytelling is as limitless and rich an experience as the scope of the books found in the children's collection. Special themes may be chosen according to the season or occasion—hatching birds, outer space, farm activities, trains, Valentine's Day, caterpillars, etc.

Alternating presentation approaches gives diversity to the programs and creates interest for the storyteller. One week may feature a participatory story and the next week, a nonparticipatory one. In the library setting, the modus operandi is the group formation, whether large or small. Consider whether all children have a good view of the puppets and props. Is there ample opportunity for all children to interact with the puppets when participatory stories are used? Book displays and book talks are excellent extensions of the initial presentation. Puppet "actors" may be integrated with the display or book talk for further reinforcement of the story's messages.

### In the classroom

Relating stories and puppets to curricular activities provides a motivational enhancement for classroom studies. Puppets' portrayals of worldwide folktales teach children about foreign cultures and lore; book reports or book talks presented by puppets foster an appreciation for language arts; biographies of famous scientists or historical, sports, and political figures give substance to the related subject and insight into the real people who populated each era. *What's the Big Idea, Ben Franklin?* by Jean Fritz, a witty look at some little-known details of the life of this founding father, and *The First Dog* by Jan Brett, which depicts prehistoric times and cave drawing, are fascinating classroom material. Usually the classroom presentation calls for a more formal puppet approach. Overhead shadow puppets, book theaters, and the box theaters described in Part Five, Presentation Formats, are ideally suited for classroom purposes. The puppets may also be displayed in conjunction with the classroom's learning centers.

### At recreational centers

The relaxed environment of parks, youth groups, campfires, festivals, and the like provides a background for experimenting with informal puppetry ideas. Participatory stories are particularly successful in channeling the natural energies of participants toward a common goal, while fostering a sense of group identity. When sessions are held outdoors, there is opportunity for dramatizing stories in large, open spaces. The imagination knows no bounds as actions for a story such as *Fin M'Coul* by Tomie de Paola are pantomimed in a wooded area using bodi-bag or large paper rod puppets and real trees as props. Or, an ocean theme presented on the shoreline of a sandy beach clearly enhances the mood of a story like *Amos and Boris* by William Steig or the adventures of that able-bodied seaman of American tall tales "Old Stormalong."

### In institutions

Hospitals and institutions for the handicapped have a special need for puppets and stories. Often, ideas need to be adapted to meet the requirements of a particular situation or to be tailored to the limits of a certain disability. If the children are confined to bed, then presentation on a one-to-one basis is usually most effective. Portability and/or small-scale props would ease the storyteller's chore of carrying the presentation from one child to another. Story aprons and story totes make perfect vehicles for transporting puppet material. Finger puppets and small stick puppets are easy to use in the limited space of the bed. Consider also that some special children can best conceptualize with reinforced sensory experiences. For example, a visually impaired child may respond best to puppets that provide strong tactile experiences, such as a bold, woolly creature; deaf children will naturally enjoy bodi-puppets because of their adaptation to sign language around the puppet's face.

### At birthday, holiday, and other parties

Parties make ideal occasions for including puppets and stories. Since there is a lot of excitement at these events, with games, gift giving, and eating, it is important to choose material that is both short and active. Sing-alongs and short, action-packed stories are apt material to introduce. Material with themes that fit the occasion make ideal selections. *Happy Birthday, Sam* by Pat Hutchins, *Chin Chiang and the Dragon's Dance* by Ian Wallace, and *Rechenka's Eggs* by Patricia Polacco are a few examples of the many choices from the cornucopia of holiday story treasures.

### With religious groups

There is a place in all religious denominations for both Bible and morality stories using puppets. The settings may be either formal or informal, depending on the organization and size of the group. While most of the ideas in this book do not actually touch upon religious themes, almost all are adaptable in concept.

## Time

The amount of time for presenting the story affects compilation of programming material. If a presentation is to be given in a ten- to fifteen-minute session, then there is obviously little time for including children in a puppet-making activity. This time restriction will necessitate prior preparation of all the puppets and props by the storyteller. Participation by the children in the actual story will also have to be kept to a minimum. A sound-participation story might be easily included, whereas action stories that require more time should be saved for sessions with sufficient time for planning the actions with the children. Trying to accomplish too much in too little time can only cause unnecessary pressure upon the storyteller. Twenty- to forty-minute story sessions are reasonable average lengths for children with good attention spans; many of the ideas suggested in this book can easily fit into this time span. Simple puppet-making activities such as attaching pictures to sticks or making balloon string puppets can be accomplished in a limited time period. Thus a session of thirty minutes could be equally divided to include both a simple puppet-making project and a presentation activity. More complex puppets such as bodi-puppets or overhead shadow puppets require extended work periods for construction. For such projects, it would be ideal to construct the puppets during one session and present the story in a consecutive period.

## Age Groups

### Preschool children

While children of all age levels are fascinated with puppets and take delight in their inclusion, preschoolers are a unique audience since they are in an impressionable, believing stage of development. They generally accept the puppets as real characters, believing what they say and putting great trust in their inherent natures. It is especially important for the adult, in working with these young children, to be keenly attuned to this sensitive aspect of young children when using puppets. The puppet characters should be true to their nature at all times, especially in the general course of conversation and interaction, and should be used within a consistent framework so as not to confuse the children. A puppet with wicked characteristics one moment should not

transform into an entirely good one the next moment, unless the plot calls for it to do so.

Keep in mind also the short attention span of this age group when selecting material. It is better to plan a program around two or three short stories, songs, or activities than to present one long story, which might cause restlessness. Building into the presentation maximum interaction between children and puppets will enable the storyteller to prolong the group's concentration. Remember, young children do not fare well if placed in passive roles for too long, so be sure to include sound and action stories in your repertoire. Furthermore, promoting this type of interaction seems to foster a feeling of closeness with this age group. Young children are sometimes inhibited when it comes to expressing their emotions—touching and cuddling puppets can enlarge this experience and cement a tight bond with the story. In such a case, furry, huggable creatures are a bonus, since they naturally invite affection. Animal and woodland stories that feature this type of character will be a popular part of the story collection.

Repetition is a very important concept in dealing with young children. Because the stories are new to them, younger children rarely tire of hearing the same story over and over again. They relish discovering new meanings or varied cadences each time the story is told. If there is opportunity for repetition in a participatory story, be sure that all the children have a chance to relate to the puppet or have some contact, no matter how small the part.

Popular story themes for preschoolers commonly seem to fall at two extremes: those that exude a warm, cozy feeling and those that reflect a wicked or mischievous theme. Warmth seems to prevail in the many books about animal creatures; it usually conveys some strong moral issues while, at the same time, giving young children a sense of security in expressing messages about sharing and caring. At the other extreme, stories about wicked, mischievous characters offer an acceptable means by which children can vent any aggressive emotions they might feel in a less threatening way than if they were to do it without the benefit of the "bad" puppet character's guise.

### Primary-age children

While they still want to believe and trust in puppets, children in grades one through three are fully aware that the actions of puppets are controlled by somebody else. These primary children, instead of actually believing, may wish to "pretend," and this shared sense of pretending becomes a secret between the storyteller and children. The rich imagination of children helps them to visualize the story's background and to fill in the voids whenever necessary—a deep, brooding forest with frightening beasts lurking in every corner or a candy land with lollipop trees and houses of gingerbread and jelly beans. The storyteller will enjoy selecting stories that will further enrich the children's fertile imaginations to serve as a background for puppet activities. Margaret Mahy's *17 Kings and 42 Elephants*, richly illustrated with lush jungle scenes, and Sibyl Hancock's *Esteban and the Ghost*, a story about a brave boy's adventure in a haunted castle, are perfect vehicles for exploring fantasy. Diversity in story material, rather than repetition, should be a criterion for selection of primary grade material—the sea, outer space, and city and rural life are all subjects which may open up horizons for these expanding minds.

The attention span of this age group will vary tremendously. It is wise to plan a mixed diet of both story approaches and story types, making sure to blend participatory and nonparticipatory stories. While preschoolers do not mind having a story or approach repeated, the primary grades prefer variety. If repetition is desired for reinforcement purposes, the same subject matter may be repeated using new presentation methods. For example, one week Hans Christian Andersen's *The Ugly Duckling* can be presented with the storyteller using a single lead puppet; the next week it could be repeated in a participatory setting using rod or string puppets, and so on. Another possibility is to maintain the general story line but to change the characters with each repetition; in this way, the new characters and their associated characteristics make it almost a new story each time.

### Intermediate-age children

The children in grades four through six require altogether more sophisticated material in both story and puppet selection. They are old enough to appreciate longer folktales and myths, and their widening sense of curiosity has taken them beyond the local radius. An easy acquisition of knowledge and a quest for adventure seem to guarantee enough for a story to have appeal. Technology and science fiction have opened up exciting new vistas. *2095* by Jon Scieszka and *Aliens Ate My Homework* by Bruce Colville have futuristic themes that appeal to this age group. With the students eager for stories that take them into the realm of the unknown or the fantastic, it is recommended that programming balance the technical and science fiction collections with the traditional folktales in order to let students experience the richness of both these worlds.

The children in this age group will enjoy testing many of the concepts in this book firsthand, while performing as storyteller for their peers or for children in lower grades. It is especially recommended that the teacher let students present book talks to the group. Older children are particularly motivated when asked to work in teams. Overhead shadow presentations are an excellent puppet medium for team work. One child can narrate the story while other team members animate the characters. Children in this age group are often very performance oriented and are quite adept at assembling the components of a puppet presentation.

They enjoy and seem to thrive on creating minute details of costuming, scenery, and props to accompany a given story.

Intermediate-age children, with their prolonged powers of concentration, make an intent audience when presented with nonparticipatory stories. If participatory stories are selected, consider those stories that combine creative dramatics activities with large spaces for presentations, such as those found outdoors or in a gymnasium. Bold stick puppets or suggestive costuming attached to the child will be enough to simulate the idea of the character and assist in interpreting its actions. Also of interest are puppets that can achieve clever animation, such as string puppets.

The many factors that influence selection of material may at first appear complex, but try always to think in the simplest terms. It is important to begin where you are, rather than to plunge too soon into complicated and difficult puppet presentations. As a storyteller, you most likely have already developed a particular style in presenting children's literature. The simple addition of one or two puppet characters woven into the existing presentation method offers an easy way to extend your art.

## SUGGESTED TITLES FOR USING THE PUPPET IN STORYTELLING

Anderson, Hans Christian. *The Ugly Duckling*; illus. by Troy Howell. Putnam, 1990.
The ugly duckling is ignored and teased until he realizes that he is a beautiful swan.

Brett, Jan. *The First Dog*; illus. by the author. Harcourt, 1988.
A hungry Paleowolf befriends Kip, a cave boy, in a story that explains how dogs became domesticated.

Coville, Bruce. *Aliens Ate My Homework*; illus. by Katherine Coville. Pocket, 1993.
When a miniature spaceship lands, the small crew draws Rod Albright into a series of extraordinary adventures.

de Paola, Tomie, reteller. *Fin M'Coul*; illus. by the author. Holiday, 1981.
An Irish folktale about a couple who use their wits to outsmart the giant Cucullin.

Freeman, Don. *Bearymore*; illus. by the author. Viking, 1976.
A circus bear has problems when he tries to hibernate and plan a new act simultaneously.

Fritz, Jean. *What's the Big Idea, Ben Franklin?* illus. by Margot Tomes. Coward, 1976.
A well-detailed biography revealing fascinating tidbits about this famous statesman-inventor.

Hancock, Sibyl. *Esteban and the Ghost*; illus. by Dirk Zimmer. Dial, 1983.
Esteban spends Halloween in haunted Grey Castle and helps a ghost redeem himself.

Hutchins, Pat. *Happy Birthday, Sam*; illus. by the author. Greenwillow, 1991.
The chair Sam's grandfather gives him for a birthday present proves to be an invaluable gift.

Jacobs, Joseph. "Lazy Jack," in *English Fairy Tales*; 3d ed. rev. Putnam, n.d.
Jack's foolishness makes a princess smile.

Lionni, Leo. *Swimmy*; illus. by the author. Pantheon, 1963.
A school of fish protects itself by banding together. A Caldecott Honor book.

Mahy, Margaret. *17 Kings and 42 Elephants*; illus. by Patricia MacCarthy. Dial, 1987.

Seventeen kings with their forty-two elephants encounter an exotic collection of animals as they parade through the jungle.

Milne, A. A. *Winnie the Pooh*; illus. by Ernest Shepard, colored by Hilda Scott. Dutton, 1974.

The classic about Winnie the Pooh and his friends.

Nash, Ogden. *Custard and Company*; illus. by Quentin Blake. Little, 1985.

Collection of humorous poems by Ogden Nash.

Osborne, Mary. "Stormalong," in *American Tall Tales*; illus. by Michael McCurdy. Knopf, 1991.

Recounts a few of the adventures of the tall-tale American sailor, Alfred Bulltop Stormalong.

Polacco, Patricia. *Rechenka's Eggs*; illus. by the author. Philomel, 1988.

Easter eggs decorated in the Ukranian style by an old woman are broken by a wounded goose she has sheltered. How the eggs are replaced makes a warm, satisfying story.

Potter, Beatrix. *The Tale of Peter Rabbit*; illus. by the author. Warne, n.d.

The classic story about Peter Rabbit and his adventures in Farmer McGregor's garden.

Scieszka, Jon. *2095*; illus. by Lane Smith. Viking, 1995.

Fred, Sam, and Joe, also known as the Time Warp Trio, travel 100 years into the future where they encounter robots and their own grandchildren.

Steig, William. *Amos and Boris*; illus. by the author. Farrar, Straus, 1971.

A warm story about the friendship between a mouse and a whale who meet during a sea mishap.

Tashjian, Virginia. *Juba This and Juba That*; illus. by Nadine Bernard Westcott. Little, 1995.

Includes a collection of chants, riddles, poems, and fingerplays.

Wallace, Ian. *Chin Chiang and the Dragon Dance*; illus. by the author. Atheneum, 1984.

A young Chinese boy is afraid to dance in the Chinese New Year's parade.

Williams, Barbara. *Albert's Toothache*; illus. by Kay Chorao. Dutton, 1974.

When Albert, a turtle, complains about a toothache in his big toe, only his grandmother understands his problem.

Williams, Vera B. *More More More, Said the Baby*; illus. by the author. Greenwillow, 1990.

Three short stories about family love featuring families of different races. A Caldecott Honor book.

Zolotow, Charlotte. *Mr. Rabbit and the Lovely Present*; illus. by Maurice Sendak. Harper, 1977.

A rabbit helps a girl put together a special present for her mother based on colors and fruits. A Caldecott Honor book.

*Chapter 2* # ADAPTING THE STORY FOR PUPPETS

**T**ODAY WE ARE experiencing a golden age in children's literature. The merging of talented artists and gifted authors has made available to the general public a generous sampling of good stories, offering an unprecedented collection of tales with appeal to a wide and varied audience. These tales range from traditional fairy tales and folklore to modern spin-offs, in which the imagination has no limit and absurdity no boundary. The end result is a superb compilation of some of the finest art available, well deserving of museum recognition.

## WHICH BOOKS, WHICH PUPPETS?

With this treasure trove of material the storyteller has a rich and varied repertoire from which to choose in pairing books with puppets. How one begins to make choices and what makes a particular story especially suitable for a certain type of puppet is a highly individual matter. Every teller of tales has a distinct story style. While some storytellers prefer the presence of friendly, folksy characters like the creatures in A. A. Milne's *Winnie the Pooh* and Arnold Lobel's *Frog and Toad*, others enjoy a more dramatic, stylistic approach such as Gerald McDermott's *Arrow to the Sun*. Further, there are those who feel a special affinity to story poems as found in Shel Silverstein's *Where the Sidewalk Ends* or his vignettes *The Giving Tree* and *The Missing Piece*. In short, one should begin where one is comfortable and then gradually move toward new domains, as confidence grows and proficiency develops.

Beyond personal taste in choosing a particular story genre, there are other factors to consider when selecting a puppet story to share with a group.

### Simple and Strong Action

The first criterion is that the story have a clear and simple action line. Upon this sound foundation characters and plot ultimately hinge, as does the structure for a successful puppet presentation. Excellent examples are seen in such traditional favorites as "Little Red Riding Hood," "The Three Billy Goats Gruff," and "The Little Red Hen." Modern tales such as Eric Carle's *The Very Hungry Caterpillar* and Leo Lionni's *Swimmy* have similar strong and direct plots. They share an element of powerful simplicity that has elevated each to the status of a popular classic.

Stories that have a more complex theme should be avoided or should be attempted only after gaining much experience in storytelling. "Cinderella" and the *Wizard of Oz* serve as examples of stories with intricate action lines that might easily frustrate the novice storyteller using puppets.

The cumulative story, structured on a repeated action by a series of characters, results in an ever growing refrain that makes it one of the easiest types for the beginning storyteller to adapt for sharing with puppets. This story's center core of action is simple yet forceful, making it highly suitable for the inclusion of puppets. Such examples as "I Know an Old Woman Who Swallowed a Fly" and "The Three Billy Goats Gruff" are immensely popular with young children, who seldom tire of their repetitive pattern. On the other hand, a steady diet of exclusively cumulative stories does not offer adequate creative challenge for the storyteller; therefore, mixing story types is indeed preferable.

## Strong Lead Characters

Identification with one or two lead characters is a key to successful puppet presentations from both the storyteller's and the audience's viewpoints. Many authors take great pride in developing appealing central characters to weave into their tales. Some all-time favorites are featured in A. A. Milne's *Winnie the Pooh* and Dr. Seuss's *Cat in the Hat,* whose characters possess distinct personalities and peculiar idiosyncrasies. Such strong characterizations serve to link other characters, dialogue, and story plot. While the action line may change, especially in a story series, the central character remains essentially stable in its reaction to or relationship with other characters and/or action in the story.

## Minimum Number of Characters, Props, and Visuals

Certain stories are too complex in terms of number of visuals required and volume of characters involved to consider for effective puppet adaptation. An example is the popular Babar series, in which Jean and Laurent de Brunhoff document the many travels and adventures of Babar the elephant, most of which involve an elaborate cast of characters and multiple short episodes for visual interpretation. While such stories lend themselves well to creative storytelling, they are not suitable for the beginner to approach with puppets.

In general, the beginner should avoid stories with diffuse story lines and static action; weak lead characters; or a multiplicity of characters, props, and visuals.

## DEVELOPING TECHNIQUE

Since the primary focus of this book is directed toward informal puppet presentation, it is important to learn how to simplify the physical preparation of puppets and props. The amount of time and labor involved in this preliminary preparation is dependent solely upon the individual's time and wishes. There are many options available in preparing puppets and story setting adaptations which may be adjusted to the storyteller's available time. Bear in mind, however, that the quality of the end product does not hinge upon the artistic execution of the completed puppet, but rather upon the interpretative handling of the puppets and the visuals. For example, a rudimentary stick puppet with a character's picture simply taped onto it and then manipulated imaginatively can surpass a more elaborately crafted puppet used with less imagination.

*Enthusiasm* and *ingenuity* are essential for insuring an effective and enjoyable puppet presentation. Enthusiasm is already assumed, but ingenuity needs to be more fully explored. Ingenuity, in this case, refers not to artistic talent but rather to a commonsense outlook of being open-minded and flexible. One must look at each story with a critical eye and make requisite changes to devise a workable presentation.

Many stories are either too complex or too simple to present with puppets without some adaptations. The following factors need to be considered in planning appropriate adjustments.

## Using Essential Elements Only

Not every character or image in a story requires explicit expression with puppets or props. It is better to withhold some characters or props to allow the audience a fuller appreciation of the imagery presented, rather than to bombard them visually with more than they can assimilate and enjoy. Carefully scrutinize the story and decide which characters and props would be most beneficial in achieving the greatest impact.

Consider the length of time in which the image makes its appearance. It is hardly worth investing time and effort to create a prop or puppet that enters only briefly unless it is crucial to the story's message or creates a special effect. Develop a sense of what your audience will find most appealing and select visuals accordingly.

Learn to space these visuals evenly throughout the story presentation. There should be a certain amount of time between the appearance of props and other visuals; if too many images appear in a cluster, eliminate the unimportant ones and introduce appropriate images later in the story. This pacing will not only help make the story more manageable to present, but it will also allow time for the storyteller to relax during the presentation itself.

### Increasing Involvement Where Needed

Stories that have minimal dialogue and/or imagery offer an opportunity for the storyteller to make extended use of a visual when there is the opportunity, and they offer time to "play" with the action and build it into a well-rounded segment. An example is the inclusion of a mixing bowl and spoon prop in "The Little Red Hen," in which a three- to five-minute dramatization would allow the development of a full-scale bread-making episode that children would find appealing. As originally written, this particular segment has a duration of only a few seconds when narrated. The challenge here is not abstraction, but rather development and expansion of an existing scene.

## ANALYZING THE STORY

Each story has its own unique format, as well as specific characteristics and merits, that makes it suitable for a particular method of presentation. A story should be viewed critically in terms of what will and what will not work. The storyteller will quickly develop a facility for judging optimum book, puppet, and presentation technique combinations. The beginner should follow the guidelines previously mentioned to search out books that combine strong action core lines with effective and memorable lead characters. Analysis charts, such as the one shown on page 17, give a basis for selection by summarizing the story's composition and its potential for puppet-story presentations.

### Selecting a Presentation Format

"The Little Red Hen" provides us with content for exploring possibilities for its adaptation into a puppet presentation.

The Red Hen herself serves as a focal point around which the actions of the story pivot. In choosing a format, select any type of puppet that allows maximum animation of the Red Hen, such as a flexible-body hand puppet or bodi-puppet. The hand puppet is useful for the storyteller in conjunction with a story apron and lapboard. While the apron hides the props, the lapboard serves to support the props while in use. The bodi-puppet is suited to dramatizing the story with children participating as the characters. Obviously, a larger playing space will be necessary when children take on the parts of the characters. Both methods are described in detail in Parts Four and Five.

In either case the storyteller may play the part of the Little Red Hen while utilizing the group to help manipulate the puppets or play the secondary roles. Since the visuals required by the story are relatively simple and few in number, the strength of the story presentation in this example depends more upon the actions of the characters than upon the visuals.

## STORY ANALYSIS CHART
## FOR PUPPET PRESENTATION

TITLE: _The Little Red Hen_

SETTING/TIME: _Barnyard / daytime_

KEY ACTIONS: _The wheat is planted, cut, threshed,_
_ground into flour, baked into bread_
_and eaten by Red Hen._

NARRATION/DIALOGUE: Sparse ___X___ Moderate_____ Abundant_____

LEAD CHARACTERS:

Character's Name _Red Hen_ Personality Type _Industrious_
_Determined_

SUPPORTING CHARACTERS:

Character's Name _Pig_ Personality Type _Lazy_
_Cat_ _Proud_
_Duck_ _Thoughtless_

PROPS/VISUALS: Few_____ Moderate ___X___ Many_____

Key Props/Visuals _seed & wheat_
_mixing bowl & spoon_

Secondary Props/Visuals _thresher_ _sack of flour_ _oven_
_mill_ _bread ingredients_

## STORY ANALYSIS CHART
## FOR PUPPET PRESENTATION

TITLE: _____

_____

SETTING/TIME: _____

_____

KEY ACTIONS: _____

_____

_____

_____

NARRATION/DIALOGUE: Sparse _____ Moderate _____ Abundant _____

LEAD CHARACTERS:

Character's Name _____ Personality Type _____

_____ _____

_____ _____

SUPPORTING CHARACTERS:

Character's Name _____ Personality Type _____

_____ _____

_____ _____

PROPS/VISUALS: Few _____ Moderate _____ Many _____

Key Props/Visuals _____ _____ _____

_____ _____ _____

Secondary Props/Visuals _____ _____ _____

_____ _____ _____

_____ _____ _____

(Permission granted to reproduce chart for individual's nonprofit use.)

## Setting

The major action of "The Little Red Hen" takes place in the domain of the barnyard. If the storyteller uses the story apron and lapboard technique, the setting can be easily illustrated by placing either a toy barn or a makeshift box barn on the lapboard. A felt rectangular patch with neat rows drawn on it can be laid out on the lapboard to indicate the wheat field. These items can be replaced with other scenic suggestions as the story progresses—a salt-box mill, a toy or box oven for baking the bread.

If the storyteller employs a participatory approach, the set needs to be increased to the larger space of the room. Each scene may be defined simply by designating spaces in the storytelling area. The wheat field may be represented by a rug, the barn by a table, the mill by a chair, and the kitchen by a table. Or, if time permits, children may be asked to draw a background mural or to construct the barnyard props of barn, mill, and wheat field. The participants, using bodi-puppets, can then perform the story's actions in front of the mural.

## Focusing on Key Actions

In any story as concise in format as "The Little Red Hen" the storyteller has the option to design and capitalize on specific action segments that will be most exciting for presenting with children. Several points of action may be considered for in-depth focus during the story presentation.

*Dramatize the laziness of the duck, pig, and cat characters.* Perhaps they are snoring loudly while sleeping in the sun, the cat languidly grooming its whiskers and the duck its feathers. Or, to add a humorous touch, the characters can be concentrating on a game of jump rope or hopscotch.

*Expand the wheat-growing episode.* The Red Hen can determinedly set forth to plant a seed, carefully tending and watering it. When the wheat pops out of the ground and grows to its full height, the Red Hen can watch with great satisfaction. A wheat prop made from a rope with paper wheat kernels attached can be pulled up out of a flowerpot, or a child starting from a curled position on the floor can pretend to be the wheat and grow slowly on cue.

*Create an appealing bread-making scene in Julia Child's style.* Children love to bake and will enjoy going through the actions of playing chef in the kitchen. Flour, water, salt, and some yeast, along with a few measuring devices are all that are needed to create an interesting bread-making demonstration. The Little Red Hen might ask volunteers from the audience to help knead the bread or to add some real or imagined items to the mix—raisins, peanuts, sesame seeds, etc. Since there will be no time to actually bake the bread, a ready-made loaf might be pulled out of the oven on cue.

These opportunities for in-depth focus will help involve the children to a greater degree in the story plot, especially a story of short duration. Age levels of groups will also determine how much expansion is required. Older children are capable of experimenting with expandable ideas and will particularly enjoy elaborating on the basic plot. Younger children, whose attention span is shorter, may be best involved in a presentation that adheres more rigidly to the original story line.

## Narration and Dialogue

Since there is minimal dialogue in this story, dramatization and miming of actions are most important. To emphasize each action, the storyteller may wish to exaggerate the action and to add prop visuals as suggested above.

Adaptations may also be made by adding dialogue as a means of enlarging upon the story. For example, when the Little Red Hen asks the animals for assistance and each responds with the negative, "Not I," she may ask, "Why not?" The reply by the characters would be true to their natures—Duck: "It will ruffle my feathers"; Pig: "I just ate and I'm much too full to move." Or the Little Red Hen can sing a song while growing the wheat or threshing it. One example is, "This is the way I thresh the wheat" sung to the tune of "Here We Go Round the Mulberry Bush." An educational element can be added if the Little Red Hen explains to the group how wheat is threshed and ground into flour.

## Characters

Since the Little Red Hen is the primary character required to dramatize this story, it is necessary that the selected puppet convey actions easily. Both the flexible-body hand puppet and the bodi-puppet meet this criterion. Both types are capable of articulating the hen's actions such as mixing bread or hoeing the ground. Since the duck, pig, and cat play passive roles these could be portrayed by almost any other puppet type—a stick, paper-bag, or finger puppet. To enliven the entire presentation, children could be encouraged to create animal sounds to accompany each character. If you wish, the entire group may be asked to participate and other animals added to the basic three such as a goat, dog, horse, or mouse. You might even consider replaying the story in another setting, perhaps utilizing jungle or sea creatures.

## Props and Visuals

This particular story incorporates some props unfamiliar to many children. The thresher and mill may need to be explained to children prior to the story. Bodi-puppets allow for the use of large-scale or life-size props such as a real hoe or mixing bowl. With small-scale presentations a makeshift hoe can be made from a dowel with a cardboard blade section attached. Consider involving group members by letting them serve as scenery. Two children with hands extended overhead and touching can create the shape of a barn; a single child can play the mill, using arms for the windmill spokes; and a line of children can represent a row of wheat in the field. All these ideas add new visual interest and also variety, especially when repeating the presentation for reinforcement.

## Alternate Presentation Settings

An entirely different story format suggestion for "The Little Red Hen" is a miniature tabletop theater, incorporating a groundscape of a barnyard setting as the principal scenic element and stand-up box or walking finger puppets capable of performing the required actions. These ideas are more fully described in Part Five.

The reader will soon discover in exploring story potential for puppet presentations that most stories will offer a broad range of story types that fall somewhere between two polarized zones: those that are simplified such as "The Little Red Hen" and those that are quite complex such as *Horton Hatches the Egg* by Dr. Seuss. As a rule it is far easier to condense than it is to add. The storyteller will learn, with practice, to modify content by abstracting and streamlining or by extending the story content. Whichever avenue one decides upon will depend on the original story and the storyteller's need to adapt it for a suitable puppet presentation.

Asbjornsen, Peter C., and Jorgen Moe. *The Three Billy Goats Gruff*; illus. by Marcia Brown. HBJ, 1957.

Popular picture-book edition of the well-known story.

Brunhoff, Laurent de. *The Story of Babar, the Little Elephant*; illus. by the author. Random, 1960.

After running away from his home in the jungle, Babar takes up residence in Paris.

Carle, Eric. *The Very Hungry Caterpillar*; illus. by the author. Putnam, 1969.

A caterpillar eats too much of the wrong food before spinning a cocoon and emerging as a beautiful butterfly.

Grimm, Jacob. *Little Red Riding Hood*; illus. by Trina Schart Hyman. Holiday, 1983.

A handsome picture-book retelling of an old favorite. A Caldecott Honor book.

Lionni, Leo. *Swimmy*; illus. by the author. Pantheon, 1963.

A school of fish band together for protection. A Caldecott Honor book.

Lobel, Arnold. *Frog and Toad Are Friends*; illus. by the author. Harper, 1970.

Five adventures introducing those two special friends, Frog and Toad. A Newbery Honor book. Also *Frog and Toad Together* (1972); *Frog and Toad All Year* (1976); *Days with Frog and Toad* (1979).

McDermott, Gerald. *Arrow to the Sun*; illus. by the author. Viking, 1974.

Based on a Pueblo Indian myth, the account of a boy's search for his father, the Sun. A Caldecott Medal book.

Milne, A. A. *Winnie the Pooh*; illus. by Ernest Shepard, colored by Hilda Scott. Dutton, 1974.

The classic adventures of Winnie the Pooh and his friends Christopher Robin, Kanga, Roo, Piglet, and Eeyore.

Seuss, Dr. *Cat in the Hat*; illus. by the author. Random, 1957.

A most unusual cat turns a dreary afternoon into an adventure for two children.

Seuss, Dr. *Horton Hatches the Egg*; illus. by the author. Random, 1968.

The faithfulness of Horton, an elephant, is rewarded when a unique baby hatches from the egg on which he has been sitting.

Silverstein, Shel. *Where the Sidewalk Ends*; illus. by the author. Harper, 1974.

An appealing and very popular collection of poems.

Zemach, Margot. *The Little Red Hen*; illus. by the author. Farrar, 1983.

A little red hen does all the work necessary to bake a loaf of bread while her lazy neighbors just watch.

# THE PUPPETS

**P**ART TWO DESCRIBES the most important kinds of puppets for the informal storytelling this book advocates, how to make and acquire a useful puppet collection, and the simple visual, manual, and vocal techniques the storyteller must develop to use with puppets.

Chapter 3 discusses the basic kinds of puppets useful in storytelling activities and provides patterns and construction techniques for those puppets. Target audiences and appropriate storytelling situations are described for each puppet type.

Building a useful collection of puppets is the focus of chapter 4. Considerations for collecting puppets useful in a broad range of situations for particular age levels are presented. How to go about buying ready-made puppets and how to acquire a stock of materials for making puppets are discussed. Sources of patterns and a list of suppliers are given.

In chapter 5 the storyteller learns how to create a character for a puppet. The physical characteristics of the puppet in hand, the storyteller's imagination, and the possibilities of manipulating the puppet and giving it a voice combine with the story itself in the development of a particular character. Some short exercises for the storyteller who is learning to handle puppets are provided.

Open-box theater with stick puppets for *Amos and Boris*

*Chapter 3*

# GENERAL PUPPET TYPES AND STYLES

CHOOSING THE "RIGHT" puppet to fit a particular story should be more than just a guess or a feeling. It is important to be conscious of the influences and factors from two basic sources: the story and the physical space in which the story is to be presented. These factors also become integrated into the storyteller's concept of the desired effect that the story will have on the audience.

## PUPPET TYPE

Puppet type is determined by the way the puppet is manipulated, for example, with the fingers, hand, or body; by rods; or with strings. Thus, the names of these puppet types reflect the method of operation—finger puppets, hand puppets, bodi-puppets, rod puppets, and string puppets.

The story itself often gives clues to what puppet type to choose. Folktales such as "The Teeny Tiny Woman" and "The Old Woman Who Lived in a Vinegar Bottle" are both obvious candidates for finger puppets. Miniaturization is the key here for making a selection from the many different puppet types; smallness of the main character is the quality which makes these stories unique. At the opposite

**Finger puppet and cutaway vinegar bottle for "The Old Woman Who Lived in a Vinegar Bottle" in miniature (above). Large stick puppet of the giant for "Jack and the Beanstalk."**

extreme is the story "Jack and the Beanstalk" in which the giant and his wife are presented in exaggerated form as bodi-puppets or large rod puppets, either being appropriate.

Sometimes more subtle or abstract factors in a story may help determine the choice of puppet type. For example, the factors of time and distance as shown in the Babar series by Jean and Laurent de Brunhoff or in *Amos and Boris* by William Steig might best be interpreted through small paper rod puppets in conjunction with an open box theater. Changing of sets could illustrate the concept of either time or distance. Puppets could be moved along the top performing edge of the box to indicate traveling. Simple scenic changes could represent the different points of arrival—a jungle or a city.

Whether a story relies primarily on action or dialogue is yet another element influencing decision. *Raven: A Trickster Tale from the Pacific Northwest* by Gerald McDermott, a story that centers around a great deal of action, would be effectively presented with puppet types that can perform intricate movements, such as the hand puppet or bodi-puppet. On the other hand, *Pierre* by Maurice Sendak, a story that relies heavily on dialogue, would be suitably presented by the talking-mouth hand puppet.

The physical space of the storytelling area also helps in determination of type of puppet. If an entire story is to be told from a seated position by the storyteller it may be favorably told and dramatized in a small, confined area, such as over the lap, using hand puppets, small rod puppets, or finger puppets. These puppets can all perform maximal actions in minimal space. If, however, participatory stories involving children and a broad space for actions are to be explored, then larger, bolder forms of puppets, such as bodi-puppets, large rod puppets, or string puppets, would be more appropriate. This larger space expands possible puppet presentations to include slapstick, humor, dance, large actions, and creative movement participation by the children.

There are several puppet types that fit in particularly well with children's stories.

## Stick or Rod Puppets

Perhaps the simplest puppet for the storyteller to use is the rod or stick puppet. The base of this puppet is a cutout picture or a three-dimensional form, made from such novelty items as small toys, stuffed bags, or paper plates with features added. The form is attached to a stick or other rod control such as a cardboard tube, blunt skewer, or drinking straw. The stick puppet is easily constructed and manipulated, and can provide the storyteller with a wide variety of characters for even the most heavily cast story. The puppet can achieve such movements as short hops, long glides, and graceful dancing.

Stories or rhymes such as "Hey Diddle Diddle" which include both animate (dog, cat) and inanimate (moon, dish, spoon) characters especially suit the rod puppet. Songs such as "Old MacDonald" also adapt well when extended to include new characters not normally part of the song. Consider adding such animals as an elephant, mouse, kangaroo, etc., so as to involve all members of the group.

Stories that depict a clearly defined travel sequence with strong action line, such as Leo Lionni's *Swimmy*, "Little Red Riding Hood," and Arlene Mosel's *The Funny Little Woman* allow for strong participatory use of stick puppets. Participants holding rod puppet characters may be positioned at strategic points around the room. Each space represents a story location in which the actors are cued to move. These spaces may be specific localities such as the woman's house, the house of the Onis, and the river in *The Funny Little Woman*. Alternatively, these may be general, less defined spaces, which show different physical movement within one general setting. An example of the latter would be the change from one part of the ocean to another in *Swimmy*.

Stories with an enormous cast, such as Wanda Gág's *Millions of Cats*, Peter Spier's *Noah's Ark*, and Roald Dahl's *The Enormous Crocodile*, can make good use of the rod puppet also. A story with a large cast invites the participation of the entire group, each child using a rod puppet. Children who have duplicate characters, as in *Millions of Cats*, simply perform as a unit.

This type also lends itself well to stories in which all the children participate, for there is little skill needed to

Cardboard stick puppets represent the three Jizo Sama for *The Funny Little Woman* by Arlene Mosel.

present a basic upright posture or single movements by the puppets. An example is the folktale previously discussed, "The Little Red Hen." While sitting in the storytelling area, children may hold up puppets of the appropriate story characters and, in a satisfied, lazy voice, may repeat the response, "Not I."

The rod puppet, however, is limited in its ability to express action and emotion. To compensate for this, the storyteller must use compelling and unusual voices and facial expressions to convey feelings and meanings.

## Construction of a Basic Stick or Rod Puppet

### Materials

Two paper plates or soup bowls (large or small)

Cardboard towel tube

Construction paper

Scrap fabric and trim

Cotton and yarn

Fabric square, 12–18″ square (optional)

Cardboard (optional)

Coat hanger wire or dowel (optional)

### Procedures

*Head*  Put the two plates together and staple around outer edges, leaving an opening to insert towel tube.

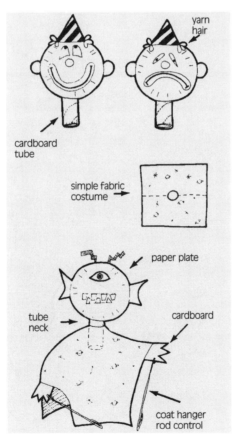

Variations of basic stick puppet construction—glad/sad clown (above) or, with addition of fabric, outer space creature (below)

Glue tube between the plates to serve as a neck and hand grasp. Create a face on one plate side with coloring medium, or add paper features. Cotton, yarn, or fringed paper make excellent hair or manes. A turnaround puppet can be made by creating a face on both sides, perhaps glad on one side and sad on the other.

*Body*  If a body is desired, cut out a large square of fabric and slit a hole in the center the same size as the tube. Insert tube in hole and slide the fabric up to the top of the tube, close to the head area, and glue or tape in place. This simple body serves to cover the hand that controls the puppet. Older children will enjoy adding small cardboard hands to both sides of the fabric square. Attach a length of straightened coat-hanger wire or thin dowel to each hand for controlling additional actions with the puppet's hands.

*Operation*   Firmly grasp the tube with the hand just below the puppet's head and move the puppet about. If extra rods are controlling the puppet's hands, then hold the ends of these rods with your free hand. Both hands of the puppet can then be manipulated together with a swaying back-and-forth motion, or one hand only may be mobilized for gestures such as waving.

## Finger Puppets

Finger puppets are a natural way to introduce nursery rhymes, simple poetry, and uncomplicated stories. Draw features on a finger with washable marking pens and you have an instant puppet. Small pictures cut from coloring books, greeting cards, or magazines attached to fingertips or a glove with double-stick tape are another source. More elaborate puppets may be constructed from felt with pom-pom noses and plastic craft eyes, and other features may be added. *The Tale of Peter Rabbit* by Beatrix Potter is ideal for finger puppets. Consider incorporating the glove into the story as part of the scenery. A felt carrot garden patch could be attached to the palm of a glove with Velcro for Farmer McGregor's garden. Or, a tree drawn on the entire glove pro-

vides branches for the finger puppet monkeys to sit on as you recite the poem "Five Little Monkeys" by Laura Richards. *See* "Finger Stories" in chapter 14 for other variations of finger puppets.

## Construction of a Basic Finger Puppet
### Materials

Felt or nonwoven interfacing fabric, such as heavy-weight Pellon

Colored felt scraps

Yarn

Plastic craft eyes (optional)

Sequins and trims

Button, bead, or miniature pom-pom

### Procedures
*Body*   Using felt or interfacing fabric, follow pattern (p. 29) and cut out a front and a back body piece. With right sides together, sew around entire outside edge of pieces, leaving bottom open for finger. Turn right side out.

*Features*   Glue or sew on small felt features. Pom-poms, buttons, or beads make appealing noses. Pom-poms can also be used for bunny tails. Yarn is suitable for tails, beards, and hair. Small plastic craft eyes give life to the puppet, but these are optional. For extra durability, consider machine stitching felt features onto body pieces before sewing the body together. If white interfacing fabric is used, features can be drawn on with colored marking pens.

**Variations of characters for basic finger puppet—goat, duck, woman**

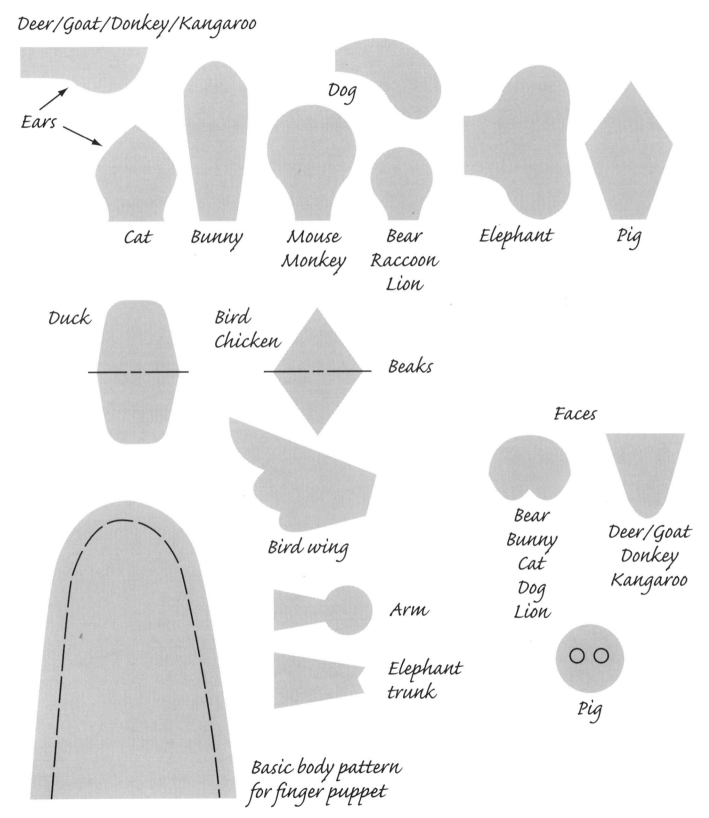

Deer/Goat/Donkey/Kangaroo

Ears

Dog

Cat   Bunny   Mouse   Bear   Elephant   Pig
Monkey   Raccoon
Lion

Duck   Bird   Beaks
Chicken

Faces

Bird wing

Bear
Bunny
Cat
Dog
Lion

Deer/Goat
Donkey
Kangaroo

Arm

Elephant
trunk

Pig

Basic body pattern
for finger puppet

Instant finger puppets made by attaching paper images to fingertips with double-stick tape

**Operation**    Place puppet over finger and explore small bending motions and wiggling actions of fingers. Some puppeteers prefer to turn the hand around and have puppets face the backside of hand. Finger dexterity is more versatile in this position and puppets can actually disappear out of sight when bent down into the palm area.

## Hand Puppets

The traditional hand puppet is probably the best-known type of puppet. Hand puppets basically fall into two categories, those with flexible bodies and those that have a talking mouth. It is unusual to find both features built into a single hand puppet. Therefore, when

Five little monkey finger puppets sitting in a decorated tree glove

choosing a hand puppet, decide which is essential to the puppet's role, action or speaking.

### Flexible-Body Hand Puppet

The hand puppet with flexible body and movable arms has the ability to interpret a wide range of emotions and actions from subtle to exaggerated. This type of puppet would be an excellent choice for portraying the futile attempts of Hildilid to chase away the night in *Hildilid's Night* by Cheli Duran Ryan. The Hildilid puppet must be able to sweep, scrub, scour, shake her fist, and even dig a grave! The flexible-body hand puppet, then, is the best choice for any story in which characters are involved in action sequences such as picking up an object, mixing a cake, writing a note, or sweeping the floor.

When choosing a flexible-body hand puppet, be sure to select one that fits comfortably over the hand and is easy to manipulate. If the puppet has a separate head with a neck tube, this too should feel comfortable. A head that is too cumbersome or weighty will be awkward to manage, and no amount of skill can entice such a puppet to function well.

A good basic puppet pattern that can be transformed into many characters is included in this chapter. Making a set of puppets from this pattern is an economical way to start a versatile puppet collection. Change the eyes, ears, and nose to create those characters you need.

Small hats of all types—police, fire, straw, Mexican, top, crown, and ten gallon—can be purchased at toy or craft shops. Hats can also be cut from material and attached to the puppet. These can quickly change the personality of a puppet.

Simple costume pieces, such as an apron, cape, or vest, may be attached to the basic body. Props such as wooden spoons, toy rakes, and magic wands also greatly enhance a puppet's character. Such props may be purchased in large discount and craft stores, or may be made from cardboard or other materials.

## Construction of a Basic Hand Puppet with Flexible Body

### Materials

Felt, velour, polyester knit, heavy
    cotton, fake fur, or heavy-weight
    interfacing fabric

Assorted fabrics and trims

Assorted felt

Plastic craft eyes (optional)

Yarn, dish or floor mop, shag fur or shag bathroom rug

Pom-pom or button

### Procedures

*Body*   Fake fur makes excellent animal characters. Print fabrics (cottons or double knits) can also be interesting and might be considered for a flowered pig, checkered alligator, striped zebra, or calico cat. Features and decorating can be drawn on the surface of white interfacing fabrics with colored marking pens.

Variations of characters for basic hand puppet with flexible body—witch, king, monkey, elephant

Cut out a front and a back body piece, following pattern. With right sides together, sew around entire outside edge of pieces, leaving bottom open to insert hand. Turn right side out and hem bottom edge.

*Hair*   A wig can be made from shag fur or bathroom rug material. Cut out front and back wig pieces and sew, right sides together; turn right side out and tack to puppet head. A mop, yarn, or fringed felt also make excellent hair. Consider dyeing the mop a color before attaching to head.

*Features*   Sew or glue on various features. Cheeks can be made by gluing pink felt circles onto the cheek areas. A mustache or beard made from fringed yarn or fake fur would be a nice touch for a Santa Claus or lumberjack. A pom-pom or button serves well for a nose. You may wish to use one of the nose patterns in this section and create a stuffed nose with material that matches the face. A large bead or wadded felt wart would add character to a witch puppet. Add a felt trunk for an elephant.

*Costumes and hats*   Cut out a front and a back costume or hat piece following the basic pattern. Sew pieces, right sides together, around outer seam lines; turn right side out and hem raw edges. Decorate with trims, sequins, and beads; add a pocket to costume, if desired.

*Animal ears*   The size, shape, and positioning of ears will help determine the character. Try long ears for a bunny, large round ones for a monkey, and floppy ones for a dog. Prepare ears before sewing the body pieces together. Ears with furry backs to match the animal's

Hats

lady

farmer

chef

police

body, lined with pink or tan felt, are attractive. Cut out a front and a back ear piece and sew with right sides together; turn right side out. Pleat ears at base and pin between head area of puppet before sewing body together; proceed with instructions for sewing body together.

*Tails*   Pom-poms, braided trims, or yarn make appropriate tails for animals. A pipe cleaner would be good for curling into a pig's tail. A tassel added to the end of a cord makes an excellent lion's tail.

*Operation*   Refer to chapter 8, Anything Puppets, and experiment with the best hand position to hold and move the puppet.

## Talking-Mouth Hand Puppet

Stories with farm animals who "moo," "quack," or "oink"; a big bad wolf who displays a threatening row of teeth; or a character who talks a great deal would be best interpreted with talking-mouth puppets. The frog in "The Frog Prince" and the wolf in "The Gunniwolf" are good examples.

It is perfectly acceptable to utilize both types of puppets within one story to increase variety and interest. For example, in "The Gunniwolf" the wolf may be a talking-mouth puppet while the little girl is represented by a flexible-body puppet.

Patterns for a round and a pointed talking-mouth puppet are included here. By adding different facial features and ears these patterns can be used to create a variety of puppet characters.

**Hand Puppet Pattern**

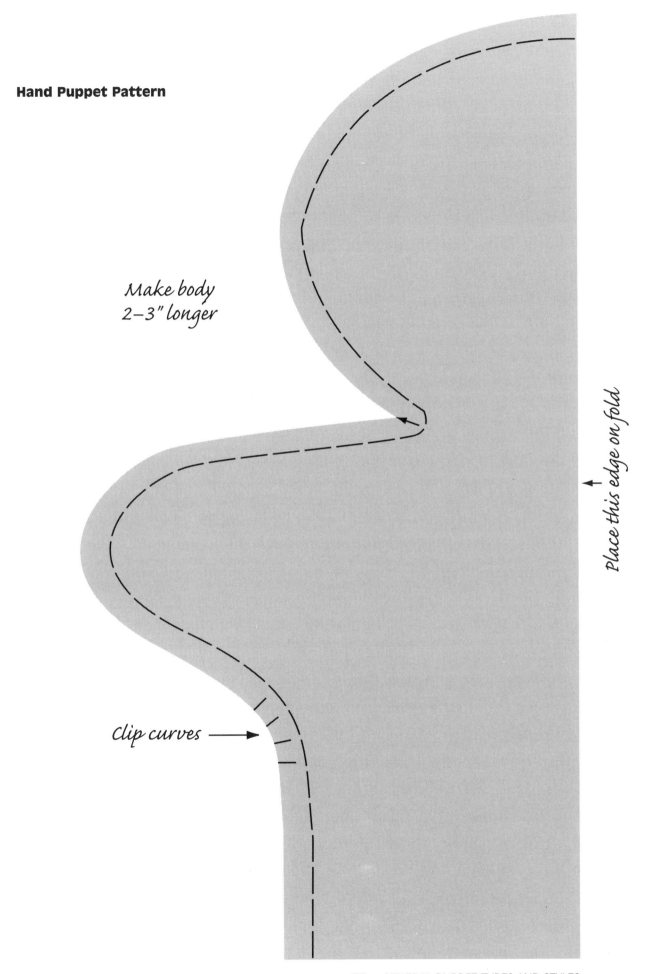

Make body
2–3" longer

Clip curves →

Place this edge on fold ↑

**Basic Costume Pattern
for Hand Puppet**

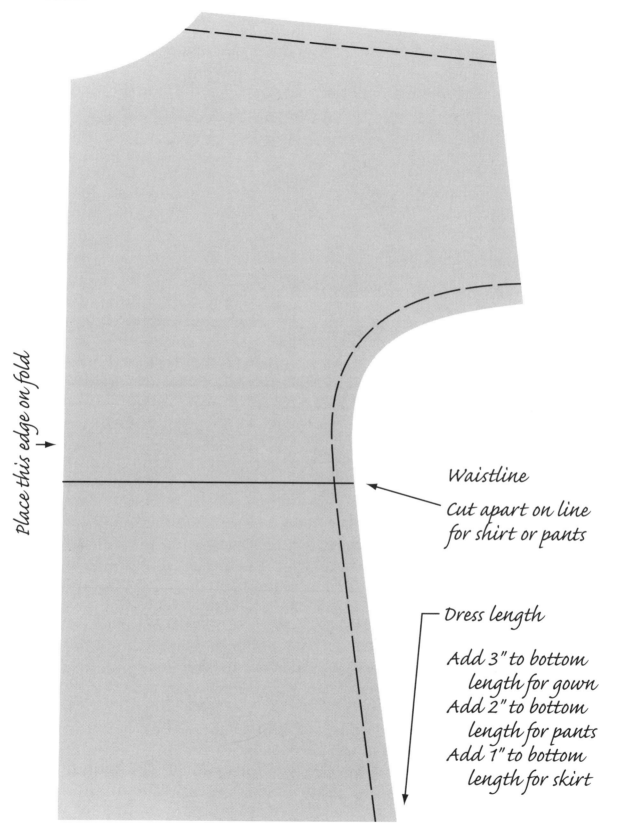

Place this edge on fold

Waistline

Cut apart on line
for shirt or pants

Dress length

Add 3" to bottom
length for gown
Add 2" to bottom
length for pants
Add 1" to bottom
length for skirt

**Wig, Mustache, and Beard Patterns for Hand Puppet**

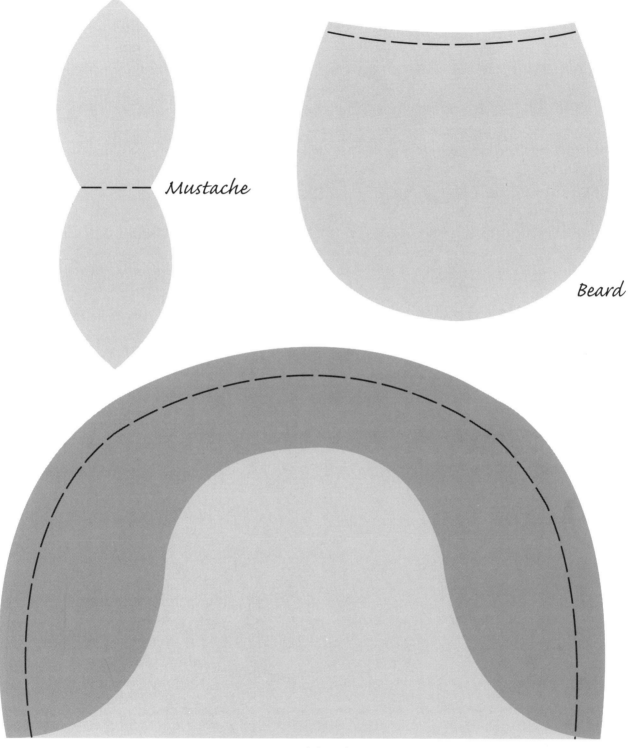

Mustache

Beard

Front and back wig

**Ear Patterns for Hand Puppet**

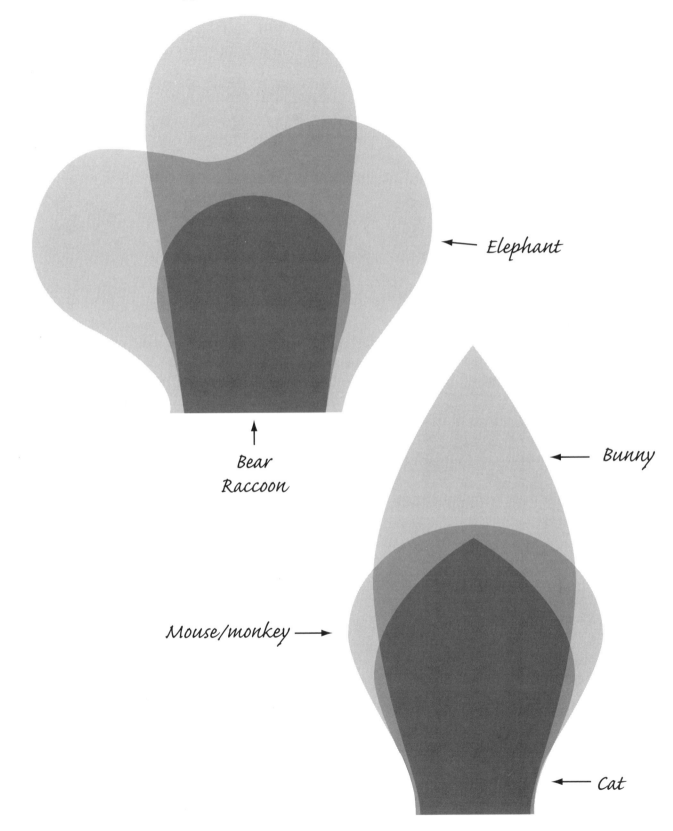

← Elephant

↑
Bear
Raccoon

← Bunny

Mouse/monkey →

← Cat

**Nose and Face Patterns for Hand Puppet**

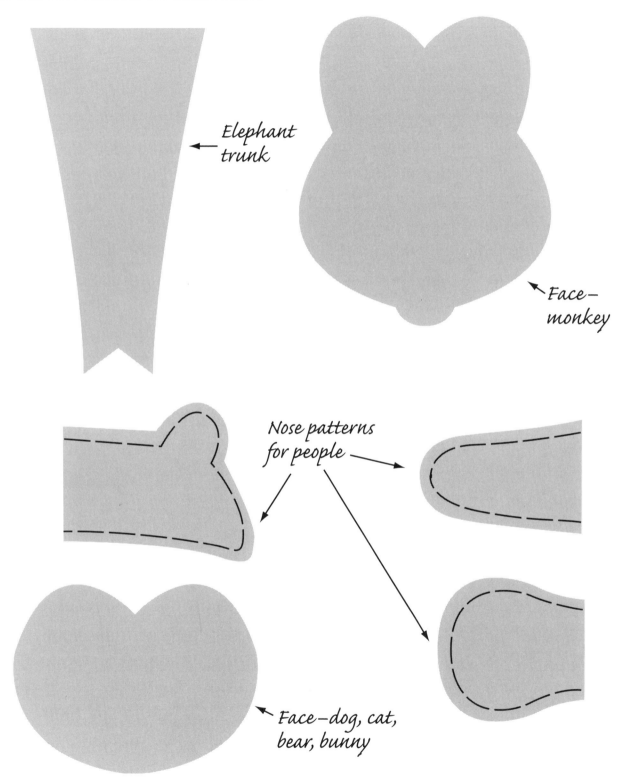

Elephant trunk

Face—monkey

Nose patterns for people

Face—dog, cat, bear, bunny

## Hat Patterns for Hand Puppet

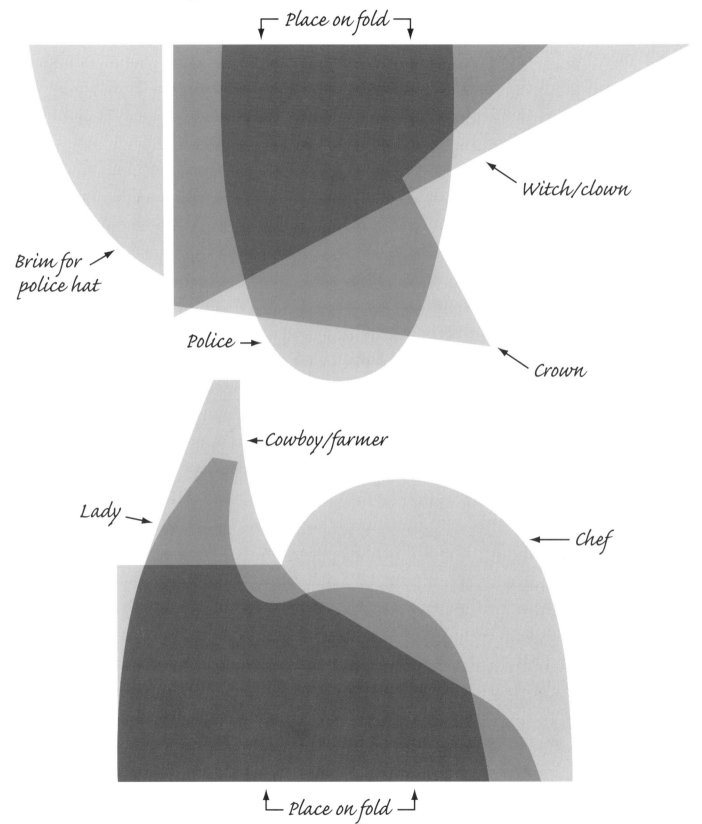

Place on fold

Witch/clown

Brim for
police hat

Police →

← Crown

← Cowboy/farmer

Lady →

← Chef

Place on fold

## Construction of a Basic Hand Puppet with Talking Mouth

### Materials

Felt, velour, polyester knit, fake fur, heavy cotton, or other sturdy fabric

Plastic craft eyes (optional)

Red or pink felt, velour, or double knit

Assorted felt and fabric

Pom-pom or button

Yarn

### Procedures

**Body** For fabric suggestions, refer to previous flexible-body instructions. Cut out front and back body pieces, extending pattern length 4 inches or more (even longer for a caterpillar or snake) depending on desired finished length.

**Talking mouth and assembly** Place pattern on fold and cut out mouthpiece, from red or pink fabric. Pin and fit mouth to body pieces, right sides together. Sew mouth edges. Turn entire puppet right side out. Note: If felt is

Variations of characters for basic hand puppet with talking mouth— pig (left) and frog (right)

used for mouth, consider lining mouth so felt will not puncture.

**Features** Add felt ears, legs, arms, eyes, and other features. Pom-poms or buttons are suitable for noses. Shag fur, yarn, or fringed felt make excellent hair. A pom-pom, rope braid, braided yarn, or other trim can be used for a tail.

**Operation** Put hand firmly inside mouth, with fingers in up-per sections and thumb in lower, and open and close hand. See chapter 5 for synchronization of dialogue with mouth action.

**Example of character for basic hand puppet with pointed talking mouth— wolf**

**Body Pattern for Construction
of Basic Hand Puppet
with Round Talking Mouth**

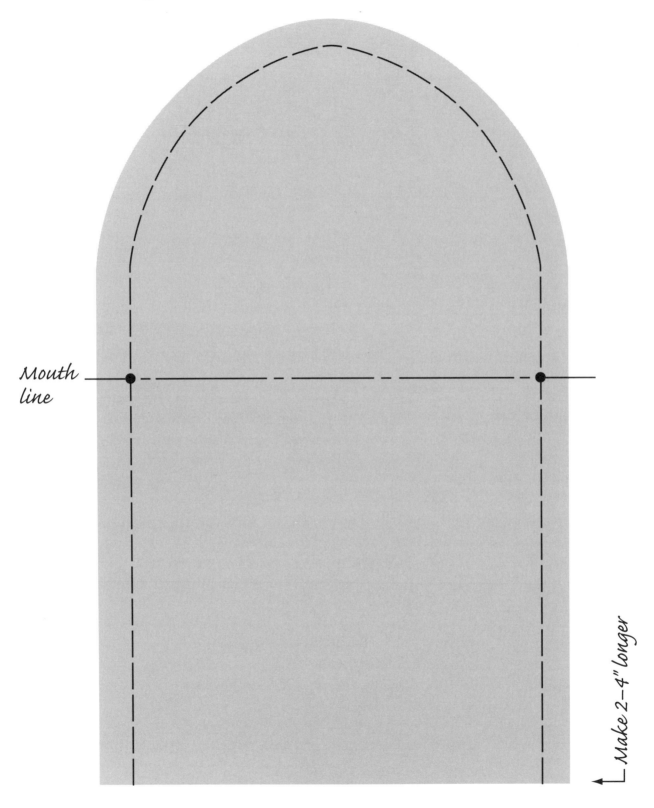

Mouth
line

Make 2–4" longer

**Mouth Patterns for Round
Talking Mouth (Top)
and Pointed Talking Mouth**

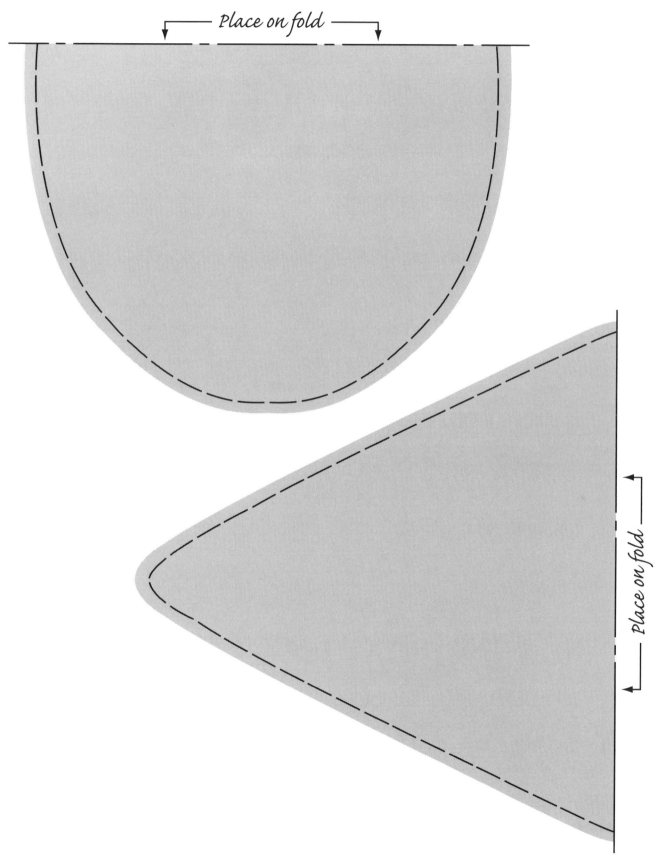

*Place on fold*

*Place on fold*

**Body Pattern for Construction
of Basic Hand Puppet
with Pointed Talking Mouth**

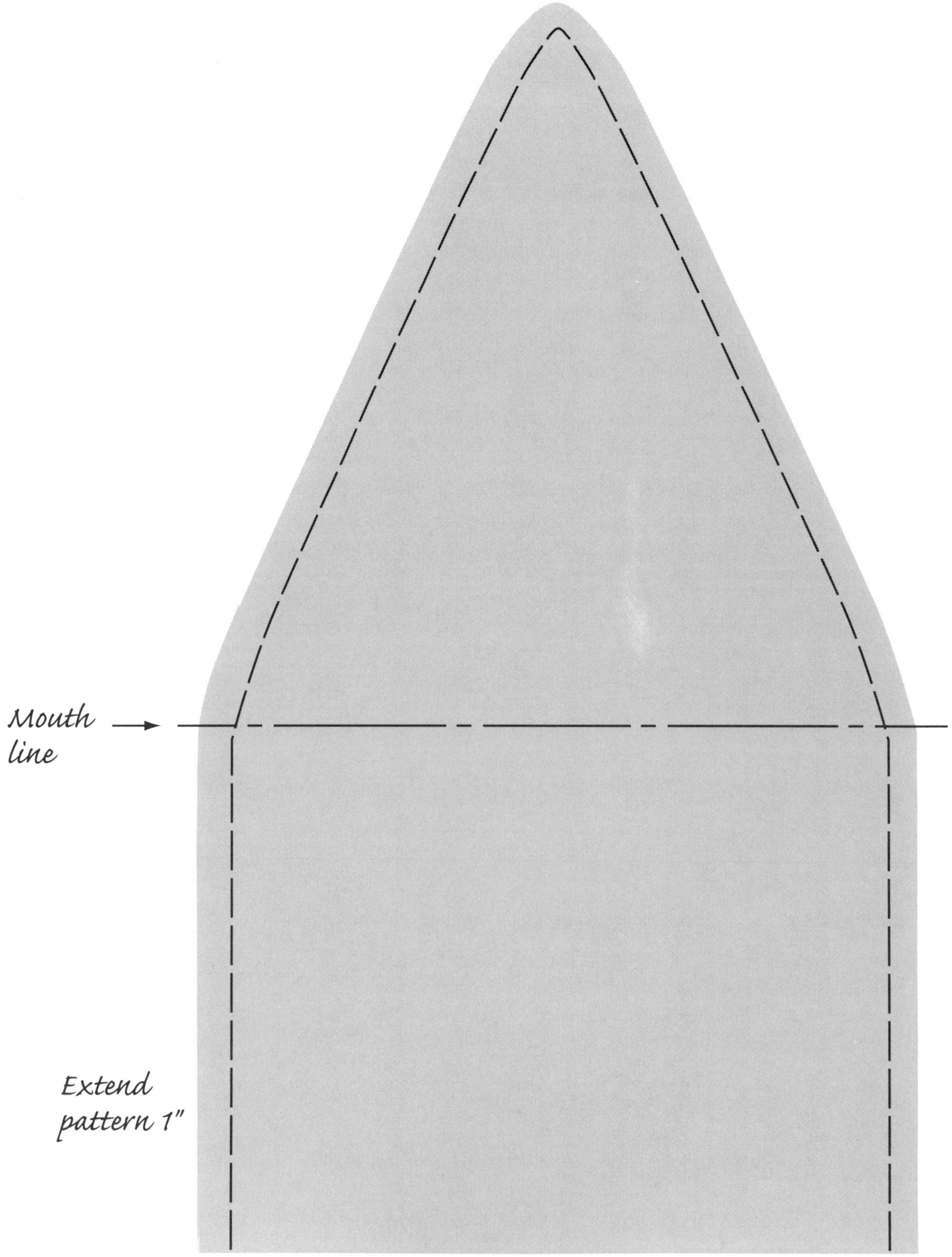

Mouth
line →

Extend
pattern 1"

## String Puppets or Marionettes

A string puppet, or marionette, is perhaps the most difficult style for the novice to use when portraying emotions or expression. This type of puppet requires advanced skills, as well as a finely crafted and well-balanced marionette in order to achieve a credible presentation. The strings, which operate each moving part, cause a delayed action effect when transmitting a specific movement from the control area to the moving puppet part. Some spontaneity in expression is therefore lost. Although children greatly enjoy playing with this form of puppet, we do not recommend the traditional marionette for the novice storyteller who is intent upon

**Half-pint milk containers make up the components for Little Bo Peep and her sheep string puppets**

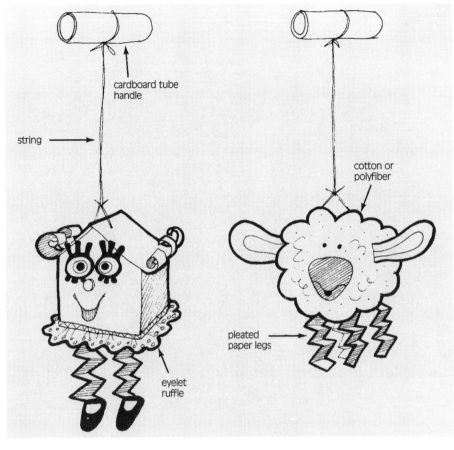

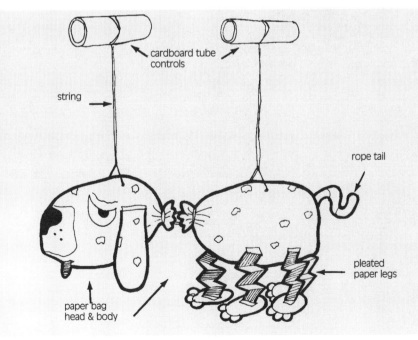

**Example of a basic horizontal paper-bag string puppet**

exploration of expression in storytelling through puppets.

Simplified versions of the string puppet, however, are exciting to explore for visual reasons, and elementary children are able to operate such simple puppets. Children enjoy experimenting with a variety of string puppets because of their fascination with the mechanical aspects of animation, and for that reason the incorporation of these puppets into the story hour is worthwhile. A cast of balloon string puppet animals from "Henny Penny," bobbing along through the forest to tell the King the sky is falling, makes a delightful parade and a readily understood story. These puppets are quickly made by attaching paper faces, tails, ears, and feet to balloons with rubber cement. Glue or tape a continuous piece of yarn or twine to the head and tail of each animal to form an operating control.

As a more grandiose alternative, imagine the impact of a four-foot-tall string puppet, with stuffed paper bags for the head and body, strung together with cardboard towel tubes serving as the arms and legs and several strings for controls. On a smaller scale, appealing and unusual versions of Little Bo Peep and her sheep may be constructed from half-pint milk cartons or small boxes and attached to a single string for young children. Picture the scene of ten plus string-puppet sheep emerging from their hiding places and following Little Bo Peep home. What a spectacle for children (and adults) to view and of which to be a part!

## Construction of a Basic String Puppet

### Materials

Small or medium paper bags

Newspaper

String

Construction paper

Scrap fabric, felt, and trims

Cardboard tubes or dowels

**Example of a basic vertical paper-bag string puppet**

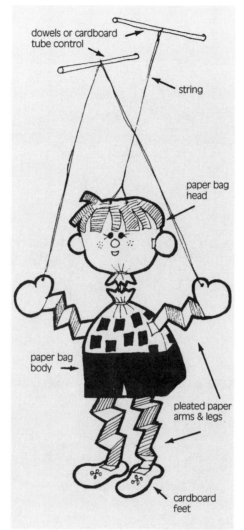

- dowels or cardboard tube control
- string
- paper bag head
- paper bag body
- pleated paper arms & legs
- cardboard feet

## Procedures

*Body and head*   Use two bags, one for the body and another for the head. Stuff with crumpled newspaper and link the necks of the bags together with string, leaving them loose jointed.

*Arms and feet*   Cut out long strips of construction paper, approximately 1½ inches wide. Pleat strips and attach to basic bag body for arms and legs. Paper hands, feet, or paws can be added to end of paper strips.

*Decorating the puppet*   Paint the puppet with tempera, acrylic, or flat latex-based wall paint, or cover with interesting fabric. (When covered with fake fur, these puppets look quite professional!) Add paper or felt features and costumes. A bow tie, sequined dog collar, ruffled tutu, comical hat, or ermined robe give special touches to the puppets.

*Assembling strings*   Experiment with the strings to find the best location for agility. The beginner should try to keep the number of strings to a minimum. A string attached to the head and one to each hand will suffice for a typical string puppet in a vertical position (person or standing animal). Tie the central head string to a cardboard tube control and the hand strings to a second tube control. A horizontal puppet, such as a dog, could have a head string attached to one tube control and body string to another.

*Operation*   Hold separate controls, one in each hand, from above and make the puppet walk along the floor. Strings can be operated separately to isolate movement or jointly for larger movements such as hops or jumps.

*Background*   A simple background for string puppets can be created by turning a table on its side or stretching a piece of mural paper between two chairs. Decorate background with appropriate scenes. Puppeteers can stand behind the background while operating the puppets in front.

## Bodi-Puppets

A bodi-puppet is a large-scale puppet that is worn in front of the body, enabling the wearer to become a particular character in a bold form of expression. It is essentially a mannequin or doll-like puppet with highly flexible limbs. The hands and feet are those of the wearer, enabling the puppet to achieve a broad range of movements, such as dancing, walking, hopping, lifting an object, clapping the hands, or throwing a ball.

Stories that take best advantage of this puppet form are those in which a character or characters are involved in extended activities requiring broad, changing movements. For example, the bears in *Another Celebrated Dancing Bear* by Gladys Scheffrin-Falk may learn new dance steps and then perform for the delighted audience; Little Miss Muffet may briskly stir up

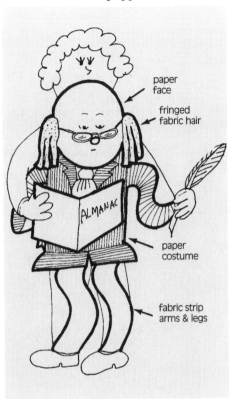

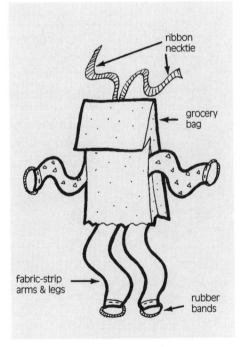

Construction of a basic bodi-puppet

some curds and whey before fleeing in near hysteria from the big spider; mighty Heracles from Greek mythology can perform the arduous task of cleaning the Augean stables; Ben Franklin may appear with a quill in his hand as he composes text for *Poor Richard's Almanac*; tall-tale heroes such as John Henry and Sluefoot Sue may enact the episodes that made them legends.

Another attraction of bodi-puppets is the appropriateness of using full-scale, everyday props. A telephone, writing pad, tennis racket, mixing bowl, and other objects found around the house can eliminate or simplify prop manufacture with this technique.

### Construction of a Basic Bodi-Puppet

Bodi-puppets may be as simple or advanced in construction as time and skill permit. One of the quickest bodi-puppets to make simply requires that a picture of the character's head be pinned onto the chest area of the puppeteer. The picture may be drawn by the child or cut from a magazine or poster. Even such a simple image is enough to suggest the character. The child's imagination fills in the details as the child becomes the puppet character. Supermarket bags also serve as an excellent base for a simple bodi-puppet as described here.

**Materials**

Supermarket grocery bag

3-foot length of 1″ wide ribbon or fabric strip

Two 3″ strips of fabric cut to length of arms

Two 3″ strips of fabric cut to length of legs

Four large rubber bands

Construction paper

Scrap fabric, cotton and yarn trims

**Procedures**

*Construction of arms and legs*   Fold over the end of each arm or leg fabric strip and slip a rubber band in each hem; staple hems to secure rubber bands in place. Staple other end of each arm or leg strip to paper bag as shown.

*Neck ribbon*   Staple center of ribbon to top center of bag.

*Decoration*   Use a rich assortment of materials and coloring medium to add character, pattern, and texture to the bag. A cutout paper face can be added to flap of bag to change its shape for more advanced designs.

*Operation*   Tie the neck ribbon around the puppeteer's neck. Attach the rubber bands to the puppeteer's wrists and ankles and proceed to experiment with movement using the puppeteer's body to express the puppet's actions.

## Overhead Projector Shadow Puppets

Although shadow puppets do not fall into the general category of other puppet types mentioned previously that rely on specific finger, hand, or body control, they remain a definite and popular puppet form that relies strongly on visual image. In a sense they most closely fit into the category of rod puppets since

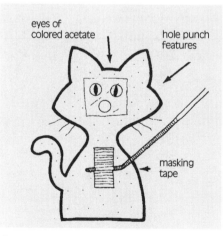

eyes of colored acetate

hole punch features

masking tape

**Construction of a basic overhead shadow puppet—cat**

they are essentially the same, a two-dimensional cutout image on a rod or stick. The major difference is that this puppet type is viewed in silhouette with a light shone from behind it making the visual aspect far more exciting than the ordinary rod puppet. Most shadow performers work directly behind a large vertical viewing screen. This often requires a special light, screen, and viewing setup. The overhead projector is much easier to use and just as dramatic.

Exciting effects can be achieved with puppets cut from thin tagboard or file folders, taped onto a drinking straw or florist's wire, and then placed on an overhead projector. Stories with simple settings and a variety of characters who move through the setting look very professional when viewed in this manner.

One of the finest attributes of the overhead shadow puppet technique is that it produces such intriguing visual effects. Bold use of color can be achieved with colored acetate (book report covers) laid over the glass: for example, blue to create an underwater kingdom for a story such as *Swimmy* by Leo Lionni; vibrant yellows, greens, and blues to represent the Caribbean setting of *The House That Jack Built* illustrated by Jenny Snow; or green for a forest setting in "Hansel and Gretel." Other physical effects can be achieved with the use of perforated materials such as lace, screening, or burlap. Paper doilies or cutout snowflakes make an excellent background for a snow scene to accompany *A Snowy Day* by Ezra Jack Keats. String and yarn can also be used to make patterns for spider webs for E. B. White's *Charlotte's Web* or lines of varying shapes for Ed Emberley's drawing books.

Cumulative stories and folk songs have themes that are simple and repetitive. In addition, they require little or no scenery, making them a natural for the overhead

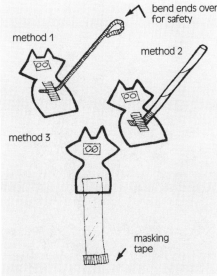

**Three methods for rod control with overhead shadow puppets: (1) florist's wire holder; (2) drinking straw; (3) clear acetate**

method 1

bend ends over for safety

method 2

method 3

masking tape

technique. Each repetition of a chorus can be accompanied by a puppet visualization of the words for cuing purposes. During *Frog Went a-Courtin'* a frog puppet could hop across the screen with a sword and pistol dangling from his belt. Accompany the chorus of the "Drinking Gourd" song with silhouettes of slaves moving slowly toward a representation of the Big Dipper constellation, or have a girl driving a wagon drawn by six horses race across the stage during "She'll Be Coming Round the Mountain."

Sharing poetry with children via the overhead puppet technique provides an opportunity to explore the imagery, rhythm, and language of a poem. Children will share the plight of the cat in William Carlos Williams's "Poem" as it climbs so carefully over the closet only to finally step into an empty flowerpot. The visual image of the cat blundering into the flowerpot adds a new dimension to the poem.

## Construction of a Basic Overhead Shadow Puppet

### Materials

Light tagboard, file folder, or other stiff paper

Thick florist's wire or drinking straws

Clear acetate (book report cover)

Colored marking pens for acetate (or waterproof marking pens)

Double-stick cellophane tape

Sharp knife, such as an X-Acto knife (for adult use), or embroidery scissors

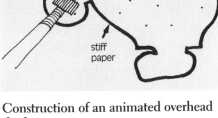

yarn hair

drinking straw

paper fastener

masking tape

stiff paper

**Construction of an animated overhead shadow puppet**

Hole punch and paper-fastener brads

### Procedures

*Body* Cut out character image from paper. Cut eye slits and other features with X-Acto knife, embroidery scissors, or hole punch. Attach a florist's wire, straw rod control, or acetate strip to back of puppet using one of the following methods:

*Method 1.* Using florist's wire, bend end of wire and tape end to back of puppet. (Bend opposite end of wire down for safety.)

*Method 2.* Using drinking straw, wrap a piece of masking tape around end of straw. Let tape extend half an inch at end of straw and attach tape extension to back of puppet with another piece of tape.

*Method 3.* Using clear acetate strip, lay tip of strip flat on back of puppet and attach with double-stick tape. Add a piece of folded masking tape on end of acetate for hand grip.

*Features* For moveable features, hinge body parts together by punching holes where joints meet and securing with a paper fastener. Attach wire, straw, or acetate rod controls to both body and moving parts sections for animating. To incorporate colored details on characters, cut out decorative holes in the basic puppet, such as spots on a leopard or eyes on a cat. Colored acetate can be overlaid on the holes with double-stick tape, resulting in a leopard with orange spots or a cat with green eyes.

*Operation*  Lay the puppet image flat on the overhead glass with rod control bent to one side, away from path of light. Move the puppet along the glass surface using the perimeter of the glass as a frame of reference. When manipulating controls, keep hands as much to the side as possible to avoid blocking out the light source.

There are two ways to use the space on the overhead glass. The bottom of the glass can represent the ground along which all the characters walk. The upper part of the glass would then represent the sky and creatures that fly would move in that space. This approach is best utilized when there is a definite distinction between the characters, as in the fable "The Wind and the Sun." Or the whole area of the overhead glass can be considered the ground, or the sea, or the sky, and characters can move about the space at will. This second method is suitable when all the characters inhabit the same type of space.

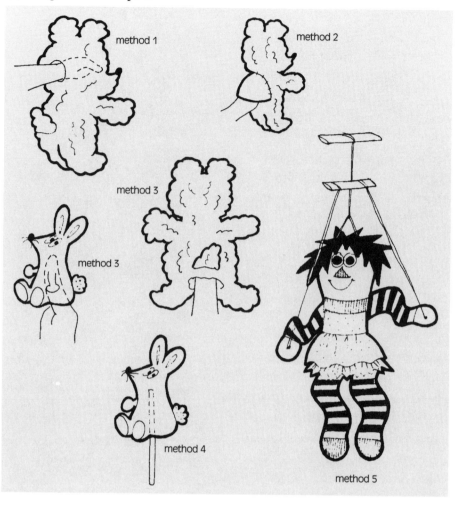

method 1

method 2

method 3

method 3

method 4

method 5

## Converting Stuffed Toys into Puppets

Excellent sources for puppets are converted plush toys and other stuffed creatures. Gift, toy, and department stores, particularly around holidays such as Christmas and Easter, abound with a fine selection of novelty toys and stuffed animals from which to choose. Many are soft, cuddly, popular creatures such as bunny rabbits, teddy bears, dogs, and cats—creatures that often reflect a warm style conducive to woodland stories or that serve well as appealing host puppets. Also look for tiny stuffed animals such as mice and chicks for finger puppets. Dolls and soft sculpture open up other possibilities for casting people in stories.

The performance capacity of each individual toy, which will depend wholly on its construction, will be limited unless the arms or mouth can be made to move. However, physical appearance and personality compensate for this restriction. Following are several methods to convert a stuffed toy into a puppet:

1. Cut a hole in the back of the toy's head and remove some stuffing to provide space for your hand. Consider slitting the mouth of the toy and sewing in a mouthpiece if the head area is large enough for a talking mouth.

2. Sew an inverted pocket on the back of the toy in which to tuck the hand for holding.

3. Cut a hole in the bottom of the toy, removing enough stuffing to provide space for your hand or finger.

4. Insert a wooden dowel to convert the toy into a simple rod puppet. Coat-hanger wire or thin dowels could also be attached to the back of the toy's hands or arms, if loose jointed, to make it capable of additional movement. If this is done, some stuffing may need to be removed from the elbows or shoulder joints to facilitate smooth movement.

5. Attach strings to the arms and legs of dolls and animals to animate them for an impromptu marionette. Tape the strings to a cardboard tube control.

## PUPPET STYLE

After a puppet type or form is chosen the storyteller must decide on the style of the puppet. Puppet style refers solely to the physical materials and characteristics of the puppet itself, which include many possibilities. These may range from the highly realistic, as seen in puppets converted from plush toys, to the abstract, as in some paper shapes on rods. Puppets can also be an exaggeration of reality—they may be extremely tall, preposterously fat, or ridiculously small, all attributes children find appealing.

The style of the puppet decided upon is greatly influenced by ethnic background, historic period, and story setting. The story *Bringing the Rain to Kapiti Plain* adapted by Verna Aardema would be well represented by large, bold angular shapes on sticks to reflect the geometry of African art. An altogether different style is exemplified in *Strega Nona* by Tomie de Paola, which carries a strong cultural theme that may best be illustrated with highly traditional puppets in authentic costumes of Italy. A gentle woodland story such as *Bread*

A plush-dog hand puppet, an abstract sun stick puppet, and an Indian ethnic string puppet show contrasting puppet types and styles. (Hand puppet by Dakin, photos by Michelle Owen)

*and Jam for Frances* by Russell Hoban may call for a soft, realistic badger to enhance its warm nature and woodsy theme.

Often puppet style is a purely personal choice, a choice based on one's own interpretation of a story. Goldilocks, who is traditionally cast as a sweet but inquisitive little girl in "The Three Bears," may take on a completely different interpretation in the form of a comic character with overly long arms and outrageous golden curls, resulting in a touch of absurd comic-drama. If you are considering a style contrary to the usual interpretation of the story, it will be to your advantage to detail your desired effect and to consider both puppet type and puppet style with this expectation in mind.

By understanding the unique characteristics of basic puppet types, the storyteller can choose the one most appropriate to convey a story and to enhance its style.

## SUGGESTED TITLES FOR
## GENERAL PUPPET TYPES AND STYLES

Aardema, Verna. *Bringing the Rain to Kapiti Plain*; illus. by Beatriz Vidal. Dial, 1981.

How Ki-pat brought rain to the Kapiti Plain is told in this rhythmic African tale.

Christelow, Eileen. *Five Little Monkeys Sitting in a Tree*; illus. by the author. Clarion, 1991.

Five little monkeys tease Mr. Crocodile and disappear one by one. A natural for telling with finger puppets.

Dahl, Roald. *The Enormous Crocodile*; illus. by Quentin Blake. Knopf, 1978.

A group of animals foils a crocodile's plans to make lunch of some children. Each child uses a rod puppet to mime the action. Storyteller assumes role of the crocodile.

De Brunhoff, Jean. *The Story of Babar, the Little Elephant*; illus. by the author. Random, 1967.

The first book in the popular series about the little French elephant.

de Paola, Tomie. *Strega Nona*; illus. by the author. Prentice-Hall, 1975.

A humorous retelling of an Italian folktale about a "grandmother witch," her magic pasta pot, and a foolish lad who create havoc for the village. A Caldecott Honor book.

Du Bois, William Pène. *Bear Circus*; illus. by the author. Viking, 1971.

A group of koala bears create an amusing circus, much to the delight of their friends.

Gág, Wanda. *Millions of Cats*; illus. by the author. Coward, 1928.

A childless couple want a cat but almost get more than they can handle. A Newbery Honor book.

"The Frog Prince," in *Best-Loved Folktales of the World* selected by Joanna Cole. Doubleday, 1982. Pp. 95–98.

The Grimm tale about a frog who turns into a prince.

Hoban, Russell. *Bread and Jam for Frances*; illus. by Lillian Hoban. Harper, 1964.

One in a series of stories about Frances, an adorable badger, and her family and friends.

Hogrogian, Nonny. *One Fine Day*; illus. by the author. Macmillan, 1971.

A cumulative story set in motion by a fox who steals milk from an old woman and has his tail cut off. A Caldecott Medal book.

*House That Jack Built*; illus. by Jenny Stow. Dial, 1992.

The Caribbean is the setting for this version of the rhyme "This is the House That Jack Built."

Keats, Ezra Jack. *The Snowy Day*; illus. by the author. Viking, 1962.

>A quiet story centered around a boy's enjoyment of a walk in the snow. A Caldecott Medal book.

Langstaff, John. *Frog Went a-Courtin'*; illus. by Feodor Rojankovsky. Harcourt, 1955.

>A picture-book version of the folk song about Frog who woos and marries Mistress Mouse. A Caldecott Medal book.

Lionni, Leo. *Swimmy*; illus. by the author. Pantheon, 1963.

>A group of fish discover that there is safety in numbers. A Caldecott Honor book.

Litzinger, Rosanne. *The Old Woman and Her Pig*; illus. by the author. Harcourt, 1993.

>Cumulative tale of an old woman who buys a pig but can't get it home because the pig refuses to go over a stile in the road.

McDermott, Gerald. *Raven: A Trickster Tale from the Pacific Northwest*; illus. by the author. Harcourt, 1993.

>Raven steals light from the Sky Chief and brings it to earth. A Caldecott Honor book.

Mosel, Arlene. *The Funny Little Woman*; illus. by Blair Lent. Dutton, 1972.

>The adventures of a courageous woman who chases her rice dumpling into the underworld are enacted in this Japanese folktale with vivid characters and a strong plot. A Caldecott Medal book.

Potter, Beatrix. *The Tale of Peter Rabbit*; illus. by the author. Warne, n.d.

>The classic story about Peter Rabbit and his adventures in Farmer McGregor's garden.

Ryan, Cheli Duran. *Hildilid's Night*; illus. by Arnold Lobel. Collier/Macmillan, 1986.

>An old woman struggles in vain to chase away the night. A Caldecott Honor book.

San Souci, Robert D. *Larger Than Life*; illus. by Andrew Glass. Doubleday, 1991.

>Recounts the adventures of five legendary American heroes: John Henry, Old Stormalong, Sluefoot Sue, Strap Buckner, and Paul Bunyan.

Scheffrin-Falk, Gladys. *Another Celebrated Dancing Bear*; illus. by Barbara Garrison. Collier/Macmillan, 1991.

>Max and Boris, two bears, are the best of friends. Boris becomes as famous as Max, a celebrated star of the Moscow Circus, when Max teaches him how to dance.

Sendak, Maurice. *Pierre*; illus. by the author. Harper, 1962.

>A boy's "I don't care" attitude leads to amusing complications.

Spier, Peter. *Noah's Ark*; illus. by the author. Doubleday, 1977.

>Caldecott award-winning rendition of the journey of Noah and the animals who accompany him. A Caldecott Medal book.

Steig, William. *Amos and Boris*; illus. by the author. Farrar, 1971.

>A mouse and a whale develop a mutually beneficial friendship.

White, E. B. *Charlotte's Web*; illus. by Garth Williams. Harper, 1952.

>The runt of a pig litter is befriended by a little girl, a clever spider, and a resourceful rat. A Newbery Honor book.

# Chapter 4

# BUILDING THE PUPPET COLLECTION

ONCE YOU HAVE taken the plunge into storytelling with puppets, you will find it advantageous to begin collecting puppets in a systematic manner. A first step may be investing in a few sturdy, washable puppets of good quality. You can supplement this beginning collection with puppets you make, and you can purchase others as finances permit. However, analyze your needs to determine which characters to acquire first. Factors to consider in compiling your puppet collection include: (1) ages of the children and the types of stories you plan to tell and (2) who will be using the puppets.

## INTEGRATING PUPPETS WITH STORIES

An easy way to begin is with the familiar. Very likely you already have a collection of stories you share with children of different ages. List these titles by appropriate age groups and give some thought to how you might integrate puppetry into the telling. Following are general considerations for integrating puppets with stories.

### Preschool Children

Stories for preschool children contain people and animal characters from the everyday world. A majority of the stories deal with one concept and with happenings or feelings children face daily. Hand puppets, made of soft material or fur that is pleasant to touch will complement most stories for this young age group. A furry puppet bear may introduce the story of "The Three Bears," help the children count each bear in *Teddy Bears 1 to 10* by Susanna Gretz, or play the bear's part in *Ask Mr. Bear* by Marjorie Flack. Thus, one puppet has versatility for several different stories. The projected mood of the story will, naturally, be a consideration in deciding upon types of puppets essential for your puppet collection. Warm, humorous rhymes and verses offer an ideal opportunity to introduce finger puppets. You may seat the children on the floor in a semicircle and have them recite Mother Goose rhymes as you simply hold the puppets in front of you. Adding a lapboard permits important simple props, such as the houses in "The Three Little Pigs," to be used effectively when telling stories.

Finger puppets may effectively be employed to introduce a story by hiding them in the pockets of a story apron. Ask a child to investigate the pockets to discover the puppets. Then you can manipulate them to introduce the story. Finger puppets may be made from felt, double knits and other soft materials, or fake fur. Varieties of finger puppets are available commercially from the manufacturers listed at the end of this chapter.

Puppets to be used by the preschool and kindergarten child must be very lightweight, simple to operate, and highly durable. A flat hand or mitt puppet that only requires the child to insert a hand into the mitt permits the gross hand movements of the child to operate the puppet adequately. Such hand puppets would have to be scaled down to fit the child's hand and, therefore, would be inadequate for the storyteller's larger hand.

### Primary-Age Children

Primary-age children are developing an interest in the world around them, and their favorite stories reflect that interest. Animal stories are still appealing. These children enjoy humorous characters and more complex stories. Puppets for this age group do not have to be as realistic as those utilized for younger children. Human clothing may be added to the basic puppet: bow ties on wolf puppets, top hats on rabbits, glasses for a horse puppet.

Hand puppets that require simple manipulation can be successfully handled by primary children. Small talking-mouth puppets are popular with this age group. Sock puppets are also a favorite of this group since humorous attributes are easily added to these puppets, while manipulation involves large hand and finger movement. Simple string and rod puppets also will be enticing to this age level.

## Intermediate-Age Children

The intermediate-age child has an interest in fantasy, historical and science fiction, as well as realistic stories. Imaginary and horror creatures have a unique fascination for this group.

Both representational and novel puppet characters will find favor. Characters from outer space, middle earth, and the world of fantasy have broad appeal to this age group. Opportunities for telling tales from mythology are also plentiful, and the large rod puppet is a good choice to portray such strong, unbending characters.

Bodi-puppets adapt well to dramatizing the exaggerated exploits of tall-tale characters. To portray the adventures of the larger-than-life characters of Paul Bunyan and his blue ox, Babe, the children may wear bodi-puppets while miming the actions with cardboard props. Maps of the United States and Canada over which the mighty logger can stride may be placed on the floor.

Puppets that transform from one character to another will fascinate children in this age group. A frog that turns into a prince or a vampire that turns into a bat—a novelty type puppet made with a smaller box character that pops out of a larger box character—would be fun to introduce.

Larger talking-mouth puppets are enthusiastically used by children in this age group with a little introduction. They also enjoy experimenting with puppets that are mechanically operated, such as string puppets, rod puppets with movable parts, and overhead shadow puppets. Sock puppets, when student made and endowed with creative personalities, are also excellent to add to the puppet collection.

Examine your list of stories and detail puppet characters needed for each story. Compile the results and create a priority buying list. There are two possible approaches to collecting puppets for storytelling. One is to buy specific puppets for specific stories. Here the storyteller buys puppets that were made to accompany a particular story, such as "Beauty and the Beast," which some commercial companies offer. The second approach is to buy a general collection of puppets and to adapt them by adding physical props and interchangeable costuming. In this way a single puppet may be used in many stories. For example, a little girl could play the part of Little Red Riding Hood simply through the addition of a red cape; Rapunzel, by adding long, yellow yarn hair;

Novelty puppet. A small-box frog pops out of a larger-box prince to show transformation from one character to another.

and a princess, with the addition of a crown and a simple robe. This approach allows the storyteller more flexibility and obviously stretches the puppet budget further.

## BUILDING A BASIC PUPPET REPERTORY

A basic puppet collection for storytelling with preschool children might include a repertory cast of a man/boy, a woman/girl, a wolf, a few other animals, a troll/monster, plus one or two characters suggested by the list of stories to be told. Since the basic nursery stories are so important and loved, consider adding the required number and graduated sizes of characters for "The Three Bears," "The Three Pigs," and "The Three Billy Goats Gruff." For a collection to be used with older children, you may want to add an old woman and an old man since many stories feature these human characters.

When buying puppets check to see that the seams are well secured. Questions to ask yourself should consider the durability of the puppet and its frequency of use. Is the puppet washable? Does the puppet fit the child's or your hand comfortably? Do the puppets you

select have a strong appeal for you personally? It is easier to create personalities for puppets to which you are naturally drawn. A list of puppet manufacturers is included at the end of this chapter.

With some adaptations, your basic puppet group of six to eight puppets can be used to tell almost any story. A few examples of how this may be accomplished are suggested here.

1. The addition of simple costume pieces will enable the animals to play the parts of people. Put a bow tie on the dog and he can take the part of the Worst Person in the World from James Stevenson's book of that name. Add a neck ruffle and some golden curls and the cat becomes Goldilocks. Place distinctive hats on a squirrel and characters ranging from Santa to a valentine can be depicted.
2. Animal puppets may act the part of other animal characters. For example, if you need a monkey for the Indian folktale "The Monkey and the Crocodile," pin a long monkey tail on a mouse puppet and tell the story. Add an elephant's trunk to a bear puppet and you're ready to tell *Stand Back, Said the Elephant, I'm Going to Sneeze* by Patricia

A squirrel hand puppet character with distinctive hats—Mexican, Santa Claus, valentine, chef—to change character

Thomas. Children will enjoy seeing familiar characters double up and be disguised as other characters. Before the story begins announce that Baby Bear has agreed to play the role of the mouse in the next story.

3. Change the costume pieces of the people puppets to allow them to assume a variety of roles. A crown and a velvet cape added to a woman puppet turn her into a queen. Add a green vest to the man puppet and put a toy or cardboard bow and arrow in his hand and he becomes Robin Hood.

4. When characters are limited, children from the group may play the parts of people needed for a story, without puppets.

Use your basic collection in imaginative ways to glean the maximum benefit from it.

## Hand-Constructed Puppets

If financial constraints limit the number of puppets that may be purchased, consider handmade puppets. These offer the flexibility of creating exactly the right character for your needs. While puppet making can be a rich and rewarding experience, keep in mind the time required to turn your "puppet visions" into original creations. Allow for sufficient time and energy.

Patterns for a wide variety of puppets are available in puppet books, pattern books found in fabric stores, and popular craft magazines. Some sources of patterns and construction ideas are included here.

## RESOURCES FOR PUPPET MAKING

Books from which no ordering information is given can be ordered from The Puppetry Store, 1525 - 24th S.E., Auburn, WA 98002-7837. Phone: (206) 833-8377; Fax (206) 939-4213.

Backer, Karen. *Easy Puppet Patterns*; illus. by the author. n.p., n.d.

Patterns for a variety of furry creatures with talking mouths.

Cochrane, Louise. *Shadow Puppets in Color*; illus. by Kate Simunck. Plays, 1972.

An introduction to an exciting and unusual form of shadow puppetry. Plays and puppet patterns for three traditional shadow plays are included.

Hunt, Tamara, and Nancy Renfro. *Pocketful of Puppets: Mother Goose*; illus. by Nancy Renfro. Nancy Renfro Studios, 1987.

Colorful booklet containing many ideas for creating puppets from Mother Goose rhymes coupled with presentation techniques. Other titles available in this series.

Keefe, Betty. *Fingerpuppets, Fingerplays and Holidays.* Special Literature Press, 1984.

Twelve original fingerplays centered around popular and "should be" popular holidays. Many finger puppet patterns are included.

Long, Teddy Cameron. *Make Your Own Performing Puppets*; illus. by the author. Sterling, 1995.

Directions for a variety of appealing puppets are included: sock, hand, shadow, bag, and marionette. Suggestions for constructing buildings and backdrops could easily be applied to tabletop theaters.

*Making and Using Puppets in the Primary Grades* (videocassette) by Susan Barthel, Bruce Chesse, and the Oregon Puppet Theatre. Puppet Concepts, 1992.

A lively presentation of puppet making activities geared for the primary-age child. A teacher's guide is included.

Masson, Anne. *The Magic of Marionettes*; illus. by the author. Annick Press, 1989.

A "how-to" guide that clearly explains all aspects of creating and using marionettes.

Paludan, Liz. *Playing with Puppets*; illus. by the author. Plays, 1975.

One of the best books on varied and colorful sewn puppets. Well illustrated with colored photographs. Includes many patterns and construction techniques.

Pittman, Jeanne. *Fanciful Furry Finger Friends*; illus. by the author. Pittman Puppet Productions, 1983.

Instructions and patterns for making an assortment of animal finger puppets. Other booklets available contain directions for sea and shore creatures, dinosaurs, and nativity characters.

Renfro, Nancy. *Puppetry and the Art of Story Creation*; illus. by the author. Nancy Renfro Studios, 1979.

The first half of the book describes simple techniques for developing stories and scripts. The second half is filled with unique ideas for creating simple puppets from inexpensive materials.

Renfro, Nancy, and Bev Armstrong. *Make Amazing Puppets*; illus. by Bev Armstrong. Learning Works, 1980.

A book filled with lots of clever, easy-to-make puppet ideas, including trick puppets, puppets you can wear, and cardboard marionettes.

Rottman, Fran. *Easy to Make Puppets and How to Use Them: Children and Youth*; illus. by the author. Regal, 1978.

Designed for leaders working with puppets in the church, vacation Bible school, day camp, scout groups, etc. Many patterns are included. By the same author: *Easy to Make Puppets and How to Use Them: Early Childhood*. Regal, 1978.

Scholz, Claire E. *Some Puppet Patterns and Stuff*; illus. by the author. Dragons, 1976.

Instructions and patterns are shown for a basic, movable-mouth puppet that can be expanded into other characters.

Sims, Judy. *Puppets for Dreaming and Scheming*; illus. by Beverly Armstrong. Learning Works, 1988.

Directions for constructing mouth, stick, finger, and shadow puppets. Ideas for staging manipulation, voices, and puppet uses make this an excellent resource for adults.

Wallace, Mary. *I Can Make Puppets*; illus. by the author. Owl, 1994.

Clever ideas for creating puppets with props, hands, and scrap materials.

Warren, Jean. *1\*2\*3 Puppets*; illus. by Cora L. Walker. Warren Publishing House, 1989.

A collection of ideas and puppet patterns to make for working with young children.

Wright, Lyndie. *Puppets*; photos by Chris Fairclough. Franklin Watts, 1989.

Ideas for easy to make bag, plate, finger, plastic-bottle, and other puppets. Also included a brief history of puppetry.

### Materials

For making your own puppets, it is necessary to have a wide variety of materials from which to choose. The fabric selected for a puppet should complement the puppet's personality or role. Rich-looking materials such as velour, brocade, and gold trim or braid suggest royalty. Terry cloth, fake fur, striped and dotted double knits all work well for animal characters. Shimmering metallic fabrics are effective for underwater creatures as well as those from outer space. Lace and netting can be used to suggest the ethereal effect desirable for angels and fairies. A number of materials are suitable for puppet hair. Yarn, polyester or cotton batting, and fake fur will produce realistic-looking hair. Fringed paper, mops, raffia, twine, string, and rope produce a rougher and more uneven effect. Strips of burlap or twisted rags produce a coarse, colorful hair style.

## Features

The *eyes* of a puppet greatly influence the style and mood of the finished character. Materials applied as eyes vary, depending on desired effect. Before permanently attaching eyes to a puppet, place the selected choices on the puppet's face to see if the proper look is achieved. Large, bulging eyes can be made with table-tennis balls, corks, egg-carton sections, paper muffin cups, milk bottle tops, and marbles. For small, delicate eyes experiment with sequins, beads, straight-pin heads, or pearl buttons. Felt and other materials may be cut and layered to produce a variety of eye shapes and sizes. Other materials suitable for eyes include paper, paper fasteners, buttons of all shapes and sizes, tinfoil, pom-poms, and plastic craft eyes. Fringed trims make excellent eyelashes.

*Noses* do a great deal to add character to puppets. A cork or table-tennis ball painted red becomes just the right nose for a clown. Simple, cute noses for children or feminine characters or whimsical animals can be made from pom-poms, beads, or buttons. Shapes cut from sponges, polyfoam, egg cartons, and cardboard make interesting noses. Thread spools, bottle caps, thimbles, and other such items also are possibilities for nose designs. Stuffed fabric noses, sewn from fabric that matches the puppet's face, are fun to explore and can produce unique solutions. A long, crooked stuffed nose would be perfect for a pirate or witch; a round, fat one for Santa or a gnome; an elongated, thin nose for Pinocchio.

*Cheeks and mouths* can be cut from felt materials. Red cording or braiding can outline a mouth shape. White rickrack, zigzag cut felt, or pieces cut from white plastic containers make excellent teeth. The mouth, like the eyes, offers some of the best opportunities for enhancing character. Experiment with different shaped mouths for achieving expression. A clown might have an exaggerated, large upturned smile; Goldilocks a cute little pout; and a lion fierce, exposed jagged teeth.

Buttons or felt circular shapes placed flat against the puppet head or protruding from the head create two distinctive *ear* styles. Pipe cleaners twisted into bizarre shapes make ears worthy of the most fantastic character. Warts, chins, hair, and other features can be constructed from fabric trims, feathers, rickrack, felt, and fake fur, as well as many of the materials previously described. These features may be attached with white glue, fabric glue, rubber cement, or an electric glue gun. (The glue gun is not for children to use.) In addition, features may be drawn on with felt-tip markers, fabric crayons, or paint. Tempera paint, textile paint, acrylic paint in a tube, and flat-latex wall paint all work well. Try outlining the features with a dark or contrasting color to heighten the shape and call attention to the expression.

Consider interchangeability of features for expanding the expression potential of a puppet's character. By sewing on pieces of Velcro in the eye and mouth areas, features can be quickly changed to fill new roles or moods within the story. By switching the mouth of Chibi from *Crow Boy* his transformation from a sad to a contented character can be portrayed.

A summary listing of materials and tools for making puppets and features follows.

## Tools and Supplies

Basic tools and supplies include: sharp scissors (for adults only), sewing machine, white glue, fabric glue or rubber cement, masking and cellophane tape, needle and thread, hole punch, stapler and staples, ruler, paper fasteners (large and small sizes), rubber bands.

In addition to a sewing machine and a good pair of scissors, two other tools are a must for the puppet-making enthusiast. The electric glue gun, available at most hardware and discount stores, is used with all-purpose glue and has invaluable uses as a substitute for the thread and needle. When the gun is plugged in, a small nylon pellet melts and is then applied to the surfaces to be glued, drying quickly and forming a high-strength joint. This tool requires care in handling in order to avoid contact of the hot material with your fingers. It is a tool for adults only to use, not children.

The second recommended tool is a sturdy, long-nose, hand-grip type stapler, of the kind used in check-out counters at stores. An excellent model is the Arrow brand #P–22 model.

## Fabrics

The following are very useful: felt, synthetic fake fur, netting, lace, velour, metallic fabric, suede cloth, felt, upholstery samples, terry cloth, burlap, cotton, double knit, dotted swiss. Keep in mind that conventional felts are inferior materials for puppet making. They do not wear well nor are they washable. A polyester felt product has recently appeared on the market which is proving to be a boon to the puppet maker. This felt substitute has superior qualities in both strength and washability. Inquire at your local fabric store about these fabrics, some of which sell under the brand names of Phun Phelt and Poly Felt.

## Trims

A few common and versatile trims include: rickrack, ribbon, drapery pom-poms, metallic trims, eyelets, braiding.

## Craft Items

A wide range of craft items is available, including feathers, raffia, yarn, pipe cleaners, sequins, beads, twine, plastic eyes, pom-poms.

## Throwaways

The following may be found in most households: egg cartons, cereal and other food boxes, plastic milk containers, yogurt cups, Styrofoam, plastic-bubble packing material, old socks, cardboard tubes, lipstick and toothpaste boxes, and egg-shaped hosiery containers.

## Odds and Ends

Keeping one's eyes open will, with a little searching, produce the following: old costume jewelry, mops, dishcloths, pot holders, umbrella ribs, drinking straws, table-tennis balls, bells, wallpaper books, string, pipe cleaners, florist's wire, nylon stockings, yarn, cotton batting or fiberfill, paper cups and plates, paper bags of all sizes, wooden skewers, stick-on and gummed reinforcers and stars, letter envelopes, clothespins, corks, sequins, beads, clear and colored acetate sheets.

## Community Resources for the Puppet Collection

To build a puppet collection when funds are not in the budget, outside sources must be tapped. Groups such as Friends of the Library or PTA groups might be solicited for funds. Donations of time, materials, and money can be sought from a variety of sources.

Set up a barrel or box and request contributions of materials suitable for use in puppet making. Parents, coworkers, and community organizations are all possible sources. Local merchants, dressmakers, and tailors are often willing to contribute scraps or to sell materials at cost. Post or distribute a notice asking for a broad range of materials. When it becomes known that you are interested in puppets, you will undoubtedly become the recipient of a great many cast-off toys, old puppets, and a variety of scrap materials. Accept everything you are offered. With some imagination you can turn most of these donations into unusual puppets.


## PUPPET MANUFACTURERS AND DEALERS

The following list presents a wide assortment of puppet manufacturers and dealers across the country. Some of these suppliers sell wholesale and retail; others sell only wholesale. However, with a minimum order that may range from $100 to $200 some will sell to the noncommercial purchaser. A free catalog and individual ordering policies may be obtained by writing to these suppliers.

Applause Inc. (Retail)
6101 Variel Avenue, P.O. Box 4183, Woodland Hills, CA 91365-4183

Hand puppets include animals, Lamp Chop, Muppet, and Disney characters. Three storytime mitt puppets sized for adult hands include Little Red Riding Hood, This Little Piggy, and Goldilocks.

Country Critters, Made in Kansas (Retail & wholesale)
Box D, Burlington, KS 66839

Features soft, plush puppets, including several types of bears, raccoon, lamb, and other cuddly animals. A selection of extra-large puppets is also available.

Creative Instructional Puppetry (Retail)
3425 Witmer Parkway, Des Moines, IA 50310

Charming, handmade felt hand puppets depicting children's favorite characters. Holiday characters; Mother Goose friends; zoo, circus, and farm animals; and community workers are also offered,

individually or in sets. A complete listing is available for special orders.

Dakin & Co. (Retail & wholesale)
P.O. Box 7746, Rincon Annex, San Francisco, CA 94120

This well-known toy company produces an extensive line of hand puppets and plush toys made of soft, cuddly fabrics that includes most animals popular with children.

Folkmanis (Wholesale)
1219 Park Avenue, Emeryville, CA 94608

A selection of twenty-three cuddly, furry wildlife creatures, some of which have baby offspring, is offered. Includes seals, bears, rabbits, squirrels, and other woodland animals.

Mary Meyer Mfg. Co., Inc. (Wholesale)
P.O. Box 275, Townshend, VT 05353-0275

Distributes a large selection of soft toys as well as an extensive collection of award winning two-finger finger puppets. The selection includes over forty animal puppets, a few character puppets, and storytime packages. A small number of three-finger finger puppets and puppet display racks are also available.

One Way Street, Inc.
Box 5077, Englewood, CO 80155-5077

Puppet scripts, cassettes, stages, and a variety of puppets, including ventriloquists' puppets, are offered by this supplier. Focus is on Children's Ministries resources.

Pakaluk Puppets (Retail & wholesale)
P.O. Box 129, Fredericksburg, TX 78624

Stocks a colorful, well-designed line of original hand puppets that includes most popular animals (with cute talking sock mouths) and basic people. Features large rod-action puppets and a small sock puppet line that is especially appealing.

Puppet Safari (Retail)
326 W. Eleventh Street, National City, CA 91950

Offers a collection of hand and finger puppets that will appeal to storytellers and educators. Mother Goose, the three billy goats Gruff, a troll, witch, wolf, Santa, bears, and pigs are all available.

Nancy Renfro Studios (Retail)
3312 Pecan Springs Rd., Austin, TX 78723

Over three hundred handcrafted, washable, durable puppet characters for use in storytelling, show production, library, and classroom are offered. Selection includes people puppets of various flesh tones and almost every type of animal, holiday, and fairy-tale character. A large "Old Lady Who Swallowed a Fly" puppet and the characters she swallows is the most popular item from this company.

## SUGGESTED TITLES FOR BUILDING THE PUPPET COLLECTION

Flack, Marjorie. *Ask Mr. Bear*; illus. by the author. Macmillan, 1932 (1958, 1966).

A bear suggests the perfect gift for Danny to give to his mother.

Galdone, Paul. *The Monkey and the Crocodile*; illus. by the author. Seabury, 1969.

A picture-book version of the Indian Jataka tale.

Gretz, Susanna. *Teddy Bears 1 to 10*; illus. by the author. Macmillan, 1986.

The route teddy bears follow from dirty to clean makes a delightful counting book.

Stevenson, James. *The Worst Person in the World*; illus. by the author. Greenwillow, 1978.

The ugliest creature in the world has a great effect on the behavior of the worst person in the world.

Thomas, Patricia. *Stand Back, Said the Elephant, I'm Going to Sneeze*; illus. by Wallace Tripp. Lothrop, 1990.

Everyone takes cover when the elephant finally sneezes.

Yashima, Taro. *Crow Boy*; illus. by the author. Viking, 1955.

Chibi, a lonely Japanese boy, is treated as an outcast by his classmates until a sensitive teacher helps him to earn the respect of the students. A Caldecott Honor book.

# Chapter 5     DEVELOPING PUPPETS FOR STORYTELLING

CREATING A DESIRABLE and workable character for a puppet is an aspect of puppetry that is both enjoyable and essential. "Character" refers to the specific impression a puppet conveys in its story or helping role. Although "personality" is part of a puppet's character, that by itself is insufficient. Now let's look at some considerations in planning the character of the puppet.

For most informal storytelling, only a basic foundation of the puppet's character is necessary to give the story form and interest. The usually complete character development seen in animated films, for example, is not necessary for our purposes. Yet we should plan and practice sufficiently so that the puppet fits into the story role or the helping role appropriately and consistently.

Puppet characterization is a composite of many internal and external characteristics. To sum up any particular character on the basis of a simple descriptive term such as "mean" or "nice" is only the most elementary beginning and does not present a clear enough picture of its true personality. Such a broad description is, of course, a start from which we must develop more specifics.

Let's take the wolf in "Little Red Riding Hood" as an example. The Big Bad Wolf may be a mean wolf, but we can also round him out further, making him more interesting by saying that he is also nervous and conniving. These new elements enrich the character. We now have a wolf who is not only mean, but also one whose nerves are constantly in tatters and who thoroughly enjoys employing novel tactics such as those he tries in "Little Red Riding Hood."

## SPECIFIC CHARACTER TRAITS

As we progress into the study of specific character traits for developing puppets, we will also be developing traits for three popular story characters as examples of actual personality development. These story characters are Little Red Riding Hood and the Old Man and Old Woman in *Millions of Cats* by Wanda Gág. In the case of Little Red Riding Hood a comparison is made between two opposing examples, a traditional and nontraditional character (versions 1 and 2). The following character traits or attributes will be examined: personality, physical shape, movements, voice, and idiosyncrasies. A chart may serve as a way of developing traits for your puppets. (See completed Character Traits Chart in this chapter on p. 66.)

## Personality

Personality refers to the values, beliefs, and philosophy of living which a person—or puppet—consistently expresses. These are internal characteristics, to be sure; the only way one knows what is part of a specific puppet's personality is by the frequency and consistency with which these values and beliefs are expressed. Therefore, it is important to remember to "show" your audience the puppet's personality; the audience doesn't know the puppet as well as you, the puppeteer, do.

An old-looking puppet who expresses young, modern ideas is revealing part of a personality. For this to be believable, however, that puppet must convey these modern ideas at least two or three times and in a consistent manner. If the puppet states modern ideas one moment and old ideas the next, a "spell" is broken, and the audience may become confused in the process of readjusting to the character. "Keeping in character," then, is a primary goal for the storyteller, which can be best achieved through practice of decided personality characteristics.

The shaping of a puppet's personality will be determined by the story intent, its interpretation by the storyteller, and the storyteller's personal style. While one person will enjoy creating a character with an offbeat personality, another may prefer a more straightforward portrayal. While straightforward interpretations are usually easier to crystallize, nontraditional personality types might also be experimented with. However, no matter how simple a puppet's personality may appear to be, some previous thought should be given to its formation and refinement.

The following illustrates two personality examples of the same character in a search for descriptive terms.

### Contrasting Personalities for Little Red Riding Hood

| VERSION 1 | VERSION 2 |
| --- | --- |
| Sweet | Sassy |
| Naive | Know-it-all |

The first version portrays the traditional interpretation of the sweet little girl; the second is that of a sassy child. The events of the story and the interactions of the other characters with the main character will be determined differently in each version. A sweet, naive little girl's response to the questions of the bad wolf will more likely be honest and direct, whereas the know-it-all child will have some evasive ideas of her own. She will not be quite as gullible as in the former version and, more likely than not, will know how to take care of herself in the dark brooding woods while maintaining the lead in controlling the wolf's behavior.

As other traits, such as physical shape, movement, voice, and idiosyncrasies, are considered, two very distinct characterizations for Little Red Riding Hood may emerge.

For now, however, let's discuss other considerations in personality development. In developing characters for any given story, building an interesting personality into each main character adds depth and credibility to the story. Contrast between the main characters also helps the child recognize the protagonist and antagonist of the story.

For example, Little Red Riding Hood and the Big Bad Wolf are obviously easy characters for building contrasting personality types. Such contrast makes for easy casting of characters when it comes to adapting puppets to the story.

There are, however, many instances in children's literature in which the two strong leads have similar personalities. Notable examples include the celebrated characters in *George and Martha* (two hippopotamuses) by James Marshall, the Frog and Toad series (two frogs) by Arnold Lobel, and *Millions of Cats* (old man and woman) by Wanda Gág. As storytellers who are free to adapt the story for puppet sharing, we have the opportunity to develop strong dramatic interest by building contrasting personalities into the presentation.

For example, in the original story of *Millions of Cats*, the Old Man and the Old Woman are both defined in similar terms as sweet and kind people. Wouldn't it make a more colorful puppet presentation to portray them with contrasting personalities?

### Contrasting Personalities for Millions of Cats

| OLD WOMAN | OLD MAN |
| --- | --- |
| Jolly | Cantankerous |
| Quick-witted | Forgetful |

Here we are laying a foundation for stark contrast, however basic it appears. No longer do we have two sweet and kind people as the story originally assumed but, rather, a visualization of more distinct characters is beginning to take form—a humorous Old Woman is juxtaposed to a cranky and absentminded Old Man. Each of these characters will affect the other's personality in marked ways. The Old Woman, being jolly and quick-witted, will probably take the lead of the two, humoring along any negativism that arises from her cranky spouse. The Old Man, being forgetful, could add to the events of the story as he constantly misplaces things or thoughts. Perhaps he forgets to bring the one remaining cat home at all!

Remember that contrast makes for more interesting presentations and this, incidentally, will make personality development of the main puppets easier for you. By planning the personality traits in advance for each puppet, you will prevent indecisiveness while laying out a stalwart foundation upon which to build the story presentation.

## Physical Shape

The physical shape is a consideration over which you may have little or no control. This, of course, depends on whether you are making the puppet from scratch, adapting a ready-made puppet, or utilizing the puppet as is from your basic collection. If you are constructing the puppet specifically to fit a particular character, it is to your advantage to develop its personality on paper first. Knowing what the puppet is like internally will naturally be of great assistance in

**Character traits comparison of versions 1 and 2 of Little Red Riding Hood**

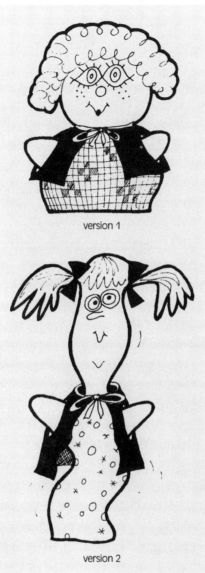

version 1

version 2

deciding what it should look like externally.

When an existing basic puppet is being used for a specific story character, shape-changing ideas may be temporarily employed. For example, cotton batting may be stuffed inside a hand puppet to emphasize girth; an additional skirt or body piece may be added to a short puppet's body to give the impression of height or slenderness.

Little Red Riding Hood has two possibilities in shape exploration for our two original versions.

### Contrasting Shapes for Little Red Riding Hood

| VERSION 1 | VERSION 2 |
|-----------|-----------|
| Round | Skinny |
| Short | Tall |

The shape of the character alone does not tell us very much. It becomes significant only as it is combined with other personality traits, particularly the puppet's internal qualities and the way it moves in conjunction with the shape. It would have been just as easy to create a shape for our sweet and naive version of Little Red Riding Hood that is skinny, squarish, or long waisted. This physical characteristic only becomes an extension of the internal one and helps us to determine how the puppet should move. For instance, a sweet and naive, round little girl may suggest movement that is much bouncier than if she had been classified as a sassy, skinny girl, whose movements could take on other patterns such as awkward or jerky.

### Contrasting Shapes for <u>Millions of Cats</u>

Notice the ease in contrast which shape allows for in *Millions of Cats:*

| OLD WOMAN | OLD MAN |
|---|---|
| Fat | Thin |
| Bottom-heavy | Tall |

Such things as humor or exaggeration can also be expressed in shape definition. For example, the suggestions above could be reversed, with the Old Man being short and small in shape to contrast with an overly cumbersome wife, creating an effect contrary to the stereotyped views of couples. In many cases general terms, such as thin and tall, can be used to describe a character's basic shape. Specific terms, however, are more fun to explore and can add unusual interest. A big-nosed giant, knobby-kneed girl, or long-necked cat all have comic qualities that intrigue an audience.

## Movement

Much about the character of the puppet can be told by its movement. All movement conveys messages to the audience—from the simple "yes" nod to the more abstract expressions such as "happiness" suggested by lively up-and-down movements of the body. These ideas along with the way a given character actually ambulates in space (walks, runs, hops) round out the puppet character into a total personality. Once a movement and style have been allotted a puppet, they should remain consistent throughout the presentation. The wolf who hovers close to the ground and moves with short, creeping motions should remain so throughout the story unless a contrasting effect or emphasis is desired. Such a case might be if the wolf is suddenly startled, causing him to make a long leap into the air or across the playing space.

Movement possibilities for the three characters being examined follow.

### Movements for Little Red Riding Hood

| VERSION 1 | VERSION 2 |
|---|---|
| Bouncy | Awkward |
| Agile | Loose-jointed |

It appears that the design of the puppet's movement is influenced greatly by the previously established personality and shape traits given the character. It would be hard to visualize the movements of a sassy, tall, and skinny Little Red Riding Hood as slow or heavy. If she did not pursue awkward or loose-jointed movements as recommended above, then she could possibly fit other appropriate alternative movement patterns, such as jouncy, shuffling, or skipping.

### Movements for <u>Millions of Cats</u>

| OLD WOMAN | OLD MAN |
|---|---|
| Heavy | Wobbly |
| Smooth | Uncertain |

Here we have contrast between two distinctly opposing movement patterns. A fat, bottom-heavy person who moves in large, heavy, but smooth movements, while shifting weight from one spot to another, is next to a more fragile character who shakes at every limb and is uncertain of each step he takes. These are movements of more subtle detailing that add depth and interest to the character, as opposed to using more common descriptive terms such as slow and fast.

## Voice

The voice completes the personality and gives the character as much coloration as its movements or physical shape. A voice can be as simple in quality as being high or low in pitch. As in the shaping of all the puppet's characteristics, it can retain additional subleties that create richness. A sputtering speech pattern, growly timbre, or tantalizing squeals expand voice repertoire and give individuality to the character. Keep in mind then not only the pitch level, but the patterning of the speech, interjections of sounds, or other peculiar quirks a voice might have. Remember that vocal and visual appeal are often synonymous in creating a total impression.

### Voices for Little Red Riding Hood

| VERSION 1 | VERSION 2 |
| --- | --- |
| Singsong | Zippy |
| Soft | Loud |

It is obvious that a sweet and naive version of Little Red Riding Hood will have a voice that harmonizes with those qualities. A singsong trait is a pleasant choice for this version which can only enhance further her innate sweetness. A zippy, loud voice would certainly be appropriate for the sassy, know-it-all version. It would be hard to visualize the voices in reverse formation in these two versions.

### Voices for Millions of Cats

| OLD WOMAN | OLD MAN |
| --- | --- |
| Hearty | Feeble |
| Loud | Sputtering |

Here again the assigned voices reflect an outgrowth of the preestablished personalities while continuing to give the desired contrast. A hearty voice next to a feeble one is a dramatic contrast and one that will capture the imagination of the audience. The voices are so clearly opposite that the storyteller will find them easy to manage and the audience easy to distinguish. So often characters with voices of similar tonal qualities can become confusing for the audience in knowing exactly which character is speaking. If the audience can strongly associate a certain tone with one character and a contrasting tone with another, the roles are immediately recognizable.

## Idiosyncrasy

While at this point the character has almost everything required to mold it into a legitimate personality, the addition of an idiosyncrasy is one last element that adds a human touch and makes the personality stand out entirely on its own. This peculiar trait could fall into any of the trait categories discussed. The important point is that such an idiosyncrasy becomes that character's trademark. This does not mean the idiosyncrasy is necessarily something humorous. It means only that the puppet does something that is unusual enough for the audience to pick up on it. Note the distinguishing idiosyncrasies for the examples below.

### Idiosyncrasies for Little Red Riding Hood

| VERSION 1 | VERSION 2 |
| --- | --- |
| Talks to flowers | Trips over things |

Our sweet and naive version of Little Red Riding Hood is one of those types who could conceivably believe that flowers talk and who is drawn to their natural beauty. A talking flower might cleverly be introduced in this version of the story during Little Red's jaunt through the woods and before she meets up with the big bad wolf. In our second version, a sassy and awkward Little Red Riding Hood probably has her nose more up in the air than down and therefore never quite watches where she is walking, so she continually trips over rocks and small animals.

### Idiosyncrasies for Millions of Cats

| OLD WOMAN | OLD MAN |
| --- | --- |
| Bursts into fits of laughter | Drops cane |

A hearty character such as the rotund Old Woman could be easily visualized as one who bursts into fits of laughter, sometimes over hardly anything at all. It is simply one of these quirks which expands her effervescence. Since we have already established the Old Man as being feeble in every aspect, it is apparent that he has difficulty holding things steady, especially in the case of carrying a cane. His wife may continually pick this up for him and thus it becomes a constant concern for all.

# CHARACTER TRAITS CHART

Having gone through the several factors that comprise the puppet's characterizations, we can now combine the traits into a complete chart for each sample character. This allows us to visualize the overall picture of the puppet character we have developed, at least on paper. From here, this tangible material gives us a basic foundation upon which to build the story presentation.

**Character Traits Chart for Little Red Riding Hood**

|  | VERSION 1 | VERSION 2 |
|---|---|---|
| *Personality* | Sweet<br>Naive | Sassy<br>Know-it-all |
| *Shape* | Round<br>Short | Skinny<br>Tall |
| *Movements* | Bouncy<br>Agile | Awkward<br>Loose-jointed |
| *Voice* | Singsong<br>Soft | Zippy<br>Loud |
| *Idiosyncrasy* | Talks to flowers | Trips over things |

Note that although the first version of Little Red Riding Hood appears to have much less dramatic interest, feature for feature, than the second version, the entire personality composition remains one whose total makes either character fun to portray. However, the second version is definitely a bolder creation in style. A storyteller who appreciates broad humor would enjoy presenting the second version. Note that "endearing" would be the key word to describe the first version's overall character as opposed to "comical" for the second version of Little Red Riding Hood.

In either case we no longer see Little Red Riding Hood as a bland, nondescript, ordinary little girl. Strong images come into play and the little girl suddenly comes alive. Even a story that is weak in structure has opportunities here for gaining new power through such a tool.

**Character Traits Chart for Millions of Cats**

|  | OLD WOMAN | OLD MAN |
|---|---|---|
| *Personality* | Jolly<br>Quick-witted | Cantankerous<br>Forgetful |
| *Shape* | Fat<br>Bottom-heavy | Thin<br>Tall |
| *Movements* | Heavy<br>Smooth | Wobbly<br>Uncertain |
| *Voice* | Hearty<br>Loud | Feeble<br>Sputtering |
| *Idiosyncrasy* | Bursts into fits<br>of laughter | Drops cane |

In *Millions of Cats*, the two lead personalities are very similar in temperament. As we have developed the characters throughout this chapter, they have taken on contrasting and more interesting traits. These could serve as models for future similar story analysis and character portrayals. The preceding chart brings out this contrast clearly.

Now that the puppet has established character traits, the storyteller has a concise tool to serve as a transmitter of the tale. Remember that not every character in a story needs to be developed to the same extent. Spend time on the main characters; let the remainder serve as supporting cast. Too many characters with strongly defined personalities may tend to compete, making them ineffectual on an individual basis. In any case the shaping of the puppet's character remains invaluable in working toward the actual presentation. It is this highly creative and rewarding aspect of storytelling with puppets that is often overlooked, yet which brings special relevance and reality to the story.

# DEVELOPING VOICE AND COMMUNICATION

Discovering appropriate voice for puppets may be a new, untapped skill for many storytellers. Most of us go through life accepting and taking for granted the one voice that comes most naturally to us. Thus, it may come as a great surprise when a potential for other voices is unveiled. Not merely two or three voices, but perhaps as many as ten or more may be yet undiscovered because we simply never gave them any thought.

An excellent exercise by which to discover these untapped voices is to place a puppet on your hand and read the same paragraph a number of times. Each time focus on the essence of a particular adjective and try to communicate and interpret the passage in light of that adjective. For example, consider the following words as cues for interpretation of your chosen paragraphs:

*Happy:* indicate with excitable, up-and-down tonal qualities, or dialogue read in short, rapid gasps.

*Sleepy:* express with exaggerated slowness, stopping to yawn occasionally or permitting the voice to taper off in the middle of sentences and beginning to snore.

*Pompous:* emphasize self-assertive quality by projecting each word fully and deliberately, one at a time, with a punctuating effect.

*Silly:* interject giggles or laughter from time to time; add a flighty, nervous quality to the voice to embellish this effect even further.

An excellent aid in further helping the storyteller to find the "right" voice for the puppet is not only to "think" the voice characteristic but also to "feel" it as well. For instance, if the puppet is to convey "sleepiness," it is important for the storyteller to simulate this sense of drowsiness first, and then try to transmit this feeling to the puppet. Pomposity, likewise, can be expressed by proudly puffing out your chest, jutting out your chin (like a king or peacock) in concert with the puppet's corresponding action. Other adjectives to explore are:

| | | | |
|---|---|---|---|
| sad | fast | hilarious | jerky |
| weird | grumpy | robust | limpid |
| slow | sweet | highbrow | stuffy |
| whimpering | beautiful | mean | assertive |

This exploratory approach serves to offer the storyteller a fuller understanding of the character's current state or emotional feeling.

## Expressing Speech Through Movement

When matching a voice to a puppet, consider the puppet's physical features, size, character, etc., to see what these suggest for voice characteristics. A graceful ballerina might call for a melodious, lyrical voice, while a menacing crocodile would speak more appropriately with a clattering, aggressive voice. Whether a puppet actually has a moving mouth or not doesn't alter or limit voice possibilities. In other words, the voice requirements remain the same, regardless of puppet type. However, the physical movements which complement the voice are expressed quite differently. A puppet with a talking mouth must rely on the patterning of speech in conjunction with mouth movements for expression. However, the puppet with a mouth that is not movable, such as the standard hand puppet with flexible body or rod-type puppet, must compensate by emphasizing dialogue through the corresponding movement of other parts. Accentuated actions may be achieved with specific motions, such as a nod of the head or a twist of the body, in synchronization with dialogue.

Sometimes a word will clearly dictate to the storyteller a particular movement. A shake of the head to reinforce the word "No!" or beckoning with a paw or hand to signify "Come here!" are suitable matching gestures. Many such movements exist that will enhance any corresponding dialogue. Try expressing some of the following ideas with your puppet, pairing movement with speech:

| | |
|---|---|
| Halt! | I don't know. |
| I like you. | Ugh! |
| Go away! | Hi! |
| Be quite. | Over there. |

It may be of help to you in capturing the essence of ideas such as those listed above to actually perform the expressions yourself without the puppet.

## Expressing Speech with a Talking-Mouth Puppet

Dialogue spoken by a puppet that has a moving or talking mouth requires special patterning of the mouth's movement to parallel the physical motions of the spoken words. For some people this synchronization comes naturally and not much actual timing or preparation is required. For others, a degree of planning is necessary to insure good results. You may first wish to try an unconscious approach, whereby you focus on the general flow of the dialogue rather than each opening and closing mouth movement. Let the dialogue take a forward lead, while the puppet's mouth is activated more or less automatically. However, if you feel yourself getting clumsy or bogged down with complicated mouth movement, you may wish to try some of the following exercises for synchronizing mouth movements with dialogue.

### Principle 1
A general rule to remember with all dialogue is that the puppet's mouth should always begin a sentence in an open position (indicated as O) and end every sentence in a closed position (indicated as C).

### Principle 2
Open the puppet's mouth on the accented syllables only rather than on every single syllable. For example:

Mis–sis–sip–pi
O    C    O    C

In this instance the mouth opens and closes only twice rather than four times as it would on all syllables.

### Principle 3
Patterning can also be designed to accentuate particular words for entire sentences. For example:

There's a pup–pet–eer hid–ing in the clos–et!
   O  C  O    C O    C    O C

In this case multisyllables or more than two words can be effectively slurred over and treated as a unit of sound with one open and closed mouth movement.

### Principle 4
There will be times, also, when the patterning of the mouth movement will dictate the desired emphasis of the sentence. For example:

 I  don't  like  snow!
OC  OC  OC  OC

This patterning clearly isolates each word, making individual words stand out with penetrating emphasis.

Another emphasis may be chosen to give a little less drama:

 I  don't  like  snow!
OC  O   C   OC

This patterning creates a less harsh and softer effect and significantly changes the overall meaning of the sentence.

Repeated practice sessions in front of a mirror will help the storyteller gain new skills in matching dialogue with movement and eventually, the puppeteer-storyteller's hand will find itself responding automatically to the flow of the dialogue, and may even find new ways to color sentences with interest.

## Trying on a Voice

The voice itself plays a large role in formulating a puppet's personality. The pitch range of a voice can give contrast within a story, setting it apart from the storyteller's own natural voice. It is important to feel comfortable with a voice. One should not feel a strain on the vocal cords or an overexertion of the speech mechanism when portraying a voice. Try several voices before settling on the one that seems best for the puppet and you.

Following is an exercise to help you create voices of varied tonal range as you explore voice repertoire. Recite the rhyme using the accompanying suggestions:

*Old King Cole was a merry old soul,*
*And a merry old soul was he;*
*He called for his pipe,*
*And he called for his bowl,*
*And he called for his fiddlers three.*

*Each fiddler he had a fiddle,*
*And the fiddles went tweedle-dee;*
*Oh, there's none so rare as can compare,*
*With Old King Cole and his fiddlers three.*

Exercises to become comfortable with your voice follow:

1. Recite Old King Cole in a low-pitched voice, slowly.
2. Repeat it in a high-pitched voice, rapidly.
3. Now alternate high and low voices for every other line.
4. Recite the verse trying to explore other moods by using contrasting adjectives to denote a mood or interpretation. Consider haughty, sad, grumpy, happy, or sleepy as interpretive approaches.
5. Recite the rhyme as if you were a character observing the action, such as: a squeaky little mouse, a tired old man, a carefree child, or a grumpy monster.

When choosing a voice for a puppet be sure that it diverges markedly from your own natural voice. This differentiation helps to set the voice apart and makes it easier for children to concentrate on the puppet, while they easily distinguish your voice from that of the character.

When alternating between various voice ranges, do not be discouraged if at first it feels awkward to shift from one voice to another. This transition merely requires several short practice periods to make it seem more natural.

Ventriloquism is not at all necessary when using puppets in front of young children. This is an art that requires a great deal of practice and skill and narrows the range of voice down considerably. Children attracted by the puppet's actions and dialogue easily ignore the visible mouth movements of the storyteller. It is true that an occasional child may point out the fact that it is the storyteller-puppeteer, not the puppet, who is actually doing the talking. Gently diverting attention away from such comments or simple stating, "Let's pretend that the puppet is talking" should suffice to appease those few children who have any doubts.

## Communication with a "Nontalking" Puppet

Sometimes it may be desirable not to use any voice with a particular puppet. A shy puppet may "communicate" by nibbling fingers from outstretched hands of children or nuzzling noses with the children. Animal puppets can also participate by producing appropriate sounds without using words at all. "Buzzes" for a bee, "oinks" for a pig, or "moos" for a cow can appropriately be uttered to convey meaning without the use of words in such a way as to delight young children. Remember that there is a great range of "moos" available to a cow, and these can express connotations and meanings. Try a sad, a happy, a dejected, and an angry moo. People puppets can also become highly individualistic when a single sound track is built into their character. For example, a witch can flounce about with a repertoire of assorted cackles and screeches; an elf can respond with only whistled answers, made vocally or with a toy whistle; a fairy can "speak" with musical chords played on a guitar, harmonica, or other available instrument. Discovering a new "voice" and, as a result, a new puppet character with specific style and pitch will enhance the already existent skills of the storyteller.

## EXPLORING MOVEMENTS WITH PUPPET TYPES

All types of puppets, because of method of manipulation, have distinct ways of expressing movement. Since the basic hand puppet with a flexible body is the most popular among storytellers as a mode of expression, due to its ability to carry out intricate actions, it is studied in depth in this chapter. Before doing so, however, let's look at the other common puppet types and compare their movement possibilities.

### Stick and Rod Puppets

The simple stick or rod puppets referred to in this book are limited in terms of movement potential. Yet, basic movement can still be interpreted. A gentle bobbing up and down movement while traversing space indicates walking; a more hurried movement, running. If the puppet is a picture image, a decision needs to be made whether to create the image in a full face or side view in relation to the required movement pattern. An interesting effect can be achieved by making the character in profile to show ambulation going in one direction and then, by flipping it to the other profile, show movement in the opposite direction. However, with this type of puppet a great deal can be left to the children's imag-

ination and an image drawn in full face view can still be used to illustrate traveling in a specific direction.

Other small tricks can be explored. Turning the puppet from side to side in rhythm to its speaking of words or phrases indicates that the puppet is talking. A subtle forward-and-backward motion of the upper main body section indicates "yes," conveyed by holding the base of the rod in place while moving the puppet back and forth. "No" is achieved by holding the base of the rod while twisting it from side to side sharply. Be sure to stop these distinct but slight movements when the puppet is not talking. Other ideas to express through movement are:

*Excitement or happiness:* indicate with lively up-and-down movements.

*Anger:* show with a series of spasmodic jerks.

*Tiredness:* express with slow, lagging walking movements.

*Hi:* indicate with a simple forward flick.

*Hopping movements:* portray with stop-and-go jumps.

*Bliss:* express with graceful, swaying motions.

*Beastly:* portray with heavy, lumbering walking movements.

### Finger Puppets

The finger puppet is generally operated on the same principles for movement as the stick or rod puppet. The operating mechanism of the stick is replaced by the finger. The finger is capable of achieving additional movements of a more subtle nature than the stick, due to the fact that the finger is flexible and can bend. For example, humbleness or tiredness can be portrayed by bowing the finger. Finger puppets can also hide or disappear by bending the finger into the palm area, then pop up again in surprise, making them appealing to young children. Some storytellers find they have more dexterity for finger puppet actions if they place the finger puppets on the back of the fingers with the back of the hand facing the audience. With this method puppets can actually disappear out of view.

## String Puppets

Like the rod puppet, the modified one- or two-string puppets described in this book can also express movement in simple terms. If there is a cardboard tube or dowel hand control to which the puppet's strings are attached, it can be operated with only one hand from above. Walking occurs by gently lifting the puppet up and down as it makes a series of consecutive steps when traveling along the floor space. These puppets are naturals to include for activities that require the puppet to travel from one place to another or for dancing. These streamlined versions of string puppets are not, however, ideally suited for exploring more subtle movements such as "yes" or "no."

Some basic movements toward expression can be explored, however, in spite of their limitations. Up-and-down hops can indicate excitement or happiness. Large, lumbering movements reflect the heavy walk of an elephant. Dances can be achieved as the puppeteer moves in rhythm with the puppet. Glides through the air make string puppets perfectly suited for portraying birds, superheroes, and space creatures. If there is more than one string, movement can also be isolated. For instance, the head section of a character can rotate back and forth as if looking around, while the body section remains stationary.

## Overhead Shadow Puppets

Since the overhead glass is small in area, controlled, concise movements of puppets are most effective. Because these movements are projected onto a large screen they are naturally magnified to the viewer and create an exaggerated effect. All the images of the characters should be well defined to express their movements clearly. In planning a course of action when moving the cast across the glass area, think of the glass in terms of a stage. Characters can all enter from one side and exit from the other. A bird or plane can fly across the upper area of the glass or a bunny can pop up from an imaginary hole at the bottom. Puppets can also move around the perimeter of the space. A cow taking a stroll can walk along the base, up one side, across the sky, then back down the other side to create a silly effect. Overhead shadow puppets, being a form of stick puppet, can achieve many of the simple movements of that type of puppet—hops, walks, skips, and jumps. But the most intriguing actions occur when these puppets contain animated parts with separate controls. Hinged together with paper fasteners, an arm can wave, legs walk, elephant trunks swing up and down, rabbit ears wiggle, snakes slither (in several sections), jaw sections talk, and tree branches shake. Older children are particularly fascinated with working these special animation effects.

## Hand Puppets

The hand puppet with flexible arms is one of the most adaptable and, therefore, most universally recognized of all puppets for expressing a broad range of movements. It is capable of transmitting an elaborate combination of gestures, ranging from the most subtle to the more exaggerated. Before going into movement there are two things a hand puppet should strive for throughout a presentation—good poise and consistent posture. A puppet that tends to droop or tilt down because of a tired hand or for other reasons makes a poor tool for expression. Keep the puppet's body straight at all times unless a specific posture is required to define the character, such as a bent-over old man or listless dog. Remember to retain the posture as originally established to keep within the character. That bent-over old man should remain so for the entire presentation. The listless dog may transform into an energetic one if the text provides a legitimate reason for the transformation.

Now let's take an in-depth look at movements for the hand puppet.

**Good and bad posture for a flexible-body hand puppet**

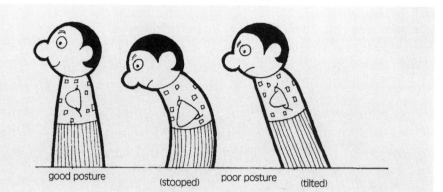

good posture    (stooped)    poor posture    (tilted)

## Exploring Hand Puppet Movements

Remember to keep the puppet's actions continuous and lively enough during storytelling to retain the children's interest, but do not let your puppet suffer from "jigolitis," i.e., movements that are unnecessarily jerky or have no relationship to the action. Create only purposeful movements that are well defined and meaningful. Such movements can be better understood when divided into the following categories.

### Small movements

Mostly confined to the fingers, these movements play an important part in expressing subtle ideas. Using fingers only, try to convey the following:

Yes!

Wave

Point to something

Tap an object

### Medium movements

Conveyed through the use of all the hand and wrist muscles, these movements express more complex ideas through larger motor actions. Try to

**Hand puppet ambulation**

express the following, involving the puppet's head and flexible arms:

No!

Look around

Bow

Stretch

### Large movements

Carried through the use of the entire arm, these movements express exaggerated ideas or give ambulation to the puppet in space. Try the following, using exaggerated motions:

Jump up and down

Fall dead (dramatically!)

Twist around

### Ambulatory movements

Ambulatory movements are best achieved by turning the puppet so that the audience sees it in the profile view.

When the storyteller, facing the audience, is in a seated position, the walking sequence segment can be expressed by moving the puppet across the front of the storyteller from right to left (if the storyteller is right-handed) and

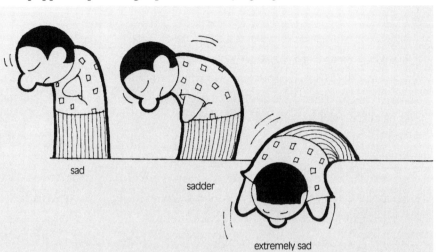

back again as far as the arm will comfortably allow without tilting. Another trick is for the storyteller to sit on a stool and actually pivot completely on the stool, in synchronization with the puppet, to give the effect of a continuous walking cycle.

Some ideas for portraying various ambulatory motions follow.

*Walking:* make small up-and-down movements as you move the puppet forward in an upright position.

*Running:* make vigorous and small up-and-down successive movements as you quickly move the puppet forward in a slightly forward tilt position.

*Hopping:* make larger up-and-down motions, clearly delineating each hop segment, as you move the puppet forward in an upright position.

## Expression

Feelings and emotions can be interpreted through the puppet by using a combination of the movements categorized above. Note the following examples:

*Happiness:* portray with lively up-and-down movements, in conjunction with spreading the arms of the puppet up and out.

*Sadness:* express by bending over the head, drooping the entire body, or swaying the head back and forth gently. Crying can be simulated by having the puppet rub its eyes.

*Anger:* indicate with spasmodic shakes of the head or body.

A puppet's transmission of varying degrees of feeling or emphasis are at the disposal of the storyteller. To indicate that a puppet is

*Sad:* bend over head slightly (small movements).

*Sadder:* droop body over and slump shoulders (medium movements).

*Extremely sad:* hang puppet over completely and make it appear to weep or sob with small jerks of head (large movements).

To express disagreement of varying intensity.

*No:* gentle shake of head (small movements).

*Stronger no:* shake body and head together (medium movements).

*Emphatic no:* strong, absolute shaking of entire body and head (large movements).

A highly recommended book for exploring further the basic movements with hand puppets is *Making Puppets Come Alive* by Larry Engler and Carol Fijan.

## Practicing movements

Spend some time alone practicing the different movements just suggested. Then proceed with the story exercise that follows, interpreting the narration through appropriate pantomime actions. Use a lapboard as a stage or use your lap and let all the actions simply take place over it.

Once upon a time there was a Little Puppet. She was very, very sad (hangs head) because she had lost a golden ring. "I will never find my ring," she said as she wept (puts hands to eyes and weeps gently). She kept getting sadder and sadder (hangs head lower and slowly rotates back and forth). Then she had an idea (taps hand to forehead)! She would go on a great search throughout the kingdom and look for her golden ring. Off she went on her journey (walks cycles as previously described). Lo and behold, she saw something glitter in the middle of the meadow (put ring prop on lapboard). The Little Puppet saw the ring and carefully picked it up (bends over and picks up ring). Now she was the happiest puppet in the world (jumps up and down ecstatically)! She ran back home (runs back to beginning position) to show everyone the wonderful ring!

Use this story exercise as a model for integrating a puppet's actions into the story's content. Make a simple analysis of the specific actions you wish your puppet to fulfill in the dialogue or narration. A duplicate copy of the story material can be annotated with red ink or cue symbols to remind you of the corresponding action desired. Once you have practiced the routine several times, the action will become more spontaneous and then can easily be enhanced with further embellishments.

## The Practice Corner

It is important to find a special place that you can designate the "practice corner." This should be a quiet place where you will not be disturbed easily, as well as a comfortable space in which you will enjoy working. A mirror where you can watch yourself perform with the puppet and view your own facial expressions would be especially beneficial in developing dramatic puppet skills. You may wish to decorate the wall with pictures of favorite storybooks and puppets as a source of inspiration for your work. Plan to practice in several short sessions rather than one long one; never attempt to practice when you are feeling tired. A high level of energy is a prerequisite for achieving successful practice sessions and obtaining maximal results.

Let this practice corner be established as a permanent work spot into which you can retreat to experiment and build up your presentation skills.

## SUGGESTED TITLES FOR DEVELOPING PUPPETS FOR STORYTELLING

Engler, Larry, and Carol Fijan. *Making Puppets Come Alive*. Taplinger, 1973.

A detailed guide to hand-puppet manipulation.

Gág, Wanda. *Millions of Cats*; illus. by the author. Coward, 1928.

Classic picture book about a lonely old man and woman who want a cat. A Newbery Honor book.

Lobel, Arnold. *Frog and Toad Are Friends*; illus. by the author. Harper, 1970.

This book introduced lovable Frog and Toad to the world. A Caldecott Honor book.

Marshall, James. *George and Martha*; illus. by the author. Houghton, 1972.

First in a series of books about the amusing adventures of two hippo friends.

# Part Three

# ROLES OF PUPPETS

**Bookworm as a host puppet**

I N ADDITION TO physical type and style considerations, there is also the need to give thought to the puppet's general role or use. There are two broad potential uses for nearly every puppet in collaboration with storytelling: serving as a host puppet or as a lead puppet. Chapter 6 defines the scope of the host puppet. Chapter 7 describes the lead puppet's participation during the story.

One important way a storyteller may use a puppet is to capture the audience's attention and to introduce or comment upon the story. The puppet in this instance is "hosting" the story hour and so the term "host puppet" comes into use. The host puppet may engage in a variety of important activities without becoming involved in the story as a character. The host puppet may welcome the children, introduce the story, comment upon and ask questions about the story. After the story is told the host may check general comprehension, understanding of plot, of characters, or other details.

The second possible use is the more common one of directly involving the puppet in the telling or drama-tization of the story through making it a character in the story. Thus the term "lead puppet" signifies that the puppet becomes an important character in the storytelling process.

It is not recommended that a puppet serve both as a host and as a lead puppet; rather, the storyteller should have two separate sets of puppets to meet the needs of these two functions. It is often confusing for young children, particularly, to become acquainted and strongly identify with a host puppet only to see this host later become a totally different character in a lead role.

While the host puppet retains the same personality forever, the lead puppet may assume varied character roles in different stories. For example, a rabbit puppet could easily play the lead in the fable "The Hare and the Tortoise," in Beatrix Potter's classic *The Tale of Peter Rabbit*, and in *Tops and Bottoms* by Janet Stevens. Assigning different roles to a puppet in this manner makes the basic puppet collection more valuable to the storyteller.

# Chapter 6     HOST PUPPETS

EMPLOYING A "HOST PUPPET" is one of the simplest and yet most effective ways of using puppets in storytelling. This puppet serves several general roles: welcoming children to the story hour; helping listeners get ready to listen; introducing the story; and aiding the story along as needed. In short, the puppet serves as a "go-between" for the children and the storyteller. It is important to select as "host" a puppet that will function in that capacity only, rather than one that will take part in the stories being told.

Any puppet with which the storyteller feels comfortable may act as a host puppet for the story hour. However, several factors make hand puppets particularly suitable to the role of host puppet. Hand puppets are flexible, fitting comfortably into a variety of physical situations. If the children sit in a semicircle around the storyteller, the puppet can be held over the storyteller's lap and can easily communicate with all of the children. With any type of hand puppet the storyteller is able to move freely around the area and respond spontaneously to comments and reactions of the children. Finally, hand puppets are capable of conveying a wider range of emotions, both exaggerated and subtle, on improvisational levels than other types of puppets.

A storyteller has the option of introducing either a nonspeaking or speaking host puppet to the children. In either case, a host puppet on the storyteller's hand encourages children to be expressive. Often the child forgets that the adult is present and concentrates wholly on the puppet. Nonverbal communication or conversation between a host puppet and a child can establish a rapport that enriches the story experience for the child and the storyteller.

A speaking host puppet can assist the storyteller through vocal communications by welcoming the children, introducing a story, commenting on aspects of the story, and even discussing personal reactions to the story with the children. The design of talking-mouth hand puppets facilitates the establishment of rapport by allowing the puppeteer to tailor comments for individual children. For example, the puppet can say, "It is nice to see you today, Diane"; "Thank you for telling me about

**A host puppet can welcome children to the story hour. (Photo of Hannah TenEyck and Kalaya Paraskevas by Michelle Owen)**

your new dog, Jeremy"; "I hope you'll come and visit again, Edgar." Or the puppet could even nibble fingers before the story hour begins as a simple gesture toward preliminary communication.

A nonspeaking hand puppet with flexible arms, communicating in a nonverbal manner, might hug or shake hands with the children as they arrive, place a birthday hat on a child, or act as a role model for the children during story time. When the story hour is over, the nonspeaking host puppet can interact with each child by passing out bookmarks, story favors, or invitations to the next story hour.

A nonspeaking host puppet doesn't speak vocally. This puppet "whispers" into the ear of the storyteller who then conveys the puppet's conversation to the children. A flexible-body hand puppet is most appropriate for this nonverbal role since it must rely on gestures, use of props, and nonvocal communication techniques.

There are two main reasons for introducing a nonspeaking host puppet into the story hour. The first is to create a warm, secure atmosphere. This is especially important if the children are young and new to group situations. Children naturally respond to a puppet who is especially defenseless and timid such as can be found in the personality of a nonspeaking puppet. They will want to love and protect it. In their concern for the puppet, young children will forget their own fears and uncertainties. As facets of this puppet's personality are

revealed, a caring relationship between child and puppet will deepen and enrich the story sharing experience.

Storytellers who are just starting to use puppets often feel more secure beginning with a nonspeaking host puppet. Also, there is sometimes a temptation for new puppeteers, who may feel nervous, to talk too much or too fast. A nonspeaking host puppet removes this temptation. With no puppet voice to worry about the storyteller can concentrate on manipulating the puppet and on developing a relationship between children and puppet. When confidence has been established a second host puppet, one that does talk, may eventually become part of the storyteller's repertory.

## DEVELOPING THE HOST PUPPET

The host puppet, whether speaking or nonspeaking, will be most effective if the storyteller develops a special feeling for it. This puppet serves as a link between the storyteller and the children in story sharing, and opens up a unique communication channel that strengthens with time. Almost any character will do—a friendly hedgehog, a cantankerous witch, a robust robot, or a shy gnome. Keep in mind the age of the children with whom you will be using the puppet. Younger children respond to a soft, cuddly character, while older children enjoy humorous, unusual personalities. Of course, it

Variety of host puppets—a friendly hedgehog, a robust robot, and a cantakerous witch (Puppets by Nancy Renfro Studios)

must also be a puppet that has a strong appeal to the storyteller.

Once a host puppet has been selected, it is important to develop a unique personality and voice for the puppet. Roscoe Wolf, a toothy, large, talking-mouth puppet, would be an excellent candidate for the position of host puppet. While at first glance Roscoe may appear fierce, closer acquaintance with him reveals the personality of a dandy who has a flair for wearing snappy bow ties and hats. In addition, Roscoe is a member of the local gourmet club and thinks nothing of wearing a chef's hat when discussing his latest epicurean adventure. This wolf beams with pleasure when children recommend books for him to read, especially books set in exotic or unusual locales.

Hoot, a large, soft, feathery owl with movable wings and beak, would be another interesting host puppet. Hoot, because of her extremely sensitive ears, is a good listener. In fact, she can hear thoughts almost as well as words. At night, when her eyesight is at its best, Hoot flies around the world searching for unusual stories to bring back to tell the children. Hoot has a particular liking for birthday cake (especially the icing flowers!) and is always delighted to be invited to share birthdays. She has prepared a version of the Owl's birthday salute which she performs at the slightest urging.

These brief sketches provide a foundation on which to build the personalities of Roscoe and Hoot. Chapter 5, Developing the Puppet for Storytelling, has many suggestions for puppet personalities.

A very special relationship develops between children and a host puppet. The host puppet easily becomes a friend since it is always present during story time. Perhaps one week this puppet might greet the children at the door, another time it could share with them a hobby or introduce a favorite book. During some stories the host puppet might just quietly listen as it sits on the storyteller's lap, in a shoe-box home, or on a window sill. Children soon will associate the host puppet with the inviting and intriguing atmosphere of the story hour. They will also look forward to seeing the host puppet along with hearing the story each session.

If you are in a seated position, use the host puppet above your lap so that you are in full view as you manipulate and speak for the puppet. Don't be concerned about the fact that the children see you. Look at your puppet and concentrate on it as you use it. If you believe in your puppet's personality so will the children. They will also look at the puppet rather than you.

The storyteller may wish to use host puppets in several ways to set the mood for a story hour:

Hoot whispers to each child that the story hour is about to begin and invites each child to come to the story corner.

Roscoe calls for attention and announces the title or theme of the story hour.

Carrying a "Travel Guide to Mexico" and proclaiming a desire to take a cruise, Hoot can introduce a story hour about traveling or folktales of Mexico.

Roscoe will quickly find himself being followed by eager children as he parades to the story area wearing a chef's hat and carrying a mysterious bag marked "Treats."

Host puppets and holidays make a perfect combination. If it is holiday time you may wish to integrate your host puppet into the theme in a particular way. A host puppet can play many roles throughout the year, including:

*Halloween.* The host puppet judges a pumpkin-decorating contest and tells ghost stories while wearing a ghost costume or colorful mask.

*Thanksgiving.* The host puppet narrates a Thanksgiving story while wearing a Pilgrim hat or recites poems dedicated to the honorable turkey.

*Christmas.* Outfit the host puppet in an elf's hat with a bell, then have the puppet share ideas for making simple gifts or lead the children in Christmas caroling.

*Valentine's Day.* The host puppet shares some original poetry he wrote for his valentine. As a treat, the puppet might give each child a candy kiss.

The special meaning of any holiday can be enhanced when a host puppet takes part in the festivities.

## NONSPEAKING HOST PUPPET

If you are uncomfortable or nervous about giving your puppet a voice, you might decide not to use a voice in the beginning. Instead, let the puppet whisper in your ear and then you relay to the children what the puppet said. The puppet might whisper, "Why are all these boys and girls here?" "What story are you going to tell?" "I'm nervous." When the puppet "whispers" in your ear, say the sentence or question to yourself. This trick adds to the puppet's believability by helping you to concentrate on the puppet's silent remarks as well as gauging the appropriate amount of time it takes for the puppet to whisper a line. It takes more time to say and listen to "I'd like to get my favorite book and share it with the boys and girls," than "What's a troll?" After listening to the puppet's whispered remarks, repeat them for the children.

Children find great delight in being allowed to share a puppet's secrets. This technique works especially well when the storyteller appears to be truly attentive to the puppet and the "whispering." In this manner the storyteller can also convey messages from a very shy host puppet to the children.

When children come to the story corner, use your nonspeaking host puppet to establish rapport. If the story hour is being held at the library, this may be a new experience for young children. The library may seem very large and certainly unfamiliar, and the children in the group may not know each other. This is especially true at public library story times. A host puppet can put children at ease while at the same time introducing them to the story time concept and to specific stories.

### Sample Plan for Using a Host Puppet

The following is a sample plan showing one way of using a nontalking host puppet to achieve the goals of introducing a story, making children feel comfortable, and inviting participation of younger children. A cuddly, soft nonspeaking hand puppet, perhaps even one that is a little the worse for wear, works well in this situation. Animal puppets such as bears, kittens, and bunnies are especially appealing. Keep the puppet out of sight while the children are being seated. It can be put in a tote, such as a wicker basket, shoe bag, or old purse. All make good homes for a host puppet. A tote adds one more facet to the host puppet's unique personality. It becomes the puppet's permanent home, the place where the puppet resides when not at story hour. Also, when the children see the tote they will know that the host puppet will soon be making an appearance. This anticipation adds to the excitement of the story time. For ideas about other homes for host puppets see chapter 20, Story Totes.

## Physical Location

Paddy Bear puppet is in an old bowling shoe-bag tote on the floor next to the storyteller. In the tote with Paddy are the following props: large comb, toothbrush, piece of yarn, hat, raincoat, picture book. Children are seated on the floor in front of the storyteller.

## Procedures

STORYTELLER: "Good morning, boys and girls. I'm so glad you came to story time today. I've brought a friend with me but he's still asleep. If you'll help me call him, I think he'll come and join us. His name is Paddy. Let's all call together in a quiet voice so we won't frighten him. Paddy, come out."

CHILDREN: "Paddy, come out."

STORYTELLER: "He's a bit shy. Let's call him again." *(Open tote and put Paddy on your hand.)*

CHILDREN: "Paddy, come out."

STORYTELLER: *(Bring Paddy out of the tote and put him against your shoulder with his back facing the children. Look at Paddy as you speak to him.)* "Paddy, all the boys and girls are here for story hour. Will you turn around and say hello to them?"

PADDY: Shakes head, "No."

STORYTELLER: *(Look at Paddy and then at children.)* "I can't understand what's the matter." *(To Paddy)* "Paddy, do you want to hear a story?"

PADDY: Nods head, "Yes."

STORYTELLER: *(To Paddy)* "Well, then, please turn around and join us."

PADDY: Shakes head, "No."

Paddy Bear's ensemble, including tote and other props

STORYTELLER: *(To Paddy)* "Why not, Paddy? What's the matter?" *(Lean toward Paddy as he "whispers" in your ear. When he finishes "whispering" look at children.)* "Paddy says he's shy and he's not sure that you'll like him." *(To Paddy)* "Paddy, these are very special boys and girls. They love stories just as much as you do. And they want to say hello to you."

PADDY: Quickly turns around, looks at group, then returns his head to your shoulder.

STORYTELLER: "Don't they look like friendly boys and girls?"

PADDY: Nods head, "Yes."

STORYTELLER: *(To Paddy)* "Why don't you say hello and see what happens?"

PADDY: Very slowly turns around and waves in a tentative manner at the children. *(Usually the children will wave back. If they don't, encourage them to do so.)* Starts to wave furiously.

STORYTELLER: *(To Paddy)* "I knew you'd like these boys and girls."

PADDY: *(Whispers in your ear.)*

STORYTELLER: *(Listens to Paddy, then conveys his message to the children.)* "Paddy says he just woke up and feels a bit scruffy. He'd like you to help him get ready for the story hour."

PADDY: Rummages around in his tote and comes out with an oversized comb. Hands comb to child.

STORYTELLER: *(To child)* "Will you comb Paddy's back?" *(Thank child as Paddy gives child a big hug.)*

As Paddy gives the comb to several children, the storyteller makes appropriate comments: "Be careful as you comb Paddy's stomach; he's very ticklish." "What a fine job you're doing." "Paddy loves to have his arms combed." Children may also be asked to straighten Paddy's ears and polish his nose with a clean finger.

Next Paddy pulls a toothbrush and some dental floss (a piece of yarn) from his tote. The children help him clean his teeth, receiving a hug for their assistance. He may also bring out a jacket, bow tie, or other article of clothing to put on to complete his ensemble.

You may add your own touches when expanding this basic idea. Perhaps you'll have Paddy try his morning push-ups. He's up to three and hopes to reach four. Children may count as Paddy does the exercises. The main idea is to capitalize on adding details that will develop the puppet's personality and endear him to the children.

The last item Paddy pulls out from his bag is the book you'll use for the first story. After Paddy hands it to you, he can sit in a special place and listen as the story is told. Paddy is a good listener and therefore a model for the children. At the end of the story hour each child can hug Paddy good-bye or whisper something into his ear.

## Other Ideas

A few other suggestions for using nonspeaking host puppets follow. Familiarity with your puppet coupled with success during story hours will surely suggest many other uses.

1. If the group is small, Paddy shakes "paws" with each child as the child tells Paddy his or her name. Paddy makes an appropriate "whispered" comment to each child. To the storyteller Paddy might "whisper," "I won't forget your name, Patty, it sounds something like my name;" or "I never met anyone named Howard before"; or other similar remarks for the storyteller to pass on to the child.

    Be sure to start this only if there is sufficient time to greet each child. Don't attempt this activity when more than eight preschoolers are present since their attention may waiver.

2. Paddy turns the pages of the book as the story is read. This helps direct the children's eyes and attention to the book.

3. This is Paddy's first story hour and he doesn't know what to do. You explain what is done and the children demonstrate. For example, ask the children to show Paddy how to sit, how to raise his hand if he has a question, and how to listen.

4. If it is a child's birthday, Paddy places a birthday crown on this child's head, thus giving very special recognition to the birthday child.

5. Before the story begins, special words from the story or the setting are explained to Paddy. As the new words become clear to Paddy, their meaning will be absorbed by the children as well. The storyteller asks the children to say the word to Paddy to help him remember it.

6. Your host puppet can be used as a logo on bookmarks, booklists, announcements of story hours, registration forms, and awards.

Paddy's role as a host puppet gives him definite importance. Therefore, Paddy is one puppet that should never be used freely by the children. He is a special guest. Also, if you choose to place Paddy in a nonspeaking role initially, he should not be given a voice later, unless you have planned the voice development as part of the character development.

## SPEAKING HOST PUPPET

Once confidence has been gained by successfully using a nonspeaking puppet with children, introduce a different host puppet that has a voice. Before sharing this puppet with the children, experiment with varied voices until you find one that fits the puppet's personality. Then use that voice consistently each time that host puppet appears. Chapter 5, Developing Puppets for Storytelling, has many suggestions for voice development.

A speaking host puppet can be used in numerous ways before, during, and after the story hour. Some of these uses are detailed here; others you may formulate with experience.

### Before the Story

The speaking host puppet prepares the children for the story hour by greeting them as they enter and by commenting on their readiness to listen as the story nears. The puppet may announce the title of the story before the children go to a specific place to sit and listen to the story. Additionally, the puppet may use props to stimulate interest in the story.

### Introducing the Story

One basic function of a host puppet is to introduce a story and to set the scene through topic discussion.

Children will look forward to the story with great anticipation after hearing the puppet mention a character or relate a scene from the story. *Two Good Friends* by Judy Delton is about Bear and Duck who are close friends. Each does a good turn for the other by sharing talents. The host puppet introduces this story by talking about special friends—those who help each other. The puppet can invite the children to tell how their friends help them and, likewise, how they help their friends.

Then the host puppet can introduce the story by saying, "In this story Bear is a terrific cook but a poor housekeeper, while Duck is a wonderful housekeeper but a very poor cook. Let's see how Duck and Bear use their special talents to help each other."

Speaking host puppets are excellent choices for introducing stories that deal with personal opinions or problems. This puppet's strength of direct communication can be used to help the children empathize with the story characters and share similar situations from their own lives. The interaction between a host puppet and a child enhances the individual involvement in the situation presented by the story.

### SUGGESTED TITLES TO BE INTRODUCED BY HOST PUPPETS

Delton, Judy. *Two Good Friends*; illus. by Giulio Maestro. Crown, 1986.

A warm story about friendship.

Gauch, Patricia Lee. *Christina Katerina and the Time She Quit the Family*; illus. by Elsie Primavera. Putnam, 1987.

One day when nothing seems to go right, Christina quits her family. After a week of doing just as she pleases, Christina decides rejoining her family is what would really please her. The host puppet can encourage children to talk about times when they have had a difficult time getting along with someone in their family and what they did about the problem.

Hoberman, Mary Ann. *A House Is a House for Me*; illus. by Betty Fraser. Viking, 1978.

All sorts of places are suggested as homes in this unique picture book. A host puppet may describe her home and ask children to describe homes of people and animals before introducing this story.

Keiko, Kasza. *The Rat and the Tiger*; illus. by the author. Putnam, 1993.

Tiger, because of his larger size, bullies his friend Rat until the day Rat finally stands up for himself. The host puppet can ask children to discuss their experiences with bullies and the way they handled the situation. After the story children can consider how they might deal with bullies in the future.

Livingston, Myra Cohn. *If You Ever Meet a Whale*; illus. by Leonard Everett Fisher. Holiday, 1992.

Collection of poems about a variety of whales accompanied by dramatic illustrations, Host puppet can tell of her recent visit to see the whales at the zoo. Children can share what they know about whales before the poems are read.

Mennen, Ingrid, and Niki Daly. *Somewhere in Africa*; illus. by Nicolass Martiz. Dutton, 1990.

Ashraf, a young boy, shares his love of the city in Africa where he lives. Host puppet can ask children to describe what they think it would be like to live in Africa. After the story children can compare their ideas with Ashraf's world.

Ryan, Cheli Duran. *Hildilid's Night*; illus. by Arnold Lobel. Macmillan, 1986.

Hildilid hates the night and does everything she can to chase it from Hexham. After an all-night struggle, she turns her back on night and sleeps all day so she can try again when night reappears.

A host puppet might tell how he feels about night-time. Children share their feelings about the night. After the story is told, children suggest and demonstrate other ways of getting rid of the night. A Caldecott Honor book.

## Using Props to Stimulate Interest

The speaking host puppet's use of a prop can generate interest in a story. Stories in which a specific object is of importance to plot development or resolution offer opportunities for host puppet involvement. The host puppet is capable of generating interest in a story via a prop in a variety of ways. It might use a prop in a manner similar to the story character. For example, a host puppet carrying a book might imitate Petunia, the silly goose, who thought wisdom would be hers just because she owned a book.

Or, a host puppet arriving at the story hour carrying a golden box is sure to arouse curiosity. When asked about it, the puppet explains that the box contains the stories from the Sky God. The storyteller can then tell *A Story, A Story*, adapted and illustrated by Gail E. Haley, to show how the stories were given to humans.

A puppet might wear something that has an important connection to a story. A pocket pinned to a puppet can lead into the story *A Pocket for Corduroy* by Don Freeman. The discussion between storyteller and puppet, focusing on the host puppet's wish to be like Corduroy, not only sets the tone for the story but develops interest in the character's problem. Pin a paper pocket on each child afterwards as a reminder of the story.

Imaginative props stimulate discussion and anticipation. Stories that contain magical elements such as the magical bone in *The Amazing Bone* are natural choices for introduction with props. Many other stories have specific objects that are of great importance. A box has a unique significance in the myth "Pandora's Box" because when this particular box is opened the world is changed forever. A stone becomes the basis for a wonderful soup as well as the keystone of the story *Stone Soup*. Search out stories which have interesting props and enhance their telling with a host puppet.

## SUGGESTED TITLES FOR USING PROPS TO STIMULATE INTEREST

Brown, Marcia. *Stone Soup*; illus. by the author. Scribner, 1982.

Three soldiers teach a hungry village how to make soup from stones flavored with a few vegetables and other contributions from the villagers' hidden cache. Host puppet can carry the stone, which becomes the basis for the soup and the story. A Caldecott Honor book. (Stone prop)

Bruchac, Joseph, and Jonathan London. *Thirteen Moons on Turtle's Back*; illus. by Thomas Locker. Philomel, 1992.

In many Native American cultures, the thirteen cycles of the moon each have their own name and story to explain the changing seasons. Each moon story in this collection is taken from a different Native American nation. The Huron describe May as the "Budding Moon," and among the Winnebago November is known as "Moon When Deer Drop Their Horns."

For many Native American people the shell of the turtle with its pattern of thirteen large scales acts as a calendar. The host puppet carrying a 12-month paper calendar can share how Native Americans use the thirteen areas shown on a turtle's back as a calendar. After the story ask children to suggest other possible names for the thirteen moons. (Calendar prop)

Carle, Eric. *Walter the Baker*; illus. by the author. Simon & Schuster, 1995.

Walter, the baker, must create a new roll through which the sun can shine three times. Host puppet can enter carrying a hard roll and complaining that it must be one of the rolls that Walter made without milk. After the story the host puppet can distribute mini-pretzels to the children. (Roll prop)

Duvoisin, Roger. *Petunia*; illus. by the author. Knopf, 1989.

Petunia, a silly goose, believes that by carrying a book under her wing she will be wise. After giving advice which has disastrous results, Petunia realizes it's not enough to own a book; one must read it as well. The host puppet might carry several books and brag about how smart she is because she has borrowed eighty-seven books from the library this week—unfortunately she hasn't read a single one! (Book prop)

Freeman, Don. *A Pocket for Corduroy*; illus. by the author. Viking, 1978.

Corduroy, a teddy bear, wants a pocket for his pants. His search for material nearly has disastrous results when he gets locked in a laundromat. But all ends well with Corduroy getting a beautiful purple pocket. Your host puppet could wear a purple pocket just like friendly Corduroy. (Pocket prop)

Grifalconi, Ann. *The Village of Round and Square Houses*; illus. by the author. Little, 1986.

This Caldecott Honor book explains why the women live in round houses and the men in square houses in a village in the remote hills of the Cameroons in Central Africa. The host puppet introduces the story by bringing in a map of Africa and explaining that in a small village in the Cameroons all live in peace together because men, women, and children have a place to be apart and a time to be together.

Host puppet can show location of Africa and the Cameroons on the map. (Map prop)

Haley, Gail E. *A Story, A Story*; illus by the author. Atheneum, 1970.

An explanation of how Ananse, the spider man, was given stories from the Sky God, Nyame. Host puppet may carry a golden box to contain these wonderful stories. A Caldecott Medal book. (Box prop)

Hoban, Russell. *A Birthday for Frances*; illus. by Lillian Hoban. Harper, 1995.

Frances, a badger, is a bit jealous of her sister, Gloria, on her birthday. How Frances overcomes her feelings about Gloria's birthday makes a warm, humorous story. The host puppet may bring a birthday present to the story hour. Children may discuss their birthdays and how they feel when it is someone else's birthday. (Birthday present prop)

Leemis, Ralph. *Mister Momboo's Hat*; illus. by Jeni Bassett. Dutton, 1991.

Mister Momboo's hat flies off his head and has a series of adventures. Host puppet enters wearing a hat and then asks children to think of all the ways a hat might be used. (Hat prop)

Levine, Abby. *Too Much Mush!*; illus. by Kathy Parkinson. Whitman, 1989.

Humorous German folktale, similar to *Strega Nona*, about a magic cooking pot which always has food in it. Host puppet can carry a pot and discuss how wonderful it would be if the pot was always full of her favorite food. Children can discuss their favorite food before the story is read. (Cooking pot prop)

Levitin, Sonia. *The Man Who Kept His Heart in a Bucket*; illus. by Jerry Pinkney. Dial, 1991.

Jack keeps his heart in a bucket to keep it from being broken. He learns the proper place for a heart when he meets a young maiden who teaches him the meaning of love. Ask children if they have ever felt sad and heartbroken. You might also discuss the wisdom of the man's plan to keep his heart from harm. (Metal bucket prop)

Steig, William. *The Amazing Bone*; illus. by the author. Farrar, 1976.

A magic bone saves Pearl, an innocent young pig, from a cruel fate at the hands of a villainous fox. A host puppet might carry a chicken bone and share the hope that it is a magic bone like the one in the story. A Caldecott Honor book. (Bone prop)

Van Laan, Nancy. *Sleep, Sleep, Sleep*; illus. by Holly Meade. Little, 1995.

A collection of lullabies from around the world. All seven continents are represented. Children can chant a section of each lullaby in the language of the culture it represents: Sh, sh, sh (Asia); Robala, robala, robala (Africa); Sha-wish, sha-wish, sha-wish (Antarctica). A host puppet wearing pajamas and carrying a blanket can ask the children what lullabies are sung to them before they go to sleep. Children can then help the storyteller lullaby the host puppet to sleep with these lullabies from around the world. (Blanket prop)

Williams, Karen Lynn. *Galimoto*; illus. by Catherine Stock. Lothrop, 1990.

Kondi, a seven-year-old boy in Malawi, is determined to make a galimoto toy out of wires even though his older brother laughs at him. The host puppet carrying a piece of wire she has found can ask the children what she can do with it. The story can then be read to provide one possible solution to this dilemma. (Wire prop)

Wright, Courtni C. *Jumping the Broom*; illus. by Gershom Griffith. Holiday, 1994.

Slaves on a plantation jump the broom during their wedding ceremony to sweep away the past and evil spirits. The host puppet can enter sweeping with a broom and then explain the symbolic role of a broom during slavery. (Broom prop)

## During the Story

A speaking host puppet is an invaluable helper during the story as well. It may reinforce good behavior, ask lead questions to check comprehension, lead the children in a chorus or poem within a story, or simply turn the pages.

The host puppet may also help the children focus on illustrations and prod them into guessing what might happen on the next page. The storyteller may invite the puppet to read or tell or make up the ending to the story. However you use it, the host puppet is certain to add to the telling and comprehension, especially for younger children.

## *Asking Questions*

A host puppet may ask critical questions with a variety of goals in mind. Single details of the story may be elicited through straight inquiry: "Who," "What," "Where," and "Why?" For example, the host puppet could ask, "Who was the first Billy Goat to cross the bridge?" or "What did the Troll say to each of the Billy Goats?"

Children may be encouraged to predict events by having the host puppet ask questions about what will happen next based on an illustration or on the facts known to that time. The host puppet, pointing to a picture, could say: "The tiny Billy Goat Gruff is crossing the bridge in this picture. Who do you think will cross next?"

Or, the puppet could break in at the appropriate time in the story and say, "We know that Veronica, the hippopotamus, is not a farm animal [in the story *Our Veronica Goes to Petunia's Farm* by Roger Duvoisin]. How do you think she'll be treated by the other animals when she first arrives at Mr. Pumpkin's farm?"

Comprehension questions check general understanding of main events and interrelationships of a story. Thus, the question, "Why did the farm animals change their minds about Veronica?" might be asked about *Our Veronica Goes to Petunia's Farm*.

"What if" questions allow the children to use imagination in changing the course of a story. Let the host puppet describe a situation that is contrary to the story action and allow a child in the audience an opportunity to suggest a new alternative, such as, "What if Veronica had been a gorilla instead of a hippopotamus?"

Reverse the roles and let the children pose some "what if" questions for the puppet to answer.

## SUGGESTED TITLES FOR <u>ASKING QUESTIONS</u>

Balian, Lorna. *The Sweet Touch*; illus. by the author. Abingdon, 1976.

When Peggy rubs her shiny plastic ring, Oliver, the genie, appears to grant her one wish. Problems develop when Oliver discovers that he doesn't know how to turn off a wish.

The host puppet ponders, "Will Oliver be able to grant Peggy's wish?" Later, when Oliver and Peggy have had enough candy and Oliver finds he can't turn off the wish, the puppet asks aloud, "How do you think Peggy and Oliver will get out of this mess?"

Duvoisin, Roger. *Our Veronica Goes to Petunia's Farm*; illus. by the author. Knopf, 1962.

The animals won't talk to Veronica, a hippopotamus, when she goes to live on Mr. Pumpkin's farm because she's a zoo animal.

San Souci, Robert D. *Sukey and the Mermaid*; illus. by Brian Pinkney. Four Winds, 1992.

In this African-American variant of the Cinderella story, Sukey meets a mermaid who loves and protects her. The host puppet can encourage students to discuss "Why did Sukey choose to leave the mermaid's home under the sea and return home?" or "What if Sukey had decided to stay with the mermaid, what would her new life be like?" A Coretta Scott King Honor book.

Steig, William. *Sylvester and the Magic Pebble*; illus. by the author. Windmill, 1969.

Sylvester, a donkey, finds a red pebble that grants his wish and sets in motion a chain of adventures. The host puppet muses, "I wonder what will happen when Sylvester's parents have a picnic on that rock, which is really Sylvester?" A Caldecott Medal book.

Steptoe, John. *Mufaro's Beautiful Daughters*; illus. by the author. Lothrop, 1987.

When the king announces that he wishes to marry, two beautiful sisters, one kind and one selfish, compete for the honor. Host puppet can ask "Why did the sisters see different snakes when they first entered the king's chamber?" or "Why did the king take many shapes during the story?" A Coretta Scott King Award winner and a Caldecott Honor book.

## Reading the Story

There are times when the reading of a story by a host puppet is very effective. This is true particularly with children who have short attention spans and have not had much experience listening to stories. A puppet reading a story will often hold the interest and attention of a slow child when reading by an adult would not. This technique helps children to increase their attention spans and to improve active listening skills. As the story is read by the puppet, it may also comment on a particular sentence or concept to reinforce an idea; ask for an explanation to gauge comprehension; or draw out a child's response to a plot twist or character action.

Stories to be read by a puppet should be short and have uncomplicated plots. Titles with one main charac-

ter are particularly suitable for reading with one host puppet. The storyteller need only use one voice, that of the host puppet.

A word of caution! Do not overuse this technique. Remember that puppets are action-oriented creatures and, therefore, should not be identified mainly with an activity that centers around straight reading of a story. This technique is acceptable as a beginning step for developing listening skills, but it will soon lose its effectiveness if repeated frequently.

## SUGGESTED TITLES FOR READING THE STORY

Bozylinsky, Hannah Heritage. *Lala Salama*; illus. by the author. Philomel, 1993.

In this African lullaby a young Masai goat herder leads his animals home to rest for the night. The host puppet might teach children how to say "Lala salama" and encourage them to repeat this phrase when needed in the lullaby. The host puppet and storyteller can share the reading of the story: host puppet reading the Swahili text; storyteller reading in English.

Dorros, Arthur. *This Is My House*; illus. by the author. Scholastic, 1992.

Simple text and colorful illustrations introduce the reader to homes that children live in all over the world. The host puppet reads the English text and the "This is my house" in the appropriate native language accompanying each illustration.

Johnson, Angela. *The Leaving Morning*; illus. by David Soman. Orchard, 1992.

A young boy says good-bye to his friends and prepares to move to his new home. A host puppet who has just moved into a new tote can tell how he prepared to move before reading the story about this boy's move.

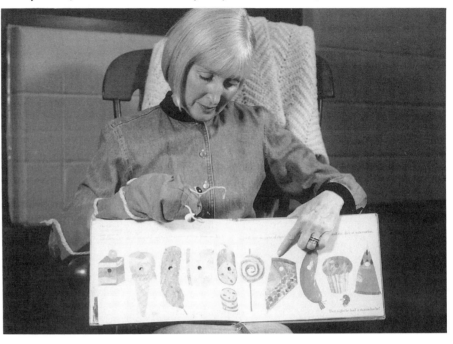

A puppet helps to focus attention on the illustrations in *The Very Hungry Caterpillar*. (Photo of Hanna TenEyck by Michelle Owen)

Lillie, Patricia. *Everything Has a Place*; illus. by Nancy Tafuri. Greenwillow, 1993.

A book with beautiful pictures and simple text showing that there is a place for everything. The storyteller can read the name of the item and the children can help the host puppet decide what the correct location is for that item.

Sharmat, Marjorie Weinman. *Mitchell Is Moving*; illus. by Jose Aruego and Ariane Dewey. Macmillan, 1979.

Mitchell, a dinosaur, announces to his friend Margo that he is moving. Margo wants him to stay next door and thinks of all sorts of ways to keep him there. When Mitchell does move, he's lonely without his best friend, who then moves, too.

A host puppet who has just moved into a new tote can share problems encountered during the move before reading the story about Mitchell's move.

## Focusing Attention

A speaking or nonspeaking host puppet is ideal for helping children focus on specific items in illustrations. With the help of the children, a host puppet can count objects in counting books, name items in alphabet books, and find hidden characters in puzzle books. *Count and See* by Tana Hoban is a counting book composed of photographs of everyday objects. A host puppet who is a good reader, but not much of a counter, appeals to the children for help with counting. As the puppet points to each object in the illustration, the children say the appropriate number.

### SUGGESTED TITLES FOR <u>FOCUSING ATTENTION</u>

Ahlberg, Janet, and Allan Ahlberg. *Each Peach Pear Plum*; illus. by the authors. Puffin, 1986.

A collection of rhymes accompanied by charming illustrations in which Mother Goose characters are hidden. As children describe where the characters are hiding, a host puppet points to them.

Anno, Mitsumasa. *Anno's Counting Book*; illus. by the author. Crowell, 1977.

First page, zero, shows a snow-covered, uninhabited world. As the reader moves to twelve, buildings, trees, and people are added in counting progression. A confused host puppet will need the children's help to discover the additions on each page.

Ehlert, Lois. *Color Zoo*; illus. by the author. Lippincott, 1989.

Geometric shapes become animal faces in this Caldecott Honor book. A host puppet can turn the pages and name the shapes.

Garne, S. T. *One White Sail*; illus. by Lisa Etre. Green Tiger Press, 1992.

A counting book that introduces children to the Caribbean. Children help the host puppet locate and count the objects in the large, bright illustrations.

Hoban, Tana. *All About Where*; photos by the author. Greenwillow, 1991.

Bright color photographs of outdoor scenes make this an interesting book to use to describe where things are located. The host puppet will need the children's help to use the correct location word when describing objects in the photos.

Hoban, Tana. *Count and See*; photos by the author. Macmillan, 1978.

Clear black-and-white photographs of familiar objects make this counting book exciting to use. A host puppet will need the children's help to get the right numbers while pointing to the objects in the photos.

Onyefulu, Ifeoma. *Emeka's Gift*; illus. by the author. Dutton, 1995.

An African counting story that presents a wealth of information about Africa through engaging text and stunning photographs. Host puppet can point to objects in the photos as children count. Children or storyteller can explain what some of the African words and phrases mean.

Tapahonso, Luci, and Eleanor Schick. *Navajo ABC*; illus. by Eleanor Schick. Simon & Schuster, 1995.

The Navajo are the largest tribe of Native Americans in the United States. Each letter in this alphabet book represents an aspect of Navajo or Diné culture. The host puppet can read the book and point out details in the illustrations. The host

puppet can also explore the glossary which translates Navajo words into English and English words into Navajo.

## After the Story

At the end of a story hour the host puppet may recommend books that follow the theme of the story hour. Brief book talks delivered by a host puppet will be met with enthusiasm. As children select books for individual reading, the puppet comments on available titles, discusses illustrators, assists with check-out, and thanks the children for coming.

After a story hour featuring animal poetry or Mother Goose rhymes, the host puppet may review some of the rhymes presented. Any type of animal host puppet would be appropriate for animal rhymes. Let's use Jennifer Giraffe as an example.

The presentation might follow this pattern. Jennifer proudly tells the children that she has learned all her Mother Goose rhymes at Giraffe School. She gaily recites the rhymes substituting the word giraffe every time an animal is mentioned: "Hickory Dickory Dock, the giraffe went up the clock. . . ."

The children will be eager to correct Jennifer by inserting the proper animal name as they repeat the rhyme. This simple activity provides listening and speaking opportunities as well as allowing the children the chance to act as teacher.

The host puppet may also compliment the children on how well they listened and invite them back to the next story time. The host puppet provides an extra reason to look forward to their future visits.

More detailed ideas to use after the story are included in chapter 22, The Story's Over; What's Next?

# Chapter 7

# LEAD PUPPETS

**A**S DISCUSSED EARLIER, a host puppet provides a special link between child and storyteller that enhances the story presentation. Children quickly identify with benign and understanding creatures such as host puppets. By capitalizing on this natural rapport the storyteller can use a host puppet to set the tone for a story hour.

A lead puppet, on the other hand, represents the main character in a story and therefore plays a more specific role. This puppet serves as a visual focus during the storytelling and helps clarify the action. In fact, the lead puppet acts out the story in one of a variety of ways as the story is told. The puppet may be used to emphasize the whole story, part of the story, or the chief character's role in a story. Its primary purpose is to draw the child into the adventures of the main character, thereby strengthening understanding and enjoyment of the literature.

Integrating a lead puppet into a story as the focal point adds drama to a story presentation by bringing the story to life visually. The inclusion of a lead puppet makes the actions and conflict of the story more immediate and personal to the audience. The emotional closeness between puppet and child is readily seen in personalities of popular stories. Paddington Bear from the Paddington books by Michael Bond, Harry the dog from the books by Gene Zion, and Louise Fatio's Happy Lion are all naturally appealing characters to which the storyteller should devote time and effort when developing characterizations.

## SPEAKING AND NONSPEAKING LEAD PUPPETS

For the lead puppet to be effective the storyteller must devote energy to developing a strong character with whom children may identify. The lead puppet concept gives the storyteller the option of portraying the character through pantomime, or of formulating a voice to suite the character's personality, or of combining actions and speaking.

Whether you decide upon pantomime or voice to help with characterization depends somewhat on the theme and action of the story. When the dialogue of the main character is necessary to convey the story line, then a lead puppet with a voice must be utilized. The poem "The Snopp on the Sidewalk" and the folk tale "King of the Cats" both require speaking lead puppets to illuminate the story line.

"The Snopp on the Sidewalk" by Jack Prelutsky is a poem ideally suited to the speaking lead puppet technique. Snopp is a lonely character who engages the narrator to keep him company for awhile. The lead character, made from a rag mop or a glove with buttons for eyes, sits on a tabletop while the storyteller recites the poem. Periodically Snopp responds with appropriate dialogue from the poem. It is important in establishing the relationship between Snopp and storyteller that the storyteller look at the puppet each time it speaks. This interaction between puppet and storyteller helps transmit the living quality of the puppet and the meaning of the poet's words.

**A glove puppet for "The Snopp on the Sidewalk"**

Another candidate for the role of a speaking lead puppet is Old Tom in the English folktale "King of the Cats." The lead character, an old tom cat, sits on the storyteller's lap quietly meowing during the first half of the story as the grave digger relates the strange events he has seen in the graveyard. The lead puppet intensifies the effect of the startling finale when it raises its head and announces in a masterful voice that he is the new king of the cats before rushing off to assume his new duties.

If, however, what a character does rather than what it says provides the impetus for plot development and resolution, a lead puppet can pantomime the action as the story is told. *The Very Hungry Caterpillar* by Eric Carle offers an excellent role for a nonspeaking lead puppet. A newly born caterpillar on its way to becoming a butterfly is so hungry that it eats everything in sight and winds up with a terrible stomachache. A diet of green leaves soon makes it feel much better. A chenille pipe cleaner may serve as the small caterpillar. A sock puppet for the large caterpillar can be turned inside out for a cocoon. Tuck a finger puppet butterfly inside the cocoon ready to emerge at the story's finale. As the story of this caterpillar with a voracious and nondiscriminating appetite is told, the lead puppet can pantomime eat-

ing the illustrations from the book or replicas of each object. This story also offers a striking opportunity to highlight a visual transformation when the lead puppet character emerges from the cocoon as a beautiful butterfly.

*Noisy Nora* by Rosemary Wells, *Hattie the Backstage Bat* by Don Freeman, and the fable "The Fox and the Grapes" are examples of other stories suitable for telling with pantomiming lead puppets. In *Noisy Nora* a mouse named Nora makes noise and pantomimes mischief in an attempt to attract attention. Only when Nora is quiet does her family give her the attention she craves. Here is a story that works well with the lead puppet concept because of the contrasting behavior of the main character herself. This contrast, between a noisy Nora rushing around making a great racket and a Nora who is quiet and still, is magnified when the actions are dramatized by the lead puppet. Obviously, a physically active hand puppet with flexible body is required here.

The storyteller can relate the tale of Noisy Nora in a natural voice leaving all the dramatics to the lead puppet. A disruptive Nora can be conveyed by banging a pot with a wooden spoon, stamping her feet, or dropping marbles. All these actions can be accompanied by a great deal of agitation and rushing about. When Nora finally settles down to become a very still, subdued mouse the striking change is highlighted. Thus, the point of the story is forcefully brought home through the lead puppet's participation.

Noisy Nora makes a strong nonspeaking puppet character and, thus, hers is a good beginning story for lead puppet involvement since the story can be told entirely in the storyteller's own voice. It is not necessary to give Nora a voice though you may choose to interject sighs, moans, and other sounds instead. Also, the actions of the lead puppet are simple to perform and amusing to watch. All the actions can be done on a lapboard or tabletop with props handy in pockets of a puppet apron or in a simple tote.

A bat puppet sitting on the edge of the book *Hattie the Backstage Bat* will immediately signal to children that a story with an unusual character and theme is soon to be shared. Hattie lives backstage in an empty theater. When a play is rehearsing, she must stay out of sight. But on opening night Hattie flies through the spotlight, saves the show, and becomes a star. Capitalize on the uniqueness of Hattie, the main character, to set the mood and introduce the story. Hattie is not only a bat, which in itself is fascinating to children, but one whose permanent home is a theater. Develop Hattie's personality by encouraging her to recreate one or two of the memorable theatrical scenes she has witnessed from her perch in the rafters. Before you begin to tell the story, place Hattie in a location designated as the theater rafters, perhaps the top of a bookcase, a display case, or a bulletin board. Save Hattie's actual participation in the storytelling until the dramatic moment when she flies into the spotlight and becomes the star of the show. It is not necessary to use a lead puppet throughout the entire story. Sometimes it is more effective to reserve the puppet's participation until the climax of the story.

## USING LEAD PUPPETS TO SHOW TRANSFORMATION

Stories in which the main character undergoes a physical or personality change provide an excellent basis for incorporating a lead puppet. Witnessing the visual transformation of a character becomes even more exciting when taken from the two-dimensional page and expressed in the three-dimensional format of puppet and props. *Dandelion, No Roses for Harry, Gus Was a Gorgeous Ghost*, and *Miss Nelson Is Missing* are all stories in which a transformation in the appearance of the main character comes about by the addition to or change of the character's clothing. *Leo the Late Bloomer* is an example of a story in which the personality of the main character is dramatically altered because psychological rather than physical change occurs.

*Dandelion* by Don Freeman features another delightful character who is a natural lead puppet candidate. Dandelion tries so hard to be well dressed for a come-as-you-are tea party that no one recognizes him and he therefore isn't allowed to join the festivities. As in the preceding examples, all the action is concentrated around one appealing character. Attaching costume pieces and wigs to the puppet as the story is told provides a fascinating visual transformation of the character.

One approach for presenting this amusing story follows.

Construct a lion puppet using a paper plate for a head; add a colorful paper body with detachable costume pieces.

Before beginning, gather or make the following items: paper sweater, jacket, and hat; envelope and letter with gold writing; two fringed paper wigs, one straight and one curly; stick for a cane; scissors; flower, real or imitation. Hide the Dandelion puppet and props.

Paper-plate puppet with detachable costume for *Dandelion* (Photo of Connie Champlin by Michelle Owen)

Introduce the story by asking the children, "Have you ever tried to be or look like someone you were not? Did you ever wear clothes that you did not feel like yourself in? Did you ever wear clothes you felt silly wearing?" Give children a chance to respond before telling them this story about a lion who tried to be someone else and got himself in trouble.

As the story begins, Dandelion slowly emerges from his hiding place. At appropriate places during the story, attach wigs and clothing pieces to the puppet with double-stick tape.

Use props when indicated in the story. After trimming Dandelion's hair with scissors, replace trimmed hair with the curly wig. When the storm arrives, remove the flower, hat, and jacket from Dandelion and exchange the curly wig for the original wig. At the end of the story bring up the flower.

To reinforce the story children may each create "just plain me" puppets by drawing pictures of their own faces on paper plates. Or they may make paper costumes for their puppet to transform "plain dress" into their own version of being "well dressed."

Harry, a dog who is the main character in *No Roses for Harry* by Gene Zion, becomes very unhappy when he is forced to wear a sweater with roses on it. All Harry's attempts to get rid of the hateful sweater end in failure until birds use it for their nest. A dog lead puppet's futile attempts to remove the unwanted sweater intensify the character's dilemma and sharpen the story's impact. Portray Harry as a paper-bag puppet wearing a paper sweater with roses drawn on it. A piece of yarn protruding from the back of the sweater can be pulled when the birds start to build their nest with Harry's sweater.

Halloween is a natural time to introduce *Gus Was a Gorgeous Ghost* by Jane Thayer. A paper tissue with a rubber band neck is transformed into Gus, a traditional-looking but unhappy ghost puppet. (See directions in chapter 14, Finger Stories.) Introduce the story with sad Gus complaining about his ordinary white clothes. During the story brighten up Gus's costume using potato prints or brightly inked rubber stamps. Individual children might also help decorate Gus's costume. At the end of the story a satisfied Gus proudly models his new outfit. Inviting children to witness Gus's transformation from a plain to a gorgeous ghost will endear this likable character to them.

In *Miss Nelson Is Missing* by Harry Allard, a disagreeable substitute teacher, who is really Miss Nelson in disguise, takes the place of pleasant Miss Nelson to give the misbehaving children in her class a taste of their own medicine. The class soon becomes very distressed by the switch and wishes fervently that nice Miss Nelson would return. A two-sided turnaround puppet made from paper plates or a paper bag can effectively show the physical transformation of Miss Nelson. The contrast in the two personalities is reinforced when Miss Nelson's dialogue is spoken in a sweet, cheerful voice while her substitute, Miss Swamp, says everything in a harsh, cackling voice. Turn the puppet to the appropriate side when each character speaks. The listeners, as well as the children in Miss Nelson's class, will be relieved at the eventual return of gentle Miss Nelson and hopeful that the awful Miss Swamp won't reappear.

Other stories in which the lead puppet's costume can be revised are *Clementine's Winter Wardrobe* by Kate Spohn and *Froggy Gets Dressed* by Jonathan London. In the first story Clementine, a cat, has a difficult time choosing what to wear for winter from her immense collection of clothes including hundreds of pairs of long johns, shirts, sweaters, socks, and other items. While telling the story, add clothing pieces to a cat puppet. Froggy, in the second title, is in such a rush to go outside and play in the snow he keeps forgetting to put on the appropriate pieces of clothing. Dress and undress a frog lead puppet appropriately.

*Leo the Late Bloomer* by Robert Kraus is about a rather low-keyed lead character who, in the form of a puppet, comes to life and helps children concentrate on the story line. A hand or rod puppet tiger combined with simple props can dramatize Leo's problems. The personality change Leo undergoes as he develops from a character who is unsuccessful at everything he attempts to a character who finally achieves mastery over his actions is an ideal situation for dramatizing with a lead puppet. The lead puppet's unsuccessful attempts to perform simple tasks during the first part of the story visually reinforce Leo's plight. The emergence of an entirely different Leo, one who is confident and successful, at the story's conclusion is strengthened when portrayed by the lead puppet.

Inclusion of props heightens interest and helps buoy the attention span of younger children. Props needed to interpret this story include: a book, paper with incomplete sketch, bib, glasses, confetti snow, picture of tree pasted on a box, and a completed drawing. To emphasize Leo's inability, use the props to show what he couldn't do. For example, to demonstrate that he couldn't read Leo holds the book upside down. Put a bib on Leo to accent the fact that he was a sloppy eater. The storyteller could put on a pair of glasses to take the role of Leo's father who watches for signs of Leo's blooming. Children could throw confetti to indicate snow falling. When Leo does finally bloom he may triumphantly read the book right side up, draw a picture, eat without his bib, and say "I made it."

## SUGGESTED TITLES FOR SINGLE LEAD PUPPETS

Allard, Harry. *Miss Nelson Is Missing!*; illus. by James Marshall. Houghton, 1977.

A disagreeable substitute takes Miss Nelson's place, and the children in her homeroom are not pleased with the switch.

Bond, Michael. *A Bear Called Paddington*; illus. by Peggy Fortune. Houghton, 1960.

Paddington, a bear from darkest Peru, finds a new home and lots of adventure in London. Other titles in this series: *Paddington Abroad* and *Paddington at Large*.

Bradford, Elizabeth. *Mr. Chang and the Yellow Robe*; illus. by Dorothee Bohlke. Garrett, 1991.

When Mr. Chang wears the yellow robe of a Mandarin he feels important. When he truly earns the right to wear the yellow robe, he learns that it is not necessary because each person is special and his ordinary robe suits him. Switch between a yellow robe and a brown robe for the Mr. Chang puppet as you tell the story.

Carle, Eric. *The Very Hungry Caterpillar*; illus. by the author. Philome, 1969.

    A newly born caterpillar on its way to becoming a butterfly is so hungry that it eats everything in sight and winds up with a terrible stomachache.

Fatio, Louise. *The Happy Lion*; illus. by Roger Duvoisin. McGraw-Hill, 1954.

    One day a zoo lion leaves his cage and, to his surprise, causes chaos as he strolls through the village. Also by the same author, *The Happy Lion in Africa*.

Freeman, Don. *Dandelion*; illus. by the author. Viking, 1964.

    A young lion's attempt to impress his friends backfires.

Freeman, Don. *Hattie the Backstage Bat*; illus. by the author. Viking, 1988.

    Hattie saves the show and becomes a star.

Freeman, Don. *Mop Top*; illus. by the author. Viking, 1955.

    Only when a young boy is mistaken for a mop does he consent to a haircut. Moppy can be made from a small box or cardboard tube using long lengths of yarn tucked inside for hair. When Moppy's hair is cut, shorten the puppet's hair by pulling the yarn from inside of the box or tube.

Galdone, Paul. *King of the Cats*; illus. by the author. Houghton, 1980.

    Retelling of the English folktale about a gravedigger who is told to deliver an unusual message which is received with great interest by his cat, Old Tom. Effectively told with a black cat puppet sitting on the storyteller's lap meowing and providing dialogue for the surprising finale.

Galdone, Paul. *Three Fox Fables*; illus. by the author. Seabury, 1971.

    A fox puppet and a bunch of real or plastic grapes are all that are needed to tell the fable of "The Fox and the Grapes." The other fables, which can be told with two lead puppets, include "The Fox and the Stork" and "The Fox and the Crow."

Henkes, Kevin. *Owen*; illus. by the author. Greenwillow, 1993.

    Owen, a young mouse, doesn't want to give up the security of his blanket in this Caldecott Honor book. Tell using a mouse hand puppet and a small, fuzzy yellow cloth for the blanket.

Kraus, Robert. *Leo the Late Bloomer*; illus. by Jose Aruego. Windmill, 1971.

    Leo, a young tiger, blooms in his own time.

London, Jonathan. *Froggy Gets Dressed*; illus. by Frank Remkiewicz. Viking, 1992.

    Froggy is in such a rush to play in the snow that he keeps forgetting to put on all of his clothes. The humor in the story will be increased as you dress and undress a paper plate puppet with detachable clothes. Use small pieces of Velcro to keep the clothing items in place.

Prelutsky, Jack. "The Snopp on the Sidewalk," in *The Snopp on the Sidewalk and Other Poems*; illus. by Byron Barton. Greenwillow, 1977.

    A poem describing the narrator's encounter with a strange, lonely creature lying on the sidewalk.

Thayer, Jane. *Gus Was a Gorgeous Ghost*; illus. by Seymour Fleishman. Morrow, 1978.

    Gus transforms himself from a plain to a brightly colored ghost.

Wells, Rosemary. *Noisy Nora*; illus. by the author. Dial, 1973.

Noisemaking and misbehaving are the weapons a young mouse uses to gain the attention of her family until she discovers a better way.

Zion, Harry. *Harry by the Sea*; illus. by Margaret Bloy Graham. Harper, 1965.

Harry, a black-and-white dog, has a series of misadventures when he is covered with seaweed while on a family outing. Cover a dog puppet with seaweed made from green fabric scraps or yarn. Tell the story using a lapboard. Also in this series: *Harry, The Dirty Dog* and *No Roses for Harry*.

## TWO LEAD PUPPETS

With experience, you may want to try using two lead puppets to pantomime a story. This technique is best suited to stories that have two major characters involved in uncomplicated actions. Start with stories that allow you to narrate as the characters mime the action. Instead of using props and scenery, especially for initial attempts, concentrate on realistically manipulating the two puppets.

One story involving two distinct characters engaged in a battle of wits is "The Monkey and the Crocodile," a Jataka tale from India. With a monkey puppet on one hand and a crocodile puppet on the other, the storyteller can narrate the entire story as the puppets pantomime the actions. When Monkey climbs a tree or Crocodile swims in the river, the scenery is imagined. The storyteller may help children see the tree by moving her eyes up the "trunk" and across the "branch" to where Monkey sits. By focusing attention on the character who is doing the action, the storyteller helps the child imagine and understand the story's setting.

Once you are comfortable handling two lead puppets in a pantomime role you may feel ready to experiment with creating a voice for each. The voice of the puppet should be consistent with the role, personality, and even the size of the character. While you may decide to narrate the story in part, allow the lead puppets to speak the dialogue to make the characters more believable. When using two puppets it is wise during initial attempts to select stories that have main characters with contrasting personalities. When first telling stories with two lead characters, give one a high voice and the other one a low voice. With practice and experimentation you, the storyteller, will be able to create voices with a variety of timbres and nuances. Chapter 5, Developing Puppets for Storytelling, has many suggestions for creating puppet voices.

Certain stories are particularly suited for two lead puppet integration. Ideal materials to use are stories where action and dialogue are divided between two characters, stories with opposing viewpoints, and stories in which traditional roles are reversed.

### Divided Actions and Dialogue

It is important to the success of this technique to select stories that have strong action and dialogue equally divided between two main characters. When necessary to the plot, less important characters may be imagined or played by the storyteller to simplify presentations.

*The Bear's Toothache* by David McPhail is an example of a story containing two strong lead characters. A boy puppet could successfully remove an aching tooth from the mouth of a bear puppet in this fanciful story, using a cardboard tooth prop. The voice of the bear should be loud and low pitched to accentuate his main dialogue, moaning and groaning. The voice for the boy should be softer and higher pitched to match his age and smaller stature. The part of the father is played by the storyteller without a puppet.

The humorous retelling of an old folktale, *Strega Nona* by Tomie de Paola, features the antics of Big Anthony, a bumbling village lad, who is able to start a magic pasta pot bubbling but is unable to halt the river of pasta when the pot overflows. Strega Nona's timely return saves the village but not Big Anthony, who must face his punishment. The roles of Big Anthony and Strega Nona contain action, dialogue, and singing, which makes them perfect choices for dual lead puppets to dramatize over the lap area. The overflowing spaghetti can be demonstrated by using yarn pulled from a pot prop.

In the Norwegian folktale "Why the Bear Is Stumpy-tailed," the action is nicely divided between the two main characters. A fox cleverly tricks a bear into believing that he can catch fish by lowering his long tail through a hole in the ice. When the ice freezes, the bear tries to pull his tail out, but he loses it and the result is the short, stubby tail bears have to this day. Attach a long, furry tail to a bear puppet with Velcro so it can be easily removed to illustrate this comic event.

## SUGGESTED TITLES FOR <u>ACTION AND DIALOGUE</u>

de Paola, Tomie. *Strega Nona*; illus. by the author. Prentice-Hall, 1975.

> A humorous retelling of an old folktale about a witch, her magic pasta pot, and a bumbling village lad who creates bedlam! A Caldecott Honor book.

de Regniers, Beatrice Schenk. *Jack the Giant Killer*; illus. by Anne Wilsdorf. Atheneum, 1987.

> The first adventure of Jack the giant killer told in a style that makes it perfect for pairs of children wearing bodi-puppets to dramatize.

Galdone, Paul. *The Monkey and the Crocodile*; illus. by the author. Seabury, 1969.

> Picture-book version of a Jataka tale about a monkey who outwits a crocodile.

Gershator, Phillis. *The Iroko-man*; illus. by Holly C. Kim. Orchard, 1994.

> A Yoruba folktale about the terrifying Iroko-man, a tree spirit, who turns those who look at him mad. When a village woman, Oluronbi, does not keep her promise to give the Iroko-man her firstborn child, he turns her into a bird. The clever solution of her husband restores the family as well as satisfying the demands of the Iroko-man. The Iroko-man and Oluronbi can be standing box puppets. To show Oluronbi as a bird, turn the box around. Create a booming voice for the Iroko-man to use for his chant and a soft, sad voice for Oluronbi. Simple cutout puppets can be used for the other characters, or children can play the parts.

Grimm, Jacob, and Wilhelm Grimm. "The Cat and Mouse in Partnership," in *Household Stories*; illus. by Johannes Troyer. Macmillan, 1954.

> A cat and a mouse unsuccessfully attempt to live together. The cat sneaks away from the mouse and eats all the fat the pair has stored for the winter. In the end, the cat devours the mouse as well. Tell this story with a talking-mouth cat puppet, a flexible-body hand puppet mouse, and a jar to represent the reserve food.

Haviland, Virginia. "Why the Bear Is Stumpy-tailed," in *Favorite Fairy Tales Told in Norway*; illus. by Leonard Weisgard. Little, 1961.

> A fox tricks a bear into believing he can catch fish through a hole in the ice. Bear's long tail is frozen off and that is why today the bear has a stumpy tail.

Lexau, Joan M. *Crocodile and Hen*; illus. by Joan Sandin. Harper, 1969.

An explanation of why crocodiles won't eat hens. To enhance the effect when Crocodile snaps his jaws shut, use a mouth puppet with a very large mouth. Storyteller assumes the lizard's role without a puppet.

McNaughton, Colin. *Making Friends with Frankenstein*; illus. by the author. Candlewick, 1994.

A collection of monstrous poems whose humor will appeal to upper-elementary-age children. Several are very suitable for telling with two lead puppets including "I've Lost My Head," "The Lady in Love," and "The Shady Character." Children will have great fun retelling these poems with puppets.

McPhail, David. *The Bear's Toothache*; illus. by the author. Little, 1972.

A young boy successfully relieves a bear of an aching tooth. Add a removable tooth to a talking-mouth puppet bear for a great finale.

Waber, Bernard. *An Anteater Named Arthur*; illus. by the author. Houghton, 1967.

Even though Arthur's mother thinks he is a wonderful son, she admits there are times when he is a problem. The humorous dialogue makes the five stories in this book fun to do.

## Opposing Views

When two opposing points of view are expressed by the main characters, lead puppets can effectively highlight the controversy. Stories abound in which this situation occurs. *Bah! Humbug?* by Lorna Balian presents a girl and a boy who hold different opinions. Marge believes in Santa but her brother Arthur does not. A lead puppet for each character brings the two views into focus, providing a proving ground for each perspective. The storyteller assumes the role of Santa. A boy puppet can lay a trap for Santa with string and bells. When the boy puppet falls asleep, the children along with the girl puppet can witness Santa's visit. Marge realizes that Arthur may be older but not always wiser. It is hoped that this understanding will not be lost upon your story listeners.

The French folktale "Toads and Diamonds" presents two sisters who have opposite views of the world due to their innate personalities. One is kind and polite, the other proud and unpleasant. Each encounters a fairy disguised as a woman in need of a drink of water and responds to her request in a manner true to character. The first sister's reward for her kindness is that of a precious stone falling from her mouth with each word she speaks. The impolite sister's reward brings a toad or snake from her mouth with each word she speaks. Talking-mouth puppets are the best choice for the two sisters. The storyteller can assume the role of the fairy requesting water. Cardboard cutouts can represent the toads or diamonds that fall from each puppet's mouth. (Hide these in your hand next to the puppet's mouth and drop them as the puppet speaks.)

### SUGGESTED TITLES FOR DRAMATIZING OPPOSING VIEWS

Aruego, Jose, and Ariane Dewey. *Rockabye Crocodile*; illus. by the authors. Greenwillow, 1988.

A Philippine folktale about two elderly boars, one cheerful and kind; one mean and selfish. Each cares for a baby crocodile in its own way and is rewarded accordingly by the mother crocodile. Tell with two lead puppets and simple group puppets to represent the fish and insects.

Balian, Lorna. *Bah! Humbug?*; illus. by the author. Abingdon, 1977.

Marge and her brother Arthur hold different opinions regarding the existence of Santa Claus.

Carlstrom, Nancy White. *I'm Not Moving, Mama!*; illus. by Thor Wickstrom. Macmillan, 1990.

A young mouse is not happy about moving. His mother lovingly responds to each complaint with reasons why she won't leave the child behind. Children in pairs, one with a child mouse envelope puppet and another with a mother mouse envelope puppet, discuss moving from each character's point of view. See chapter 9 for envelope puppet directions.

Hall, Donald. *I Am the Dog, I Am the Cat*; illus. by Barry Moser. Dial, 1994.

A dog and a cat take turns explaining why it is great to be who they are. Children in pairs share other reasons why it's great to be a cat or a dog.

Huck, Charlotte. *Toads and Diamonds*; illus. by Anita Lobel. Greenwillow, 1995.

The popular fairy tale of two sisters, one beautiful and kind, the other mean and unpleasant, each of whom receives a just reward for her behavior toward a fairy.

## Traditional Roles Reversed

Stories that capture our interest often highlight traditional role reversals. Some examples follow:

A small and physically weak character helps a larger, stronger character as in the fable "Androcles and the Lion." Many versions of this fable are available. Younger children will enjoy a modern version, *Andy and the Lion*, portraying the friendship that develops when a boy removes a thorn from the paw of a lion. In addition to a boy flexible-body hand puppet and a talking-mouth lion puppet, add a few props when telling this story: toy pliers, a cardboard thorn, rock, cage made of chickenwire, and a medal to pin on Andy.

A foolish/weak character outwits a wise/strong character. A perfect example is the English folktale "Tops and Bottoms." A farmer strikes a bargain with a goblin who claims the crops from the farmer's field belong to him. The farmer agrees to do all the work if the goblin will take only half of the crop. The year the goblin asks for the bottom half of the crop, the farmer plants wheat, which grows above ground. When the goblin asks for the top half of the crop, the farmer plants carrots, which grow below ground. Even when the goblin challenges the farmer to a mowing contest, the farmer outwits him by putting iron bars among the wheat on the goblin's side of the field. Two hand puppets with flexible bodies and a few cardboard props for the crops and scythes are all that are needed to tell this amusing tale. Cardboard crops can be poked into a sheet of Styrofoam to show how they grow, above or below ground.

Farmer and goblin act out their conflict over a garden prop made of Styrofoam.

A traditional character assumes an unexpected role. The heroine in Dennis Lee's Poem "I Eat Kids Yum Yum!" from *Garbage Delight* is an ideal example. The humor and wit of a girl turning the tables on a mighty monster become even more enjoyable if the girl puppet is small and delicate and the monster puppet is large and rough. Present the monster as a swaggering and blustering creature who sings with a gruff, gravelly voice. When the girl sings her reply in a menacing and very determined voice, the surprised monster will undoubtedly quake and shiver before making a hasty exit. The unexpected twist found in the poem is vividly reinforced and made all the more amusing by the addition of puppets because of the high contrast between the characters.

## SUGGESTED TITLES FOR DRAMATIZING ROLE REVERSALS

Aardema, Vera. *Borreguita and the Coyote*; illus. by Peter Mathers. Knopf, 1991.

In this humorous Mexican tale, Borreguita, a little lamb, outwits Coyote. To highlight the finale, the Coyote puppet needs a mouth that opens wide. Scenery can be simple; a piece of blue cloth with a yellow paper moon for one scene and a mountain from a large box with a second overhanging box as the ledge for another.

Baumgartner, Barbara. *Crocodile! Crocodile!*; illus. by Judith Moffatt. Dorling Kindersley, 1994.

The title story in this collection of stories told around the world recounts how a clever monkey outwits a crocodile and explains why crocodiles and monkeys have never been friends. Perfect for telling with a monkey and a crocodile hand puppet. Two other stories in this collection suitable for two lead puppets are "Crocodile Hunts for the Monkey" and "How the Chipmunk Got His Stripes."

Conger, Leslie. *Tops and Bottoms*; illus. by Imero Gobbato. Four Winds, 1970.

A farmer outwits a goblin who tries to claim his crops.

Daugherty, James. *Andy and the Lion*; illus. by the author. Viking, 1938.

A modern picture-book version of the fable "Androcles and the Lion."

Johnston, Tony. *The Tale of Rabbit and Coyote*; illus. by Tomie de Paola. Putnam, 1994.

A Mexican folktale in which trickster Rabbit outwits unsuspecting Coyote. This folktale explains why coyotes howl at the moon. Simple props such as a clay pot, stick, and paper ladder will add greatly to the telling.

Lee, Dennis. *Garbage Delight*; illus. by Frank Newfeld. Houghton, 1977.

Delightful collection of nonsense poems. Two poems particularly suited to the lead puppet technique are: "I Eat Kids Yum Yum!" and "Inspector Dogbone Gets His Man." Try each with two lead puppets.

McKissack, Patricia. *Flossie and the Fox*; illus. by Rachel Isadora. Dial, 1986.

In this African-American variant of Little Red Riding Hood, a spunky little girl outwits a wily fox. Perfect for telling with two lead puppets, a girl and a fox.

Paxton, Tom. *Androcles and the Lion and Other Aesop's Fables*; illus. by Robert Rayevsky. Morrow Junior Books, 1991.

Androcles, a slave, pulls a thorn from a lion's paw, earning the lion's gratitude and help when Androcles least expects it.

Stevens, Janet. *Tops and Bottoms*; illus. by the author. Harcourt, 1995.

In this variant of "Tops and Bottoms" a hungry hare attempts to outwit a lazy bear. A Caldecott Honor book.

Young, Ed. *The Terrible Nung Gwama*; illus. by the author. Collins, 1978.

In this Chinese folktale a young woman outwits a monster who devours human beings. Use a flexible-body hand puppet for the woman and a talking-mouth puppet for the Nung Gwama. The storyteller can assume the role of the peddlers who advise the woman.

## PARTICIPATION WITH LEAD PUPPETS

The ideas presented in the preceding pages detail steps for incorporating one and two lead puppets into story presentations. In these situations the lead puppet is used by the storyteller and the children are observers. But lead puppets also offer an excellent opportunity to draw children into the story through active participation. Several types of stories are well suited to this technique.

1.  Stories that require a question or answer stated repeatedly. An example is "The Yellow Ribbon," from Virginia Tashjian's *Juba This and Juba That*, which has a question that is repeated several times along with a surprise ending. The storyteller narrates and also plays the part of Mary in the story, using a hand puppet with a detachable head and a yellow ribbon tied around its neck. A child chosen from the listeners plays John and wears various hats and props to indicate different stages in John's life: baseball cap—youth; diploma—high school graduation; top hat—wedding; fedora—adult; grey wig—old age. Throughout the story John asks the Mary puppet, "Why do you wear that yellow ribbon?" At the end of the story, when Mary allows John to remove the ribbon, he and the whole audience will be amazed when the puppet's head rolls off! A more effective device for dramatizing this unusual tale would be hard to imagine.

2.  Stories in which a child assumes the identity of the lead character. In some instances the portrayal of a story can be more exciting if a child rather than a puppet is used as the lead character. To enrich the participation experience, a child can become the lead character by donning a costume and a mask and, in effect, becoming a bodi-puppet. Children love to "dress up" and become someone else. What a wonderful way to become totally involved in a story!

*Humbug! Witch* by Lorna Balian offers the opportunity for a child to assume the role of the main character with costumes in a most satisfying deception. A young girl's unsuccessful attempt to impersonate a horrible witch makes an amusing story. Dress a child in a witch costume and mask. Give the child a broom to use. The storyteller, another child, a puppet, or a stuffed toy can assume the role of the cat, Fred. As the storyteller narrates the story, the child appears from behind a bookcase and pantomimes the action: trying to look horrible; attempting to cackle like a witch but only producing a giggle; unsuccessfully attempting to ride the broom; failing to change Fred, the cat, into a hippopotamus; mixing magic potion; removing the costume piece by piece; and flopping onto a pretend bed. The addition of props heightens the visual enjoy-

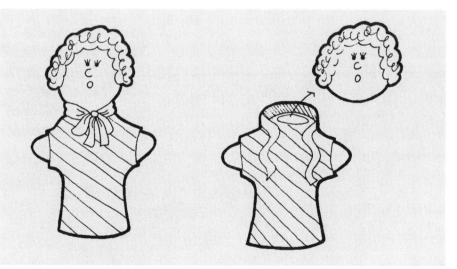

**Puppet with removable head for "The Yellow Ribbon"**

ment of this dramatization: a rug for the bed; a kettle in which to mix the potion; items such as a mixing spoon, prune pits, egg shells, rubber spiders and lizards for the potion.

*The Beast of Monsieur Racine* by Tomi Ungerer can be told in a similar manner. Two children, masquerading as a "beast," first steal Monsieur Racine's special pears and then become friends with him. Only when Monsieur Racine presents the strange animal to the Academy of Sciences do the children cast off their disguise. The role of Monsieur Racine is played by the storyteller. An old blanket can be converted into the lumpy skin of the beast and draped over two children who will play the beast.

3. Stories in which children change the appearance of the lead character by adding costume pieces. *Harlequin and the Gift of Many Colors* by Remy Charlip and Burton Supree, a story that explains the origin of Harlequin's multicolored costume, is an example. The children assume an important role by supplying the fabric pieces that are a key element in the story.

A large grocery-bag puppet serves as Harlequin. The storyteller assumes the role of Mother and also manipulates the Harlequin puppet. Children participate by contributing colored fabric pieces for Harlequin's costume. The action might follow this procedure:

Begin a story with Harlequin puppet on your hand.

Set a carnival booth made from a box on the tabletop.

Wrap a blanket of stars around Harlequin.

Hide or lay Harlequin down when children wonder where he is.

Make Harlequin appear before the booth window.

Put puppet behind your back as Harlequin runs away.

Ask children to bring up fabric scraps.

Make Harlequin reappear.

Assume role of Mother and turn cloth over in your hands.

Glue scraps to paper base costume while Harlequin pretends to sleep.

Wake Harlequin and attach costume to body front.

Show children the fantastic costume.

As a follow-up, children can make their own fantastic costumes from large grocery bags and a rich selection of fabric scraps or paint. To make the costume, cut out neck and arm holes, then slit center front of a large grocery bag. After the costumes are completed, invite children to model them. Try

Turnaround paper-plate stick puppet for *How Spider Saved Halloween*. A cardboard tube is the neck; paper or fabric strips are the spider's legs.

distributing party noisemakers and having a minicarnival or parade. You might even feature a contest for the best costume.

Many stories offer opportunities for similar inter-action between children and lead puppets:

Children can hold up sample noses for Arthur the aardvark to try as he searches for a replacement nose in *Arthur's Nose* by Marc Brown.

Fly, Spider, and Ladybug attempt to outwit a gang of bullies in *How Spider Saved Halloween* by Robert Kraus. Children can add costume pieces to a spider puppet until he finds the perfect disguise—a pumpkin. A two-sided paper-plate puppet makes a perfect spider—one side represents a black spider, the other a spider disguised as an orange pumpkin.

When the hippo in Bernard Waber's story *You Look Ridiculous Said the Rhinoceros to the Hippopotamus* dreams of changing her looks to please her friends, invite children to assist by taping the new parts to a rod or paper-bag lead puppet. Parts to be attached include a rhino's horn, monkey's tail, a giraffe-like neck, and a turtle's shell.

*Jennie's Hat* by Ezra Jack Keats provides the opportunity for children to transform a plain straw hat into a designer creation by adding paper flowers, leaves, pictures, a paper fan, and even a bird's nest complete with baby birds. A bodi-puppet worn by a child or the storyteller is a perfect base on which to place the plain hat—a large straw basket with the handle under the puppeteer's chin.

## SUGGESTED TITLES FOR PARTICIPATION WITH LEAD PUPPETS

Balian, Lorna. *Humbug! Witch*; illus. by the author. Abingdon, 1965.

A humorous story about a young girl's unsuccessful attempt to disguise herself as a horrible witch.

Charlip, Remy, and Burton Supree. *Harlequin and the Gift of Many Colors*; illus. by Remy Charlip. Parents, 1973.

Harlequin's friends make it possible for him to attend the carnival wearing a new multicolored suit.

Fox, Mem. *Shoes from Grandpa*; illus. by Patricia Mullins. Orchard, 1990.

A young girl, Jesse, gets a whole new outfit to go with her new shoes. Bring in clothes and dress up a girl as the story is told.

Keats, Ezra Jack. *Jennie's Hat*; illus. by the author. Harper, 1966.

A plain straw hat is transformed into a beautiful creation.

Kraus, Robert. *How Spider Saved Halloween*; illus. by the author. Parents, 1980.

Spider's ingenuity outwits a gang of bullies.

Mahy, Margaret. *Tortoise's Flying Lesson*; illus. by Emily Bolam. Harcourt, 1994.

The title story in this collection of folktales from around the world dramatizes eagle's attempts to teach turtle how to fly. Children add feathers to a turtle puppet. Attach pieces of Velcro to the turtle puppet's shell and to the feathers the children will attach.

Tashjian, Virginia A., comp. *Juba This and Juba That*; illus. by Nadine Bernard Westcott. Little, 1995.

Poems, riddles, and humorous sketches selected for use as story hour stretchers. Includes "The Yellow Ribbon."

Ungerer, Tomi. *The Beast of Monsieur Racine*; illus. by the author. Farrar, 1971.

Monsieur Racine, a retired tax collector, befriends a strange animal who has been stealing his favorite pears. When the beast's true identity is revealed, it startles the on-lookers.

Waber, Bernard. *You Look Ridiculous Said the Rhinoceros to the Hippopotamus*; illus. by the author. Houghton, 1973.

A hippo's attempt to change her appearance to please those around her makes her *really* look ridiculous.

Wahl, Jan. *Little Eight John*; illus. by Will Clay. Dutton, 1992.

Little Eight John constantly disobeys his mother but learns his lesson when the Old Raw Head Bloody Bones appears. Put a cap on a boy who pantomimes the actions of Little Eight John. Storyteller takes role of the mother. Give another child a large stick puppet of Old Raw Head Bloody Bones for the dramatic climax. A Coretta Scott King Award winner.

Wood, Audrey. *King Bidgood's in the Bathtub*; illus. by Don Wood. Harcourt, 1985.

A king refuses to leave his bathtub to rule his kingdom so members of the court join him in the tub. The clever Page solves the problem by pulling the plug. Children wearing costume pieces and carrying props act out the story. Set up chairs to form the tub's outline. A Caledott Honor book.

Ziefert, Harriet. *A New Coat for Anna*; illus. by Anita Lobel. Knopf, 1986.

In this story set after World War II, when supplies were short, a mother trades her special possessions to provide a new winter coat for Anna. A girl wearing an old coat plays Anna. Other children pantomime roles of the farmer shearing the sheep, the old woman spinning the wool, and the tailor measuring her. Storyteller plays the role of the mother. At the end Anna models her new coat.

## SWALLOWING PUPPETS

Stories abound in which a character swallows things—food, insects, animals, people, even dreams! Popular examples from folk literature include "Drakestail," "The Wolf and the Seven Kids," and "The Old Lady Who Swallowed a Fly." Swallowing puppets add greatly to the fun of these stories. A swallowing puppet may be made of many things—a box, a bag, even a tennis sock! The main requirement is that the puppet is able to devour or "swallow" whatever the story requires. In most cases it is also necessary for that which has been swallowed to be retrieved from the puppet, unharmed of course. Making a swallowing puppet involves more work than simpler puppets, but the delight of the children rewards you for the time spent. Three types of swallowing puppets are described in this chapter: a large paper-bag puppet for "The Old Lady Who Swallowed a Fly"; a box version for *The Clay Pot Boy* by Cynthia Jameson; and a tennis-sock puppet for *Gregory the Terrible Eater* by Mitchell Sharmat.

## Paper-Bag Swallowing Puppet

The song "I Know an Old Lady Who Swallowed a Fly" recounts the tale of an old woman who has a most unusual appetite, swallowing a fly, a spider, a bird, a cat, a dog, a cow, and who died trying to swallow a horse, of course! This popular character is a natural swallowing puppet. The puppet must have a mouth hole through which the animals are inserted as they are eaten. In addition, a slit is needed so the swallowed characters can be easily removed from the Old Lady's stomach.

Give the children appropriate cardboard cutout characters to feed to the Old Lady as the song is sung. The fly should be the smallest character with each succeeding creature a bit larger until the final and largest animal, the horse, is so big it gets stuck in the mouth of the Old Lady and chokes her.

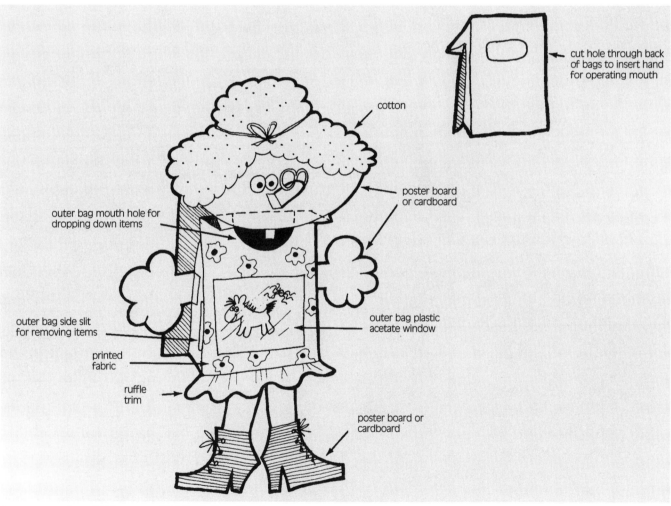

Large paper-bag "I Know an Old Lady" swallowing puppet

## Construction of Old Lady Puppet

A double-bag swallowing puppet, while requiring a longer time commitment to construct, is a large, attention-getting puppet well worth the energy expended.

### Materials

Two large grocery bags

Stiff paper or poster board

Construction paper

Clear acetate (book report cover)

Scrap fabric and trim

Yarn or cotton

### Procedures

Cut a rectangular window hole in the stomach area of one bag (outer bag).

Tape a piece of acetate to back of window hole.

Cut out a mouth hole under flap of bag.

Cut a slit on either side of bag, close to window hole, large enough for hand to pull out swallowed items.

Slip outer bag over inner bag (which has no cutouts or preparation). Fit together so bags match up perfectly.

Cut hole through the back of bags, behind mouth area, to slip hand through for operating mouth.

Staple the bags together around entire bottom edge.

Cut out a face shape, larger than flap of bag, from poster board.

Glue face to flap of outer bag. Paint on facial features or make features from construction paper. Yarn or cotton serves well for hair.

Glue a colorful piece of fabric on front of outer bag for a costume. Use trim to decorate.

Add poster board arms and legs.

Cut out various small paper animals to feed to the puppet.

### Operation

Slip fingers through back hole and move flap up and down. Drop items down mouth hole and remove them through slit near stomach. You may wish to weight items by taping metal washers or coins to the backs.

### Box Puppet

In Cynthia Jameson's story *The Clay Pot Boy*, a childless couple form a boy from clay to be their son. The boy eats everything and everyone he meets including the old woman and her spinning wheel, the old man

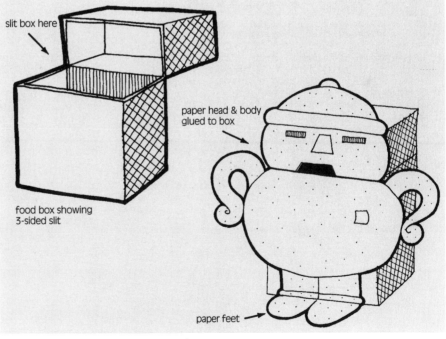

Swallowing puppet fashioned from a box for *The Clay Pot Boy*

and his rake, a barn, a rooster, a hen and her eggs, and ten tubs of milk. The Clay Pot Boy's indiscriminate feasting is finally put to an end by a Billy Goat who smashes him to bits.

The puppet created for this character must have the ability to break open so the characters inside can be removed unharmed. A cereal or detergent box can successfully form the base on which to construct a swallowing Clay Pot Boy.

### Construction of Clay Pot Boy

This is a simpler way to make a swallowing puppet, but one that is suitable for stories in which quick retrieval of objects is desirable.

#### Materials

Cereal or detergent box

Construction paper

Cardboard

#### Procedures

Slit front and three sides of box along mouth line.

Cut out a head and a body section for the Clay Pot Boy from construction paper.

Glue head to upper portion of box and body to lower.

Cut out a mouth opening slot to allow puppet to "swallow" objects.

Cut out cardboard characters to feed to the puppet.

#### Operation

Slip objects to be eaten through mouth slot. Snap box apart when Clay Pot Boy "breaks."

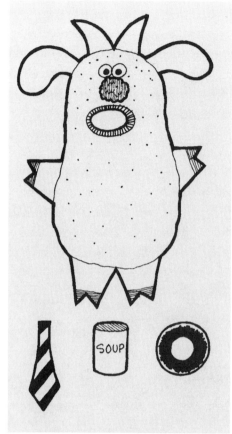

Swallowing puppet fashioned from a tennis sock for *Gregory the Terrible Eater.* Felt is used for the horns, ears, eyes, and legs. The items to swallow are paper.

### Tennis-Sock Puppet

A tennis sock altered only slightly offers a third variation of a swallowing puppet. The goat described in Mitchell Sharmat's story *Gregory, the Terrible Eater* has a unique appetite, even for a goat. Gregory prefers fruits, vegetables, and other such foods, much to the dismay of his parents. After consultation with a doctor, Gregory begins to eat a balanced goat diet.

Gregory's plight can be dramatized very satisfactorily with a sock swallowing puppet. Children can "feed" Gregory cardboard cutouts of preferred foods.

### Construction of Gregory Goat

This simply-made puppet can serve as a talking-mouth puppet as well as a swallowing puppet

#### Materials

Tennis sock with pom-pom

Felt scraps

Cardboard

#### Procedures

Use stretch opening of sock for the mouth and pom-pom for the nose features.

Slit an opening in the back of sock for your hand. Inside the back, sew a finger loop above and below the "mouth" to provide movement control.

Add felt legs, ears, horns, and eyes.

Cut out miniature cardboard food items to feed to the puppet.

## SUGGESTED TITLES FOR <u>SWALLOWING PUPPETS</u>

Chase, Richard. "Sody Sallyratus" in *Juba This and Juba That*, comp. by Virginia A. Tashjian; illus. by Nadine Bernard Westcott. Little, 1995. Pg. 48–52.

    A story from the American South featuring a bear who swallows an old man, old woman, little girl, and little boy. When he tries to eat the pet squirrel, he falls and splits wide open allowing everyone to escape. A large-box swallowing puppet makes a very satisfactory bear. Finger puppets or paper characters can be swallowed.

Chocolate, Deborah M. Newton. *Imani in the Belly*; illus. by Alex Boies. BridgeWater, 1994.

    An East African tale of Simba, the terrible King of Beasts, who swallows Imani's children as well as many villagers and animals. Imani's love for her children gives her the courage to face Simba and rescue her children. Construct a large swallowing puppet from a box or a grocery bag and use paper cutouts for the people and animals who are swallowed.

Czernecki, Stefan, and Timothy Rhodes. *The Singing Snake*; illus. by Stefan Czernecki. Hyperion Books, 1993.

    An amusing retelling of an Australian folktale about a snake who swallows a lark in order to win a singing contest. Make a paper-bag style snake swallowing puppet so that the lark can be seen inside of the snake.

Gág, Wanda. *The Funny Thing*; illus. by the author. Coward, 1929.

    The Funny Thing is an animal who loves to eat the dolls of good children. Bobo, a good man of the mountains, convinces the Funny Thing that eating jum-jills will make his blue points beautiful and his tail grow longer. The Funny Thing eats so many jum-jills that his tail grows longer and longer until he wraps it around the mountain.

    Make a Funny Thing puppet from an oatmeal box with a tail made from a sock. Pull the sock tail from the box as the Funny Thing eats jum-jills fed to him by the children.

Garrison, Christian. *The Dream Eater*; illus. by Diane Goode. Bradbury, 1978.

    A fascinating Japanese story about a Baku, or dream eater, whose favorite dish is nightmares. The Baku's hunger is satisfied by the bad dreams of the villagers. As the story is told, pull the Baku from a bag decorated to look like a river. In order to swallow the nightmares, the Baku needs a large mouth that can open and close. A large box or a grocery bag can be used as the foundation of this puppet. Children may wish to create their own bad dreams to feed to the Baku.

Grimm Brothers. *The Wolf and the Seven Little Kids*; ed. by Linda M. Jennings; illus. by Martin Ursell. Silver Burdett, 1986.

    A wolf tricks seven little goats into opening the door and then he swallows them. Quick thinking on the part of Mother Goat releases them from inside the wolf's stomach. Combine any style wolf swallowing puppet with cutouts of the little goats.

Jameson, Cynthia. *The Clay Pot Boy*; illus. by Arnold Lobel. Coward, 1973.

    A clay pot boy devours everything in sight until he is smashed to bits by a goat. As story is told, children may feed the Clay Pot Boy.

Karas, G. Brian. *I Know an Old Lady*; illus. by the author. Scholastic, 1994.

    The woman who devours a succession of animals makes a humorous swallowing puppet.

Kent, Jack. *The Fat Cat*; illus. by the author. Scholastic, 1971.

    A Danish folktale about a cat who eats everything he meets until a woodcutter slashes him open and releases what has been captured within. Make a cat puppet from paper bags or a split box as described in the preceding chapter.

Sharmat, Mitchell. *Gregory, the Terrible Eater*; illus. by Jose Aruego. Four Winds, 1980.

    Gregory, a goat, prefers foods not considered wholesome by his parents.

Sloat, Teri. *The Eye of the Needle*; illus. by the author. Dutton, 1990.

    From Alaska comes the story of Amik who is so hungry he eats everything he catches, realizing too late that he has saved nothing for his grandmother. How Grandmother uses the eye of her needle to solve Amik's dilemma makes a wonderful story. Either a box or grocery bag swallowing type puppet will make an effective Amik.

    Each time Amik swallows something the children can supply a loud "Glump" to accompany the animal's disappearance into Amik's mouth. Children can also participate by feeding the animals to Amik.

Starbird, Kaye. "Eat-It-All-Elaine," in *Amelia Mixed the Mustard*; ed. by Evaline Ness; illus. by the editor. Scribner, 1975.

    An amusing poem immortalizing Elaine, the camper who ate anything and everything within reach. Recreate Elaine's gastronomic feats using a two-bag swallowing puppet similar to the Old Lady.

Thaler, Mike. *A Hippopotamus Ate the Teacher*; illus. by Jared Lee. Avon, 1981.

    On a field trip to the zoo, Ms. Jones is swallowed by a hippopotamus, who replaces her in the classroom until the situation is remedied. A box-type swallowing puppet for the hippopotamus can devour a paper cutout Ms. Jones.

Wahl, Jan. *Drakestail*; illus. by Byron Barton. Greenwillow, 1978.

    An easy-to-read version of the French folktale about a duck who encounters many characters on the way to see the king. Hide the characters inside a box-type swallowing puppet until the finale.

# Part Four

# PARTICIPATORY STORYTELLING

Cardboard puppet for *The Little Engine That Could*

**T**HAT INVISIBLE BOND linking storyteller and audience becomes strengthened and even more unifying with active participation of the audience. When invited to join in the experience, physically or emotionally, children become involved to a far greater extent than is possible when they remain mere observers. The characters and story take on a sense of immediacy as the children try on character roles physically. In participatory storytelling everyone takes part. There is no audience because all the children are part of the experience. Thus, this technique taps the children's resources for creative expression as well as their talents for dramatic interpretation.

Four ways of including children in storytelling are presented in this part. The use of "anything" puppets to recreate individual characters or enact complete stories is presented in chapter 8. The possibilities of involving sound are explored in chapter 9. Action participation is examined in chapter 10. How to combine sound and action into exciting, multifaceted storytelling highlights chapter 11.

Children like to interpret both heroic and villainous characters, and both afford good opportunities for in-depth character study. Imagine a child's delight in giving voice to a wild creature's braying or in manipulating the gestures of a crazed king or a timid mouse. Children enjoy role-playing both realistic and imaginary characters. When children are given an opportunity to dramatize with voice and actions, the experience is heightened and, correspondingly, the educational value is increased.

Of special interest to the librarian, media specialist, or teacher who works with young children is the factor of added retention that accompanies participatory storytelling for children who might otherwise quickly forget. A typical nonparticipatory story presentation of fifteen or twenty minutes' duration may be too much for individual children with limited concentration skills. However, when a specific role or task is assigned to the group, the attention span increases due to the active involvement in the story. More importantly, the direct impact of the story upon the listeners is greater.

During participatory activities no formal stage is used; instead, the children sit in an open area and contribute to the story by creating sound effects, manipulating puppets, or playing rhythm instruments. The type of puppet utilized is of secondary importance to the child's involvement. A variety of puppets, depending on the requirements of the story, may be suitable.

An educationally sound approach to use with beginning participatory storytelling is to introduce ideas slowly, building from the simple to the more complex. One way to begin is with anything puppets—simple, featureless puppets that rely completely on the imagination of the child puppeteer for personality. Using anything puppets, the whole group may simultaneously pantomime actions of the lead character, develop dialogue for a character, improvise a scene from a story, or even dramatize the entire story.

Involving children in the creation of sounds to accompany a story is another surefire participatory technique. At first you might ask all the children to supply a preassigned sound for the lead character in a story. From there each child might invent a suitable sound effect for a character or background element in a story.

Alternatively, you may begin by asking children to use puppets only to pantomime the actions of the lead character in a story. Then the various characters of that same story could be assigned to individual children and the complete story pantomimed simultaneously in small groups. Finally, try combining sounds and actions to provide an exciting visual and auditory experience in which all children are included as a large group again, some creating sound effects, others manipulating puppets.

Initial activities are best conducted within the security of the group and only gradually should children be expected to be responsible for an individual sound or puppet character—and, even then, always as part of a group sharing situation. As the children begin to feel comfortable with simple sounds and actions, the storyteller may attempt more elaborate dramas and more diverse characterizations.

## USING PARTS FOUR AND FIVE

The standard format in chapters 9 through 21 should help the leader clarify content and presentation of each story. At the same time, the storyteller is encouraged to make whatever modifications are necessary to meet the particular needs of the group.

### Approach

This segment outlines the general roles that both storyteller and children will assume during storytelling. For example, "leader narrates story as children pantomime the actions" indicates the general responsibilities for each. A lead puppet is a constant factor, along with narration, in each story; these parts are usually managed by the storyteller.

By scanning the "Approach" segment, the leader can decide whether the particular story fits in with the objectives he or she has for a group at the time.

When not stated, it is assumed that the seating arrangement for the children will be a semicircle on the floor. The leader will typically be seated or standing before the group.

### Puppets/Props

This segment lists key "Characters/Props," along with the suggested type of puppet and specific materials for props. This list is kept to a minimum; only those elements essential to the story are included. The storyteller may easily substitute readily available materials under the "Types/Materials" subsection.

## Presentation

Organization is an important factor for insuring a smooth and successful story presentation. This segment includes four subsections that assure such an even flow, simply by outlining the sequence of activity.

"General procedures" helps the leader assign specific parts to children, including order of appearance and use of props. To increase the element of surprise for the children, the leader should try to hide props out of view—in paper bags, totes, boxes, apron pockets, or behind a person's back.

"Introduction" is the event—usually questions, discussions, description of props—used to gain the interest of the children for a specific story. Such simple beginnings help establish mood while providing a natural lead into the story.

"Story actions" are minimal directions for sequential movement of characters and props. The storyteller and children may take creative freedom in enlarging upon these actions, once they are familiar with the story.

"Follow-up" suggests additional activities to enrich the story experience through reinforcement of the plot, actions, or characters of the same or similar stories. Examples include reviewing important actions through a host puppet; constructing a simple finger puppet of a character to take home; and dramatizing part of the story.

As the storyteller gains experience, personal preferences for activities and combinations of activities for story sharing will develop. While this is natural and appropriate, it is still important to give children a variety and broad scope of story experiences.

# Chapter 8 ANYTHING PUPPETS

N "ANYTHING" PUPPET is a basic, faceless puppet that is an excellent tool with which to begin participatory experiences with literature. Its versatility, because of its facelessness, stimulates a child's imagination; it puts the child completely in charge of developing the puppet's personality. It is the child who turns this rather plain-looking piece of cloth into a character with distinct voice and movement. Since there are no set features on the puppet, the child's imagination can roam freely and without constraints. The anything puppet in this way provides great stimulation for the child's creativity. Everything the puppet becomes depends upon the child, who is solely responsible for giving it life and personality.

New stories can be created around the anything puppet. These featureless puppets may be used solely with imagination supplying the facial features and costumes. Or, one may be more elaborate and combine elements of creativity and artistic ability to design facial features and/or costumes. Either method, imagination alone or embellishment of the anything puppet, results in an adventurous journey for nearly any story and at little or no expense.

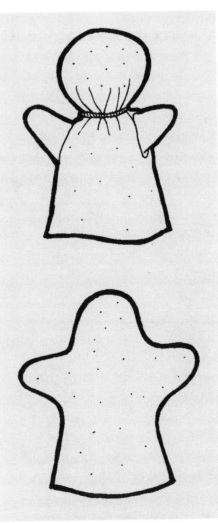

Examples of two types of anything puppets—round and flat

## MANIPULATION AND CONSTRUCTION

Anything puppets may be made from a piece of soft material, such as flannel, felt, nonwoven interfacing fabric, double knit, or cotton. There are two styles of anything puppets: round and flat. The round anything puppet is made from a piece of cloth approximately twenty inches square. Stuffing gives the head shape, a rubber band serves as a neck, and the puppeteer's exposed fingers act as the puppet's arms. The flat anything puppet is a mitt-like puppet. This style puppet is easier for young children with less developed fine motor skills to manipulate.

### Construction of Round Anything Puppet

#### Materials

Flannel, double knit, nonwoven interfacing, or cotton fabric

Stuffing—paper towels, cotton batting, or fiberfill

Rubber band

#### Procedures

Cut a 20″ square from soft fabric material and trim off the corners.

Insert stuffing, in the center of the square.

Cut two armholes for puppeteer's fingers as shown. Estimate the best location for armholes by placing index finger in head area (middle of cloth) and using rubber band for securing neck. Then indicate with marker where thumb and middle finger seem most comfortable when puppet is held upright. Cut small holes through which fingers will protrude.

## Construction of Flat Anything Puppet

The flat, mitt-like anything puppet may be easily made out of felt, muslin, double knit, and other materials. It is held by inserting the thumb in one arm, the little finger and ring finger in the other arm, with the index and middle fingers used to manipulate the head.

### Materials

Flannel, double knit, nonwoven interfacing, felt, or cotton fabric

### Procedures

Cut out a front and a back body piece following pattern in chapter 3.

Put right sides together and sew all around the edges, leaving bottom open for hand.

Turn right sides out.

Hem bottom edge if desired.

## Holding Anything Puppets

Give each child a round or flat anything puppet. Using your bare hand, demonstrate three common ways of holding a puppet:

1. Index finger inside puppet's head; thumb and middle finger through armholes.
2. Index finger inside puppet's head; thumb and little finger through armholes.
3. Index and middle fingers inside puppet's head; thumb through one armhole; little finger and ring finger through other armhole.

Allow children the opportunity to discover which of the three ways feels most comfortable for them to hold the anything puppet. Puppets should always be held with the arm bent at the elbow so that the puppet is standing up straight for good posture and not at a slant, unless the char-

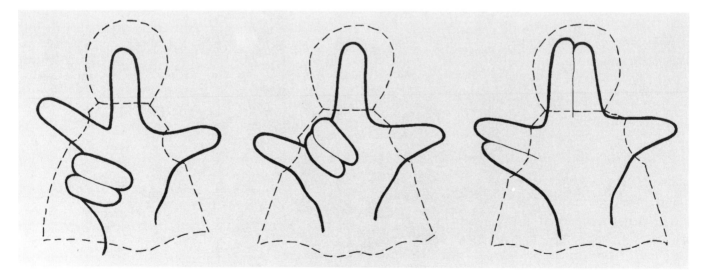

Three ways of holding an anything puppet

acterization requires it. A tired woman carrying a heavy sack or an old man trudging into a storm would both walk with a forward slant or bent posture. When the children are ready to familiarize themselves with the puppets, ask the puppets to clap their hands, nod their heads "yes," and jump up and down. Watch at this time for puppets that may not be firmly positioned on a child's hand. Make sure everyone has at least one finger in the puppet's head.

Remember the purpose for using anything puppets is to stimulate interest in good literature and memorable characters, rather than to make a puppeteer of the child. Therefore, the degree of proficiency in puppet manipulation is of less importance than the child's honest interpretation of the character's actions. Involving the child in the story is the goal.

## Warm-Up Activities

Before using the puppets with stories, a few warm-up activities should be done to familiarize the children with the puppets. Do not dictate to the children how to do an activity, but, rather, encourage them to respond naturally and imaginatively and accept their interpretation of the actions. This inspires creativity and properly ignores competition.

The warm-up activities are of two types: action/response and interpretation. The action/response activities are characterized by a leader, child, storyteller, or puppet performing an action which all the puppets imitate. "Follow the Leader," "Guess What?" and "Mirror, Mirror," are action/response activities.

Interpretation activities present a question or situation and each child must individually decide how to move the puppet to achieve the desired result. Honest, concentrated actions result when children know that their interpretations will be respected. As we make a determined effort to instill in children the belief in their own uniqueness and creativity, we encourage them to be risk takers and to explore new solutions to problems. This honest attempt to solve a problem will eliminate silliness and lack of concentration. "Come On and Join in the Game," "This Is the Way," "Sing Along," "Say Hello," and "Character Sketches" are all interpretation warm-up activities.

### Action/Response Activities

Every child should have an anything puppet when participating in these activities. There is no audience; everyone is involved in the action. The desired result is to have each individual watch what the leader does and imitate that action as faithfully as possible.

## Follow the leader

The leader, you or a child, stands in front of the group and performs an action. The leader is not using an anything puppet. The puppets imitate the leader's action. Possible actions include: bow, hop, turn around, walk, yawn, jump, sneeze, laugh, cry. Select another leader to continue the activity.

## Guess what?

Children will teach their puppet one activity, such as playing basketball, painting a wall, or shoveling snow. All props and scenery are imagined. Then, one puppet plays leader and goes before the group and pantomimes the activity. When finished, all the other puppets perform the same activity. After each action the children discuss what the puppets were doing.

A variation is to give each child a prop, such as a flower or a cup, around which to plan a pantomime.

## Mirror, Mirror

In pairs, one puppet is the leader and the other puppet is the mirror reflection. The leader-puppet performs an action which the mirror-puppet reflects, such as raising arms, hopping, turning around, etc. Then have the puppets switch roles. The whole group, divided into pairs, does the mirroring at the same time.

## Interpretative Activities

The first three activities here are songs. Children sing each song as all the puppets perform the designated actions. Each child decides how the puppet will do the required action. Individual interpretations of the appropriate movements should be encouraged.

Ask the children to suggest other actions to incorporate into the song "This Is the Way," sung to the tune of "Here We Go Round the Mulberry Bush." Actions might include: nod my head, climb the stairs, wash my hands, etc.

### This Is the Way

*This is the way I clap my hands,*
*Clap my hands, clap my hands,*
*This is the way I clap my hands,*
*So early in the morning.*

## Sing along

As your anything puppet conducts the singing, all other puppets sing, "Row, Row, Row Your Boat" or some other popular round. After singing the song once together, puppets sing in a round. Encourage children to try different voices, perhaps singing in deep voices during the unison singing and in high-pitched voices during the round.

## Say hello

Each child teaches his or her own anything puppet to talk. Allow about three minutes for children to quietly interact with their puppets. Suggest that the puppet learn to say the puppeteer's name, its own name, tell how old it is, and describe any hobbies and activities that are of interest. Then each puppet introduces itself to another anything puppet.

## Character sketches

As you describe a character doing an action, the children, using anything puppets, pantomime the action. Suggestions for practicing actions follow:

A tired, old man is walking slowly forward; he stops, yawns, lies down, and goes to sleep.

A girl is running after a fly ball; she catches it, tosses it up in the air to catch again, misses it, and chases it as it rolls away.

A boy is skipping toward a flower; he stops, looks down at the flower, picks the flower, smells it, and skips home carrying the flower in his hand.

A peg-legged pirate is walking toward his ship; he trips on a rock, falls down, picks himself up and brushes himself off, then hobbles back to his ship.

Doing a few of these warm-up activities will increase the children's awareness of their puppet's capabilities, as well as increase their sense of how to develop those capabilities. These activities will also give children an opportunity to experiment with the puppets before being asked to use them with specific stories.

## STORY INVOLVEMENT

Once the children have had an opportunity to experiment with anything puppets, the next step is to incorporate the puppets into interpreting specific stories. The following activities are designed for group puppet activity with children remaining, for most activities, in their seats. Each child has an anything puppet. All the children will participate, sometimes through pantomiming the actions of a character or using the puppet to clarify the meaning of a concept. Other times the children will work in pairs to develop dialogue for characters in specific situations.

### Pantomiming a Character

The children listen carefully to the story and, with anything puppets, pantomime the actions of a selected character, usually the main character. Any story with one central character who is involved in fairly continuous action is appropriate. For example, all the children's puppets may be Peter in A Snowy Day by Ezra Jack Keats. As you tell the story, the puppets perform the actions of Peter exploring the world of snow. All other characters in the story are imagined.

Another suitable title for pantomiming is The Chick and the Duckling by Mirra Ginsburg. This is a story about a chick who imitates all the actions of a duckling until the duckling goes swimming. The chick nearly drowns and decides not to follow the duckling for another swim.

You, the narrator, use an anything puppet as the duckling character. All the children use their anything puppets to portray the chick. As the duckling, you say and do the actions. The chicks say, "Me too," and imitate the actions. The chicks can't swim and almost drown. The next time you suggest going for a swim, all the chicks refuse the invitation.

### SUGGESTED TITLES FOR PANTOMIME WITH ANYTHING PUPPETS

Brown, Margaret Wise. *The Runaway Bunny*; illus. by Clement Hurd. Harper, 1972.

A bunny runs away and tries to hide but his mother always finds him. Children use puppets to mime actions of the bunny. Narrator portrays the mother rabbit.

Ets, Marie Hall. *Play with Me*; illus. by the author. Viking, 1955.

A little girl finds that being still and quiet is the best way to make friends with animals in the woods. The "anything" puppets portray the little girl's actions. A Caldecott Honor book.

Ginsburg, Mirra. *The Chick and the Duckling*; illus. by Jose and Ariane Aruego. Macmillan, 1972.

Chick imitates all the actions of a duckling until the chick almost drowns.

Jones, Maurice. *I'm Going on a Dragon Hunt*; illus. by Charlotte Fitmin. Four Winds, 1989.

Lead children with anything puppets on a dangerous and exciting dragon hunt.

Keats, Ezra Jack. *The Snowy Day*; illus. by the author. Viking, 1973.

A boy enjoys a fun-filled day in the snow, as puppets pantomime Peter's activities. A Caldecott Medal book.

Kraus, Robert. *Milton, the Early Riser*; illus. by Jose and Ariane Aruego. Windmill, 1987.

Milton, a panda, awakens early and sings, plays, and does all sorts of things, but no one is awake to join him. When his family and friends finally do wake up, Milton is too tired to do more than sleep. Puppets enact Milton's role.

McKee, David. *Elmer in the Snow*; illus. by the author. Lothrop, 1995.

Elmer, a patchwork elephant, leads an elephant herd on an adventure in the snow. Attach squares of colored paper to the anything puppet that represents Elmer. Children's puppets play the other elephants.

Sivulich, Sandra. *I'm Going on a Bear Hunt*; illus. by Glen Rounds. Dutton, 1973.

A young boy goes on a bear hunt but rapidly retraces his steps when he finds a bear. Group collectively portrays the youth's actions including climbing a tree, swimming across the lake, shaking himself dry, running through a swamp, and crawling inside a cave.

## Understanding Concepts

Puppets can help children understand ideas presented in "how-to" and concept books that deal with such terms as size, shape, numbers, colors, and letters. When puppets are used to express a concept introduced in a book, several results are observed. First, the child exhibits comprehension by manipulating the puppet to demonstrate understanding of the concept. Second, if the child's understanding of the concept is incorrect, the misconception will be easily recognized and can be corrected. Finally, children can experiment with different means of expressing the same concept.

For example, in *Busy Day* by Betsy and Guilio Maestro, the action words may be demonstrated by puppets. This book presents words associated with the daily activities of a clown and an elephant at the circus. When a word is read, all the puppets express its meaning through an appropriate action. To extend the learning, ask the children to suggest other means of expressing the same action. For the word "marching" the puppets might march in single file, or in pairs, as a marching band. Children might even experiment with a variety of unusual situations involving one of the action words: elephants marching in a circus parade; soldiers marching uphill; a drill team performing a maneuver. For some of these actions the children may need to move about the area with their puppets.

There are several ways of using anything puppets with a book about the concept of opposites, such as *Opposites* by Richard Wilbur.

Read both words and show the pictures. Then say the words again as the anything puppets perform each action.

Say one word and act out its meaning with your anything puppet. The children use their puppets to act out the opposite word after you say it.

Half the group does the first part of the word pair while the remaining group acts out the opposite word action.

Children work in pairs; one puppet mimes a word from the book while the partner acts out its opposite.

Still in pairs, children think of new ways to illustrate the antonym concepts with their puppets, perhaps with a short scenario or skit to illustrate the meanings.

### SUGGESTED TITLES FOR <u>ACTING OUT CONCEPTS</u>

Domanska, Janina. *Busy Monday Morning*; illus. by the author. Greenwillow, 1985.

A Polish folksong about harvesting hay presents a wonderful opportunity for anything puppets to mime the actions.

Hoban, Tana. *Over, Under and Through and Other Spatial Concepts*; illus. by the author. Macmillan, 1973.

Photographs highlight spatial concepts. Puppets may demonstrate each concept with appropriate actions in relation to objects. Then children can make up new situations to illustrate the concepts.

Hoban, Tana. *Round and Round and Round*; illus. by the author. Greenwillow, 1983.

Beautiful color photographs illustrate roundness in a variety of ways. Puppets act out the use of round objects—eating a cookie, bouncing a ball, riding a bicycle.

Koch, Michelle. *By the Sea*; illus. by the author. Greenwillow, 1991.

Presents a series of opposites using the seashore as the background. Pairs of children demonstrate opposites using anything puppets.

Maestro, Betsy. *All Aboard Overnight*; illus. by Giulio Maestro. Clarion, 1992.

Compound words are introduced in a story about a family taking a train trip. Using anything puppets, small groups act out other scenarios incorporating the compound words.

Maestro, Betsy, and Giulio Maestro. *Busy Day*; illus. by Giulio Maestro. Crown, 1978.

Bright illustrations chronicle the activities of an elephant and a clown.

Spier, Peter. *Crash! Bang! Boom!*; illus. by the author. Doubleday, 1972.

Sounds made by inanimate objects are explored. Puppets may show how to use the objects as each sound is made.

Terban, Marvin. *Superdupers!*; illus. by Giulio Maestro. Clarion, 1989.

The meanings and origins of over 100 nonsense words such as "shilly-shally" and "pell-mell" are pre-sented in words and pictures. Challenge pairs of children with anything puppets to create dramatization for the words.

Wheeler, Cindy. *A Good Day, A Good Night*; illus. by the author. Lippincott, 1980.

A cat and a robin explore day and night. Children can use puppets to act out activities done at night and during the day.

Wilbur, Richard. *Opposites*; illus. by the author. Harcourt, 1991.

A poetic look at opposites.

## Developing Dialogue

Becoming a character from a story and informally creating corresponding dialogue gives children a chance to experience the story on a personal level. It also encourages exploration of the character as well as creative use of language. Anything puppets can be used in this way to introduce children to improvisation in a nonthreatening manner. The puppets help children feel comfortable, enabling them to concentrate on what the puppets, rather than what they as individuals, are going to say or do.

Improvisation is a spontaneous activity involving all the children at the same time. There is no audience since everyone is participating. The goal is not a performance but rather an exploration by each child of the characters' thoughts, motivations, and resulting words and actions. In the story *Yours Till Niagara Falls, Abby* by Jane O'Connor, Merle and Abby are best friends. Merle is very upset because she is being sent to camp for eight weeks. Abby decides everything will be fine if she goes to camp with Merle. Abby must first persuade her parents that attending Camp Pinecrest all summer is a good idea. In groups of three, children using anything puppets can improvise the scene between Abby and her parents. Abby must think of many good reasons for going to camp. Her parents don't agree with her. What do they say?

After a few minutes of improvising dialogue, ask the members of each group to switch roles. Switching provides an opportunity to examine the situation from another point of view.

Improvisational dialogue experiences expand the dialogue in a story and enrich the language experience. A new element can be introduced by challenging the group to develop alternative plots or endings. In *Yours Till Niagara Falls, Abby*, Merle becomes ill and Abby must attend the camp by herself, with amusing results. Children can improvise what would have happened if Abby and Merle attended the camp together. Or they might want to develop Merle's character by having her attend the camp without Abby. A number of situations can be developed for exploring the characters in new situations.

Read a scene or short story to the group. Then ask children, in pairs, to use anything puppets to converse in their own words and expand the character's dialogue, adding details consistent with the character's personality.

For example, the fable "The Contest," beautifully illustrated by Bernadette Watts in *The Wind and the Sun*, tells about an argument between the Wind and the Sun concerning who is the stronger. Both agree that the winner would be the one who removes the coat from a man walking along the road below. In pairs, children portray the Wind and the Sun. One puppet acts as the Sun while the other plays the part of the Wind. When given the signal, perhaps a clap of hands, each character tries to convince the other that it is the strongest. Drawing on their knowledge of the special qualities of these natural elements, children can invent original situations proving the strength of each character. All children will be participating at the same time. After a few minutes, give another signal to end the conversation.

## SUGGESTED TITLES FOR <u>DEVELOPING DIALOGUE</u>

Andersen, Hans Christian. *The Emperor's New Clothes*; illus. by Riki Levinson. Dutton, 1991.

The popular story of the vain Emperor whose ignorance and nakedness were publicly displayed is an apt story for puppet depiction. Groups of three can enact the scene in which the weavers convince the Emperor that his invisible clothes are truly beautiful.

Craig, Helen. *The Town Mouse and the Country Mouse*; illus. by the author. Candlewick, 1992.

Using anything puppets, pairs of children take the role of Tyler, the town mouse, and Charlie, the country mouse. Each character tries to share the joys of home with the other.

Fleischman, Sid. *McBroom and the Beanstalk*; illus. by Walter Lorraine. Little, 1978.

McBroom loses the World Champion Liar's Contest because he tells the truth. Partners can work with puppets to see who can tell the biggest lie. One puppet is Heck Jones, the other is Josh McBroom.

Lobel, Arnold. *Frog and Toad All Year*; illus. by the author. Harper, 1976.

A story for each season plus one for Christmas highlights the adventures of those good friends, Frog and Toad.

The winter story, "Down the Hill," tells about Frog's attempts to lure Toad out into the snow to have some fun. With one puppet as Frog and the other as Toad, have Toad tell Frog all the reasons why he (Toad) would rather stay in bed.

Marshall, James. *George and Martha Rise and Shine*; illus. by the author. Houghton, 1976.

Five humorous stories about two good hippopotamus friends, lovable George and Martha. Read the story "The Fibber" in which George wants to impress Martha. What can he do and say to impress her? In pairs, one "anything" puppet plays George, the other Martha. Then switch roles.

Naylor, Phyllis Reynolds. *Shiloh*. Simon & Schuster, 1991.

In this Newbery Award winning story, eleven-year-old Marty befriends a dog, Shiloh, abused by its owner. How Marty saves Shiloh is a heartwarming story. Children can improvise the scene in chapter 1 when Marty tries to convince his dad to let him keep Shiloh. They can also work in pairs to recreate the confrontation between Marty and Judd, the dog's owner, that results in the bargain that allows Marty to keep Shiloh.

O'Connor, Jane. *Yours Till Niagara Falls, Abby*; illus. by Margot Apple. Hastings, 1982.

Abby Kimmel dreads the thought of spending the whole summer at camp without her best friend. How Abby survives makes a warm, witty story.

In groups of three, children can recreate the scene in which Abby tries to persuade her parents to send her to camp.

Sharmat, Marjorie Weinman. *I'm Terrific*; illus. by Kay Chorao. Holiday, 1977.

Jason Bear's opinion of himself is not shared by his friends who not only do not find him terrific but also, just the opposite, think he is overbearing. Jason learns that he does not have to be terrific all the time. Rather, if he is just himself, he's likely to be accepted.

One puppet, as Jason Bear, can try to explain to a friend why he's terrific. The other puppet, as his friend, can react to Jason's assessment of himself. Switch roles.

Watts, Bernadette. *The Wind and the Sun*; illus. by the author. North-South, 1992.

A picture-book version of the Aesop fable about the contest between the wind and the sun to decide who is the stronger. One puppet depicts the Sun while the other depicts the Wind. Each tries to convince the other of its superior strength.

White, E. B. *Charlotte's Web*; illus. by Garth Williams. Harper, 1952.

A humorous, heartwarming fantasy about a pig named Wilbur, a little girl named Fern, and a clever spider named Charlotte, who saves Wilbur from fall butchering.

The scene in which Fern convinces her father not to kill the runt of the pig litter can be improvised through the use of anything puppets with one puppet being Fern and the other her father. A Newbery Honor book.

## STORY DRAMATIZATION

Anything puppets may be used to introduce children to the elements of a story through dramatization. Puppets, in this case, become the characters from rhymes and stories. Dialogue and action are all-important in improvising a story; scenery and props are not. They are, instead, imagined. Before acting out the story with puppets, children will need to think about the setting, who the characters are, why they behave as they do (motivation), and the problem or conflict in the story.

Remember the goal is for each child to create an individual interpretation. Since the group is not performing on a stage for an audience, it is unnecessary to evaluate the improvisations with the same yardstick that would be used for a performance. The goal is to enhance the creative growth of each child, providing opportunities to explore and discover in an uncritical atmosphere. It is the process of becoming a character and experiencing the plight of the character that is important. What the child's puppet improvisation looks like is of far less importance than the growth of his or her imagination.

Mother Goose rhymes are good sources for beginning dramatizations since they are short, familiar, and offer a variety of themes.

 ## "Hickory Dickory Dock"

One excellent rhyme with plenty of action is "Hickory Dickory Dock." All puppets depict the mouse, who is well known for its climbing prowess. First, recite the rhyme together without the use of puppets. The purpose here is to familiarize everyone with the poem and to give the children a chance to think about the action.

Next ask the children the following questions:

"Where is the clock?"

"What does it look like?"

"How will the mouse run up the clock?"

"Will it succeed on the first try?"

"What happens after the mouse runs down the clock?"

These questions will help children visualize the action and add details to their dramatizations.

Now, enter the puppets. As you say the rhyme, all puppets act out the story. Some may finish before you do and some after, depending on the elaborateness of their dramatization.

### Other One-Puppet-Character Rhymes

The following familiar rhymes need only one puppet character:

"Little Tommy Tittlemouse"

"Wee Willie Winkie"

"Yankee Doodle"

"Doctor Foster"

 ## "Jack and Jill"

Next, try the sad story of "Jack and Jill." Children, working in pairs, say the rhyme together. One puppet will be Jack and the other will be Jill. Questions to think about before beginning the improvisation include the following:

"Where is the hill? The well?"

"How will the puppets show Jack and Jill tumbling down the hill?"

"What happens after they fall down the hill?"

### Other Two-Puppet-Character Rhymes

These verses require two puppet characters and work well with the group divided into pairs.

"Little Miss Muffet"

"Old Mother Hubbard"

"Polly Put the Kettle On"

"Simple Simon"

## "Humpty Dumpty"

A more complex rhyme provides an opportunity for larger group work. In groups of four to six, anything puppets can dramatize the tragic tale of "Humpty Dumpty." After saying the rhyme together suggest the following questions:

"Where is the wall?"

"Who will be Humpty Dumpty? The King's horses? The King's men?"

"What happens to Humpty Dumpty after he falls?"

Anything puppets can be converted into specific characters with stick-on paper faces and features. Shown here are a mouse (left) and a butterfly.

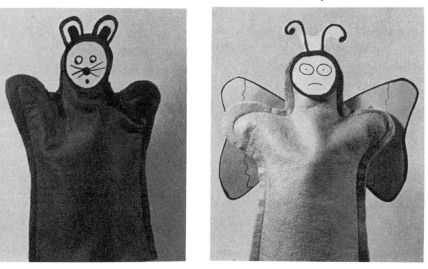

Anything puppets can be converted into specific characters with stick-on paper faces and features. Shown here are a mouse (left) and a butterfly.

"What might be done with Humpty Dumpty's broken pieces?"

Allow five minutes for groups to plan their dramatizations. After the playing, ask groups to share what happened to Humpty Dumpty. Don't be surprised if he was scrambled and eaten!

### Three- to Six-Puppet-Character Rhymes

More intricate rhymes are included here. These work best with groups of three to six.

"Georgie Porgie"

"Mary Had a Little Lamb"

"Old King Cole"

"Queen of Hearts" (Group of three)

From dramatizing Mother Goose rhymes, a transition is easily made to folktales and modern stories. Anything puppets can be visually transformed into almost any story character by the addition of a paper face. Simply attach the face with double-stick tape to the head portion of the anything puppet. Features corresponding to the designated character can then be drawn onto the face. Paper wings, tails, ears, and other additions complete the transformation from anything puppet to specific character puppet.

Mirra Ginsburg's adaptation of the Russian folktale *Mushroom in the Rain* contains a straightforward story line and simple characters who are constantly involved in the action, an excellent combination for participatory storytelling with anything puppets. A group of animals crowd under a mushroom to stay dry. The animals hide a rabbit from a hungry fox who circles the mushroom. Children, working in groups of seven, can in a few min-

utes transform anything puppets into the ants, butterflies, rabbits, mice, sparrows, and foxes required by the story. One child in each group becomes the mushroom under which the six various animals hide to stay out of the rain. As the leader narrates, children enact the story adding dialogue if they desire. Additional animals can be added to provide an opportunity for all children to be involved.

"The Bremen-Town Musicians" is another story suitable for dramatizing with anything puppets. This popular folktale by the Brothers Grimm centers around the attempts of a donkey, a dog, a cat, and a rooster to reach Bremen where they hope to become street musicians. On the way the animals rout a band of robbers and settle down happily in the forest. Anything puppets can quickly become animals and robbers. Questions for the children to consider before dramatizing the story include: "What musical talent does each animal possess?" "How will the animals frighten the robbers away from their den?" "Where will each animal sleep in the house?" "Which of the robbers will return to the house to investigate why they ran away?" As many as eight children in a group can successfully enact this story as you narrate the story line. Pause during the telling when specific actions are indicated—traveling along the road; frightening the robbers away; robbers fleeing; finding a place to sleep in the house; robber returning and being attacked by the animals.

*The Princess and the Pea* by Hans Christian Andersen provides an opportunity for children to combine actions and dialogue as they recreate this simple, humorous tale. A prince wants to marry a princess but she must be a real princess. He is convinced that a visitor to the palace is indeed royal when a pea hidden under twenty mattresses disturbs her sleep. The uncomplicated story line allows ample opportunity for creating interesting dialogue and accompanying actions. It is perfect for playing by groups of three or four. Let anything puppets assume the roles of the Prince, Princess, Queen, and, if necessary, the King. Each child can develop a unique personality and voice for a character. Children might design a series of tests for the Princess to pass. Or they might embellish the role of the Prince and his family. Some interesting questions to consider before the dramatizations begin include: "Why was the Princess traveling alone on a wet and windy night?" "How does the Prince plan to learn whether a young woman is a princess or a commoner?"

Capitalizing on the chameleon quality of anything puppets, a storyteller can quickly and inexpensively assemble a cast for any tale to be told or dramatized by the children.

## SUGGESTED TITLES FOR STORY DRAMATIZATION

Du Bois, William Péne, and Leo Po. *The Hare and the Tortoise and the Tortoise and the Hare*; illus. by William Péne Du Bois. Doubleday, 1972.

The traditional version of the popular fable and an Oriental version in which the Hare is victorious. Children use specific character "anything" puppets to enact and compare the two versions.

Foreman, Michael. *Mother Goose*; illus. by the author. Harcourt, 1991.

A beautifully illustrated collection that makes an excellent resource since it includes the most popular rhymes as well as less familiar ones.

Ginsburg, Mirra. *Mushroom in the Rain*; illus. by Jose Aruego and Ariane Dewey. Macmillan, 1974.

An adaptation of a Russian folktale about animals hiding under a mushroom to stay dry.

Hooks, William H. *The Three Little Pigs and the Fox*; illus. by S. D. Schindler. Macmillan, 1989.

Try dramatizing this Appalachian version of "The Three Little Pigs." The whole story could be dramatized; pairs of children could use anything puppets to act out the scenes between Mama and each child and each child and the Fox; or all could dramatize the scenes between baby sister Hamlet and the fox.

Langstaff, John. *Frog Went A-Courtin*; illus. by Feodor Rojankovsky. Harcourt, 1955.

Frog's attempts to woo Mistress Mouse are charmingly recounted in this picture-book version of a well-known ballad. All the children can participate in Frog's courtship and wedding using anything puppets, two portraying the bride and groom. All other puppets take the role of wedding guests. A Caldecott Medal book.

Plume, Ilse, reteller. *The Bremen-Town Musicians*; illus. by the reteller. Harper, 1987.

The Grimm Brothers' tale of four animals who set off to seek their fortunes in Bremen. A Caldecott Honor book.

"Princess and the Pea," in *Seven Tales by H. C. Andersen*; trans. by Eva Le Gallienne; illus. by Maurice Sendak. HarperCollins, 1990.

The story of a true princess who is kept awake all night because of a pea hidden under her mattress.

Rockwell, Anne. *The Three Bears and Fifteen Other Stories*; illus. by the author. Crowell, 1975.

Delightfully illustrated collection of popular folktales, many of which can be dramatized with anything puppets. Includes such classics as "The Three Billy Goats Gruff," "Little Red Riding Hood," and "The Gingerbread Man."

Shannon, George. *Stories to Solve*; illus. by Peter Sis. Greenwillow, 1985.

Fourteen mysteries from folktales around the world provide possibilities for dramatization with anything puppets. Tell each story to the group. Then have small groups of students using anything puppets act out each mystery, being sure to include in each dramatization the words or actions that explain the mystery. *More Stories to Solve* provide additional possibilities.

Zemach, Margot. *Three Little Pigs*; illus. by the author. Farrar, 1988.

Picture-book version of the very popular story can serve as a springboard for retelling the tale with anything puppets. Groups of six can portray Mother Pig, her three children, and the wolf. The sixth puppet can supply the pigs with building materials for their homes.

# Chapter 9    SOUND STORIES

SOUND EFFECTS MAY SERVE as a central and unifying theme in storytelling. Such simple sound involvement as clapping hands, making animal sounds, using musical instruments, or repeating phrases provides for active and dramatic participation by the whole group. Children may contribute sounds when a puppet is held up by the storyteller as the story is told. For some stories you may choose to develop sounds for just one character—the lead character. For example, in *Katy No-Pocket* by Emmy Payne, each time you hold up the kangaroo puppet during the story, the children respond with "Oh my! No pockets!" And when Katy finally does get pockets to carry her offspring, the audience may respond with "Hooray! Pockets!"

Other stories may lend themselves to development of sounds for several or all of the characters. For example, in "Henny Penny" each time a specific animal is held up by the storyteller the children provide the appropriate sound. The hen puppet raised over the storyteller's head is a cue for the children to say, "Cluck, cluck, cluck." The duck puppet would cue a response of "Quack, quack." All the children make the sound at the same time when the puppet is raised. The sound is ended when the puppet is lowered.

Another technique calls for each child to hold a puppet and to produce an accompanying sound, original or predetermined, at intervals during the storytelling. In this case it is necessary for each child to have a puppet representing a character from the story. In portraying "Henny Penny" a child would hold up the hen while simultaneously clucking its sound. Other children would perform the same service with the duck, turkey, goose, and rooster. The leader could supply puppets, or child-made puppets could be used. "Anything" puppets with paper features would be quick and easy to adapt for sound stories. If the group is large, it is acceptable to have several puppets representing the same character so that all the children may participate. As the story is told, children raise the puppets as a unit and make the appropriate sound or sound effect whenever the characters are mentioned. Stories that have numerous characters continually involved in the action, as well as cumulative tales and verses, are excellent choices for sound involvement, since each character in the repetitive narrative may be given a particular sound.

There are two basic philosophical approaches in determining the sounds assigned to characters in a specific story. In one, the sounds are selected exclusively by the storyteller; in the other, the children assist in developing the sounds. The storyteller may choose to select the sounds prior to storytelling when time or inexperience are factors. With experience the adult may choose to accept some suggestions from the audience and, at a later date, try the audience development techniques suggested in this chapter.

When children are to be involved in the creation of sounds for a story, they should be familiar with the plot and the characters. To accomplish this, the storyteller may choose to read the story in the traditional manner, tell the story, briefly summarize the plot and introduce the characters, or use a filmstrip or other audiovisual form of the story. These are done prior to improvising sounds for the story.

## EXPLORING SOUND

### Types of Sounds

Sounds to be used with stories can be made with the voice, found objects, or musical instruments. Vocalizations include a wide range of sounds—sentences, phrases, single words, syllables, nonsense and animal sounds. Experimenting with the range capabilities of the voice is exciting and fun for children. *Mouth Sounds* by Frederick Newman contains a fascinating collection of more than seventy sounds to make with the mouth. Instructions for making sounds for animals, musical instruments, cars, horns, honks, and whistles are included. A record with all the sounds plus directions accompanies the book. Here is a beginning list of possible vocal sound choices:

| | |
|---|---|
| Train: | Toot toot |
| Wind: | Whoooooooossshhh |
| Motor: | Whirrrrrr |
| Dog: | Grrrr grrrr |
| Door: | Crrreeaakkkk |
| Horse: | Nnnneighhh |
| Water: | Gurgle, gurgle, guzzle, guzzle |
| Train Conductor: | All Aaabooaarrrd! |

The impact of these sounds is affected by the emotion, rhythm, and timbre employed by the speaker. The role of a character in a story, the setting, and the plot all influence the type of sound to use, as well as possible vocal nuances to consider.

The action of a character may spark an idea for a sound, and onomatopoeia may aid the development of sound effects. Examine what a character does and then select a word, such as "crash" or "boom," that represents a sound associated with the action of that character. In "The Gingerbread Boy," consider "whack" for the threshers and "swish, swish!" for the mowers.

Sound effects may also be words, such as "Aim, Fire" for General Border in *Drummer Hoff* by Barbara Emberley, or "Come back" for the Little Old Woman in "The Gingerbread Boy." Animal noises are also fitting, but rather than mimicking the sound in the usual way, repeat it or use a rhythm pattern. For example, the sound effect for the satisfied pig who swallowed the pancake in Anita Lobel's version of *The Pancake* could be three quick oinks, "Oink, oink, oink!" However, in the story "The Old Woman and Her Pig," the pig balks at going over the stile and thus may be better characterized by one long, woeful, drawn out "Oooooiiinnnnnnnnnk."

Children may also provide dialogue for puppet characters as part of sound exploration. Stories in which questions are asked and the answer follows in dialogue form can be enacted effectively in this manner. Try to find or make appropriate puppets for the characters in the story. For example, telling "The Little Red Hen" will require a hen, a dog, a cat, and a mouse puppet. Divide the children into three groups; the storyteller uses the hen puppet. One child from each group holds the corresponding puppet character. When the Little Red Hen asks Mouse to help, all the children in the Mouse group reply, "Not I!" as the Mouse puppet is raised. Folk stories that have simple repetitive dialogue also lend themselves well to this approach. "Goldilocks and the Three Bears" is a good example. Here the bears' repetitive question, "Who's been sitting in my chair?" develops enthusiastic participation and character development.

"A Hole in the Bucket" from *The Fireside Book of Fun and Game Songs* is an amusing song to sing in this manner. Each child makes a puppet representing either Henry or Liza from the song. Divide the group into two parts; the Henry puppet group sings the question and the Liza puppet group responds with the answer. An entertaining effect is created when boys do the "she" part and girls are responsible for the "he" part. Other answer-back songs from the same collection include:

"Where Are You Going, My Pretty Maid?," "Lazy Mary," and "Soldier, Soldier."

Common objects when viewed with ingenuity can yield interesting sound effects:

*Jangling a set of keys:* a knight in armor

*Clapping together blocks of Styrofoam or wood:* slamming a door

*Rhythmically rubbing a paperback book back and forth across a table:* waves washing up on a beach

*Tapping a pencil on a table:* a shutter knocking against the side of a house

*Crumpling tissue paper in the hand:* a crackling fire

*Clattering two empty soup cans against a hard surface:* horses' hooves

*Shaking a coffee can containing a few grains of rice:* rain or hail

*Shaking a sheet of metal:* thunder

You may wish to set up a sound bin with a diverse collection of objects that children can use to discover new sound effects. This collection could include:

Rhythm instruments—castanets, rhythm sticks, drums, wooden blocks, triangle

A metal washboard

Pots and covers

Spoons, wooden and metal

Blocks of Styrofoam found in packaging

Plastic dishes

Various size blocks of wood

Marbles

Tongue depressors

Sandpaper

Covered containers that can be filled with small objects—coffee cans, Tupperware, boxes

Musical instruments are another area to explore when designing sounds or sound effects for a story. Short tapping beats on a drum or tambourine may indicate running. Long sounds of a cymbal or gong might provide the needed ominous tone for a ghost story. Or, a different instrument could be used to represent each character in a story. In our original example, "Henny Penny," the hen might be represented by a quick shake of the tambourine, the duck by three beats on a triangle, the rooster by five shakes of a maraca. Tone bells and the xylophone also offer the opportunity to design unique rhythms for characters, as well as providing interesting effects to enhance mood and setting. A run up the scale could underline the climactic moment in a story. A run down the scale may highlight a disaster, such as the fox eating each animal at the conclusion of "Henny Penny."

## Warm-Up Activities

The following activities may serve as "warm-up" activities. Warm-up activities are preliminary activities that help the child to explore possible sounds for use with characters during storytelling. For example, if "The Grobbles" by Jack Prelutsky is the selected poem, you may experiment with sound before the reading by first trying a variety of menacing sounds that the entire group repeats. Next ask individual students to share their interpretation of the sound a grobble makes while the whole group again imitates. In many stories this would also be a sure way of enabling the children to become acquainted with the variety of characters, as well as exploring possible accompanying sounds.

The story of *The Funny Little Woman* by Arlene Mosel offers possibilities for various kinds of sound involvement. In this story the main character has an amusing habit; she giggles. One way to involve all the children is to ask them to giggle whenever the leader holds up the finger puppet representing the Funny Little Woman.

A deeper level of involvement may be inspired by a creative dramatics approach to sound development. The basis of this simple creative dramatics exercise is to explore movement as a way to interpret a character and then to attach sound to that movement. In *The Funny Little Woman* the villains are Oni, wicked monsters who live in the underworld. Creating sounds for the Oni might begin as follows. Ask children to make themselves as small as possible in their own space. With their eyes closed, encourage them to create a mental picture of an Oni in its home in the underworld. As you provide background sounds with a tambourine, children grow into their version of an Oni. Ask children in their character as Oni to walk in the mud, swallow the river, and express anger. Start and end each activity with a signal, perhaps a drum beat, on which children move and freeze. Now, as children repeat each movement, encourage them to add sounds an Oni might make.

After this warm-up, tell the story using a Funny Little Woman finger puppet and a large stick puppet Oni. Whenever you say "The Funny Little Woman," hold up that puppet as a signal for children to giggle. When the Oni puppet is raised, each child responds with an original Oni sound. The sound ceases when each puppet is lowered. Thus, the outcome of this creative dramatics exercise is that each child develops a unique sound to contribute during story time.

## EXAMPLES OF SOUND STORIES

Three types of participation are detailed in the sound stories that follow. In the first example, "Fiddle-I-Fee," children chant animal sounds from a folk song as the storyteller hangs paper animal puppets on a clothesline. In "Jack and the Robbers," each child uses a puppet and responds with the designated sound for that charac-

ter. For the poem "The Grobbles," children create original sounds to be made each time the storyteller holds up a grobble puppet. While these are intended to illustrate various possibilities of involving children with sound, any combination could be adapted to suit the storyteller's purpose, time, and skills.

Actively involving children in the creation of sound effects for a story is an excellent introduction to more intense dramatic involvement. Freedom of expression is encouraged when all children participate together while gathered in a familiar storytelling setting. This secure, sharing environment encourages closeness both with the story and with one another, as well as providing a first step toward dramatic interpretation by combining story sounds and actions in progressive activities.

## Cat Goes Fiddle-I-Fee

*Cat Goes Fiddle-I-Fee* is Paul Galdone's delightfully illustrated picture book version of a traditional English cumulative song. Farmyard animals make a variety of unusual sounds.

### Approach

Leader, chanting the rhyme, hangs puppets on clothesline. Children all repeat appropriate sounds as each animal character is introduced by the leader.

### Puppets/Props

| Character/Props | Types/Materials |
| --- | --- |
| Cat | Paper cutout puppets |
| Hen | |
| Duck | |
| Goose | |
| Sheep | |
| Pig | |
| Cow | |
| Horse | |
| Dog | |

| Barn tote | Paper bag decorated to look like a barn |
| Clothesline | Rope or cording attached with small screw hooks or nails to a bulletin board or strung between chairs; two people also make excellent clothes poles |
| Clothespins | The spring-type kind |

## Presentation

### General procedures

Place all animal puppets in the barn tote bag. Hang the clothesline from a bulletin or flannel board in the storytelling area. Hang the puppets on the clothesline while chanting the story.

### Introduction

Discuss barnyard animals. Point to the barn tote and ask children what animals would be found inside a barn. As children suggest animals ask, "What sound does that animal make?" Tell them, "I know a rhyme about some of those barnyard animals, but the sounds they make may surprise you. After you hear each animal's sound, say it with me."

### Story actions

Take the cat puppet out of the barn tote as you begin to chant the first verse "Had me a cat, the cat pleased me. . . ." Hang puppet on the clothesline as you chant the cat's sound, "fiddle-i-fee."

Pull the hen puppet from the bag as you chant the second verse, "Had me a hen, the hen pleased me. . . ." Hang hen puppet on the clothesline as you chant, "Chimmy-chuck, chimmy-chuck."

Then point to the cat puppet on the clothesline as you and the children repeat the cat's refrain.

Repeat the procedure with each new animal, pointing to the animals already on the clothesline while encouraging children to imitate the sound of each animal as you point to it in reverse order of their emergence from the tote.

Clothesline characters for presenting *Cat Goes Fiddle-I-Fee*—cow, hen, and horse

Following are the sounds for each animal:

| | |
|---|---|
| Cat | Fiddle-i-fee |
| Hen: | Chimmy-chuck, chimmy-chuck |
| Duck: | Quack, quack |
| Goose: | Swishy, swashy |
| Sheep: | Baa, baa |
| Pig: | Griffy, gruffy |
| Cow: | Moo, moo |
| Horse: | Neigh, neigh |
| Dog: | Bow-wow, bow-wow |

## Follow-Up Activities

Add other animals to the clothesline and make up a new sound for each one.

Distribute the puppets to various children who will hang them on the clothesline as the song is sung again.

## Construction of Clothesline Paper Cutout Puppets

### Materials

Construction paper

Recycled clothing (optional)

Scrap fabric

Spring-type clothespins

### Procedures

Cut out large paper shapes of animals.

Decorate each animal with coloring medium and scrap fabric. For larger animals consider recycling children's old clothes, such as pajamas, blue jeans, T-shirts, and dresses, and attaching to basic paper animal heads.

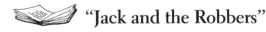 "Jack and the Robbers"

In this tale by Richard Chase, Jack, a lazy boy, leaves home to seek his fortune. On the way he is joined by a group of mangy animals who manage to frighten a gang of robbers from their den. "Jack and the Robbers" is a version of "The Musicians of Bremen" told in the Appalachian region of the United States.

## Approach

Leader narrates story and cues children for sounds. All children use character puppets and contribute sound effects.

## Puppets/Props

| Characters/Props | Types/Materials |
|---|---|
| Jack | Envelope puppets |
| Jack's Daddy | |
| Ox | |
| Donkey | |
| Dog | |
| Cat | |
| Rooster | |
| Robber 1 | |
| Robber 2 | |

## Presentation

### General procedures

Each child will need a puppet representing a character in the story. So that all the children in a large group may participate, you will need multiple puppets of each character. Explain that in the story each character has a special sound effect to make. When a character is mentioned during the story, the children with corresponding puppets hold them up and make the appropriate response.

Any type of hand puppet can be used: simple puppets the children have made, such as envelope or paper-bag puppets, finger puppets, felt mitt puppets, anything puppets with paper faces; or commercial puppets. For the example included here, construction directions are given for envelope puppets.

Introduce each story character and demonstrate the sound that identifies it. For example, hold up the dog puppet and howl, "A-woo! woo! woo!"

### Characters and Sound Effect Suggestions

| | |
|---|---|
| Jack's Daddy: | "Lazy boy!" |
| Jack: | "That's me!" |
| Ox: | "Umm–mm–muh!" |
| Donkey: | "Hee–hee–hee–haaaaaaw!" |
| Dog: | "A–woo! woo! woo!" |
| Cat: | "Meow–ow–ow–owwww!" |
| Rooster: | "Ur–rook–a–roo!" |
| Robber 1: | "Stick-em up!" |
| Robber 2: | "Crime doesn't pay!" |

You may wish to use the sound effect suggestions given, develop your own sound effects, or ask the children to help you create sound effects to be used for each character.

Distribute puppets to the children and provide time for practicing sound effects. Explain that children are to raise their puppet, make the appropriate sound effect, and then lower the puppet during the narration.

Tell the story, pausing after naming each character to give children a chance to respond. Make use of intonation and phrasing as you build to the climax of the final scene, a technique that will encourage the children to use dramatic expression in their voices as well.

### Introduction

Bring out a donkey puppet with its head hanging low and making unhappy braying sounds. Inquire of the donkey, "What's the matter?"

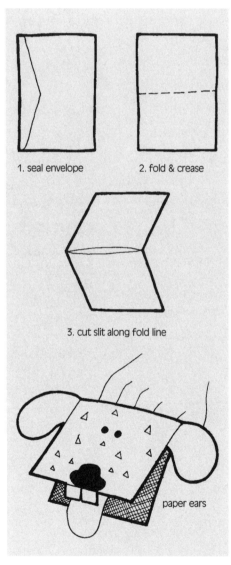

1. seal envelope  
2. fold & crease  
3. cut slit along fold line  

paper ears

**Envelope dog puppet for "Jack and the Robbers"**

The forlorn donkey responds with another sad, "Hee–hee–hee–haaaaaw!" and says, "I'm old and tired and my master no longer wants me. So I'm going to run away."

And that's exactly what that donkey did—he ran away from home. Fortunately the donkey met Jack, who had just struck out down the road to seek his fortune and they had quite an adventure.

### Story actions

One time away back years ago there was a boy named Jack [That's me!] who lived with his folks off in the mountains. Jack [That's me!] was awful lazy sometimes, just wouldn't do a lick of work. So one day when Jack [That's me!] took a lazy spell Jack's Daddy [Lazy boy!] tanned him good.

Jack [That's me!] didn't like that a bit, so early the next morning he slipped off without tellin' his Daddy [Lazy boy!] and struck out down the road to seek his fortune!

Jack [That's me!] got down the road a few miles and there was an old Ox [Um–mm–muh!] standing in a field a-bellowing like it was troubled over something.*

Continue telling the story, pausing after each character's name so the children can make their sound effects.

*"Jack and the Robbers" from *The Jack Tales* by Richard Chase. Copyright 1943, © renewed 1971 by Richard Chase. Reprinted by permission of Houghton Mifflin Company. All rights reserved.

## Follow-Up Activities

Create new sound effects for each character.

Using rhythm instruments or objects in the room, create a musical rhythm for each character. Pause in order to give puppets a chance to move to the rhythm as it is played.

## Construction of Envelope Puppets

### Materials

3¾″ × 6½″ letter envelopes

Construction paper

### Procedures

Seal flap of envelope.

Fold envelope in half with flap on underside; crease fold line.

With scissors, cut a slit along entire outer fold line.

Decorate with coloring medium and add paper ears, teeth, tongue, and other features.

### Operation

Slip fingers into top section of envelope and thumb into bottom; open and close hand to make puppet talk.

 ## "The Grobbles"

This very popular poem by Jack Prelutsky is about some gruesome creatures that lurk in hollow trees in the forest, just waiting for someone to come along.

### The Grobbles

*The grobbles are gruesome (\*)*
*the grobbles are green (\*)*
*the grobbles are nasty (\*)*

*the grobbles are mean (\*)*
*the grobbles hide deep*
*in a hollowy tree*
*just waiting to gobble*
*whomever they see. (\*)*

*I walk through the woods*
*for I'm quite unaware*
*that the grobbles are waiting (\*)*
*to gobble me there*
*they suddenly spring (\*)*
*from their hollowy tree*
*oh goodness! the grobbles (\*)*
*are gobbling m . . . (\*)†*

(\*) Children make "grobble" sounds.

### Approach

Leader recites poem and uses a lead puppet as children create sound effects without puppets.

### Puppets/Props

| Characters/Props | Types/Materials |
|---|---|
| Grobble | Spring clothespin puppet |
| Tree tote | Paper bag decorated with a tree motif |

### Presentation

#### General procedures

Hide grobble puppet inside tree tote.

Then select a child to portray main character, who will walk in front of tree.

All the other children make "grobble" sounds each time the leader raises a hand or otherwise cues the group.

†From *The Snopp on the Sidewalk* by Jack Prelutsky. Copyright © 1977 by Jack Prelutsky. Used by permission of Greenwillow Books, a division of William Morrow & Company, Inc.

## Introduction

Ask children, "Have you ever heard of a grobble?"

Next, describe a grobble to children who, with their eyes closed, imagine how a grobble might sound. On a signal, such as a brief whistle, click, or hand-clap, ask all the children, still with their eyes closed, to create their version of a grobble sound.

As you recite the poem, encourage children to recreate their sounds each time you raise your hand and to end the sound when you lower it. Practice the sounds with the hand cues before beginning the poem presentation.

## Story actions

Recite the poem, pausing after the first four lines and other lines indicated so children can create sound effects.

As you begin the recitation, the grobble puppet peeks out of hole in tree tote.

At the beginning of the second stanza, selected child strolls slowly in front of tree.

Grobble pokes head out of tree and gobbles child up as rest of group makes grobble sounds.

## Follow-Up Activities

Each child makes a grobble puppet using a spring clothespin. In pairs, children act out the poem, with one child using a puppet while the other child walks in front of an imaginary tree. Let them switch roles.

Clothespin puppet to use when presenting "The Grobbles"

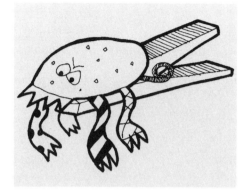

## Construction of Grobble Clothespin Puppet

### Materials

Spring clothespin

Paper scraps, material, and yarn

### Procedures

Cut out and color a simple grobble character from paper scraps and decorate with other scrap materials.

Attach to tip of upper section of clothespin.

### Operation

Squeeze back end of clothespin to make grobble gobble.

## Construction of Bag Tree Tote

### Materials

Medium-sized paper bag

Scraps of paper or felt

paper foliage

cut out hole in front and back

Paper-bag tree tote for presenting "The Grobbles"

### Procedures

Make a knothole by cutting a hole in the paper bag.

Cut a large hole in back of bag to place hand through for operating grobble puppet.

Make foliage and texture bag, with markers, paper, or felt, to look like a tree.

Hide grobble puppet inside tree tote. During poem, grobble appears in knothole.

## SUGGESTED TITLES FOR SOUND STORIES

"Bought Me a Cat," in *From Sea to Shining Sea*; comp. by Amy L. Cohn; illus. by eleven Caldecott Medal and four Caldecott Honor Book artists. Scholastic, 1993. Pp. 264–65.

Similar to "Cat Goes Fiddle-I-Fee." This version includes the music. Hang puppets on clothesline.

Carle, Eric. *Rooster's Off to See the World*; illus. by the author. Simon & Schuster, 1987.

Rooster is joined by a variety of animals as he sets off on a journey to see the world. Children add puppets to the clothesline as animals join Rooster and take them off again as each group of animals returns home.

Chase, Richard. *The Jack Tales*; illus. by Berkeley Williams, Jr. Houghton, 1943 (1971).

Includes "Jack and the Robbers," a version of "The Musicians of Bremen" told in Appalachia.

"Conjure Wives," in *Diane Goode's Book of Scary Stories & Songs*; illus. by the author. Dutton, 1994. Pp. 42–47.

An African-American tale of conjure wives whose refusal to share with a Halloween visitor results in their being turned into owls. This story offers many opportunities for sound involvement. The storyteller can use a puppet to represent a conjure wife and another to represent the visitor at the door. When these puppets are raised, children say the appropriate chorus. Or children can each create a conjure wife puppet and use it as the story is told to chant the parts of the conjure wives.

Emberley, Barbara. *Drummer Hoff*; illus. by Ed Emberley. Prentice-Hall, 1967.

A delightful tale, told in repetitive verse, of the building and firing of a cannon. Leader narrates

story as children use puppets and create sound effects. A Caldecott Medal book.

Fowke, Edith. *Ring Around the Moon*; illus. by Judith Gwyn Brown. Prentice-Hall, 1977.

Collection of rounds, riddles, tongue twisters, and other songs from the oral tradition of Canada. A section, "Answer Back Songs," includes less commonly known titles suitable for singing with puppets.

Galdone, Paul. *Cat Goes Fiddle-I-Fee*; illus. by the author. Clarion, 1985.

Picture book version of a traditional English rhyme about farmyard animals.

Hadithi, Mwenye. *Baby Baboon*; illus. by Adrienne Kennaway. Little, 1993.

Baby Baboon laughs at Leopard's attempts to catch Hare but stops laughing when Leopard catches him. Mother Baboon outwits Leopard and Baby Baboon is free to laugh again. Children create sound effects for Baby Baboon when storyteller holds up a baboon anything puppet. Or each child can create a Baby Baboon mouth or anything puppet and hold it up when creating the sound effects.

Hellen, Nancy. *Old MacDonald Had a Farm*; illus. by the author. Orchard, 1990.

The old-time favorite in picture-book format. The clothesline becomes an imaginative barnyard.

Hamanaka, Sheila. *Screen of Frogs*; illus. by the author. Orchard, 1993.

An old Japanese tale of Koji, a wealthy but spoiled man, who changes his ways as a result of a meeting with a talkative frog. Children make an envelope frog puppet and create the sounds of the thankful frogs.

Kuskin, Karla. *Roar and More*; illus. by the author. Harper, 1956.

Animals and the sounds they make are examined in words and pictures. Leader can manipulate animal puppets while children make appropriate animal sounds. Or children can control puppets as the sounds are made.

Lobel, Anita. *The Pancake*; illus. by the author. Greenwillow, 1978.

Danish tale, similar to "The Gingerbread Boy," but in this telling a pig eats the pancake. As each character is mentioned, a puppet is held up and its corresponding sound effect made.

Marshall, James. *Goldilocks and the Three Bears*; illus. by the author. Dial, 1988.

A humorous retelling of the traditional story. One child handles each bear puppet while dialogue is provided by the rest of the group. A Caldecott Honor book.

Mayo, Margaret. *Tortoise's Flying Lesson*; illus. by Emily Bolam. Harcourt, 1994.

Eight animals stories drawn from the folklore of cultures around the world. Children can create simple puppets and develop sound effects for the characters in "The Friendly Lion." Children can make an envelope lion puppet and practice a lion's roar for participation when the story "Grandmother Rabbit and the Bossy Lion" is told.

Minarik, Else Holmelund. *A Kiss for Little Bear*; illus. by Maurice Sendak. Harper, 1968.

The kiss that Grandmother sends to Little Bear travels a roundabout route before finally reaching its destination. Children hold up appropriate puppet and respond with sound effects.

Mosel, Arlene. *The Funny Little Woman*; illus. by Blair Lent. Dutton, 1972.

The adventures of a woman who chases her rice dumpling into the underworld are enacted in this Japanese folktale. Children can create sound effects for the Funny Little Woman and Oni while storyteller uses puppets to portray the action. A Caldecott Medal book.

Newman, Frederick R. *Mouth Sounds*; illus. by Marty Norman. Workman Publishing, 1980.

Step-by-step instructions for creating over seventy mouth sounds. A record of the sounds is included.

Payne, Emmy. *Katy No-Pocket*; illus. by H. A. Rey. Houghton, 1944.

A mother kangaroo is very upset because she has no way to carry her child. Assign a sound to Katy that the children make when the storyteller holds up a kangaroo puppet.

Porter, Wesley. *The Musicians of Bremen*; illus. by Kenneth W. Mitchell. Watts, 1979.

A cumulative tale about a group of animals who plan to seek their fortune in Bremen. On the way, the animals frighten a band of robbers and take over their home. Assign a sound effect to each character similar to the method described in "Jack and the Robbers."

Prelutsky, Jack. "The Grobbles," in *The Snopp on the Sidewalk and Other Poems* by Jack Prelutsky; illus. by Byron Barton. Greenwillow, 1977.

The grobbles are just waiting to gobble up anyone who wanders near their tree. Children respond to each line in the poem with grobble sounds. During a second telling children might enact the poem with grobble finger puppets.

Rae, Mary Maki, reteller. *The Farmer in the Dell*; illus. by the author. Viking, 1988.

As this popular nursery song is sung, children can add puppets to the clothesline during the first half and take them off as the characters go away.

Wahl, Jan. *Tailypo!*; illus. by Will Clay. Holt, 1992.

An African-American story about a creature who returns seeking its tail, which an old man has cut off. Each child makes an envelope puppet of the creature and uses it during the storytelling to chant the creature's demand: "Tailypo! Tailypo! All I want is my tailypo!"

Williams, Linda. *The Little Old Lady Who Was Not Afraid of Anything*; illus. by Megan Lloyd. Crowell, 1986.

A little old lady is followed through the woods by a collection of objects trying to scare her. Construct clothesline puppets and hang them on the clothesline when each object is introduced. Old clothing is a great base for most of the puppets; pair of shoes, pants, shirt, gloves, hat. Children provide the sounds for each character. At the end of the story, give each puppet to a child, put all objects together, and create a scarecrow.

Winn, Marie, comp. *The Fireside Book of Fun and Game Songs*; illus. by Whitney Darrow, Jr. Simon & Schuster, 1974.

A wide variety of songs, all fun to sing, make up this collection. A rich resource, the "Echo" and "Question and Answer" titles are particularly appealing for puppet singing.

Zemach, Margot. *The Little Red Hen*; illus. by the author. Farrar, 1983.

The Little Red Hen gets no help when she bakes a loaf of bread until it's time to eat the product of her labor. Children provide dialogue for puppet characters.

# Chapter 10    ACTION STORIES

**I**MPROVISING A STORY through action with puppets offers many possibilities for the storyteller. The story is presented in a spontaneous manner as opposed to rehearsing it again and again. Precious time need not be spent learning lines, making scenery, or practicing parts—all essential when performing a "puppet show." Thus, more time is available for additional stories and greater diversification. Everyone can easily be included, with the goal being enjoyment rather than performance perfection. Children use their own interpretative actions to "try on" characters. The group shares the story instead of performing it for an audience.

One way to get started in action participation is with the use of a popular story, such as Robert Kalan's *Jump, Frog, Jump!* in which one character repeats a single action. The frog in this story manages to avoid a series of disasters by being able to "Jump, frog, jump!" at the critical moment. While sitting in the storytelling area, children recreate the frog's jumps using simple puppets. All the other characters in the story are imagined. When the frog's jump is required, the children hold their puppets in front of them and pantomime the story action with the puppets. When the action is finished the puppets are lowered until the next action is needed. Paper-bag or cup puppets, quickly assembled to represent the frogs, are both fun and easy to make while adequately suiting the requirements of the activity.

Once children have had some experience pantomiming action at their seats, involve them in stories that require more use of space and a variety of actions. *A Rainbow of My Own* by Don Freeman can be shared effectively in this manner. Each child makes a rainbow stick puppet from one-third of a paper plate to which free floating colored paper streamers are attached. With their rainbows the children can share the fun of the main character, playing with the rainbow in a fantasy world. These puppets can move about the room to specific movement patterns suggested by the story— whirling, floating, dancing. A record can be used to provide background music to enhance this fantasy

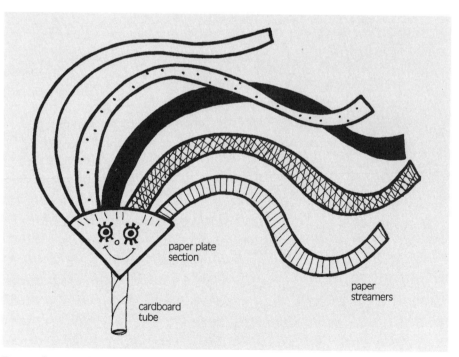

paper plate
section

cardboard
tube

paper
streamers

**Paper-plate rainbow puppet for *A Rainbow of My Own***

adventure. In addition, the music acts as an effective control signal for starting and finishing the action. When the music begins the movement also begins, and as the music fades the puppets stop their movement.

Many children's stories contain two main characters sharing the action. Examples include the Frog and Toad books by Arnold Lobel, the George and Martha series by James Marshall, and the adventures of Morris and Boris by Bernard Wiseman. These series all offer many opportunities for action with puppets. Working in pairs, each child uses a puppet representing one of the main characters. As the storyteller narrates, the appropriate puppet pantomimes the actions. For example, in *Morris and Boris*, half the children could make moose bodi-puppets and the other half bear bodi-puppets. With the puppets fastened around their necks and hung in front of their bodies, the children might act out the problems Boris encounters when he tries to teach Morris how to play games. As an extension of the story you could encourage the children to think of new activities for Morris and Boris to teach each other. Bodi-puppets are excellent puppet choices when gross movement is required since they are large and allow the child great freedom of movement.

Stories that involve a variety of characters may also provide action opportunities for whole groups of children. Additional characters can easily be incorporated into the story in order to include everyone in the sharing experience. The fable "The Boy Who Cried Wolf" moralizes the outcome of a shepherd boy who calls "Wolf!" once too often—no one believes him when the wolf really does materialize. The storyteller may manipulate the lead character puppet of the shepherd boy, as the children use puppets to mime the actions of the sheep, farmers, and farm animals. Each child will have a puppet. When a character is mentioned during the story, all children with that character will raise the puppet and perform the required action. Then the puppets

are lowered until another action is indicated. These puppets may be anything puppets, stick puppets with movable parts, or simple hand puppets, all operated by children sitting in groups around the storyteller. The array of possibilities for involving large numbers of children is limitless.

Stories such as Gerald McDermott's *Arrow to the Sun*, which incorporate a lead character who faces a series of challenges or makes a long journey, are excellent choices for the action technique. The hero in *Arrow to the Sun* must prove himself by passing through four kivas where his courage is tested by lions, serpents, bees, and lightning. A stick puppet representation of the boy will allow him to easily move through the kivas as well as through the air to the sun. Children wearing bodi-puppets or pictures may portray the Lord of the Sun, Corn Planter, Pot Maker, Arrow Maker, and villagers. Bodi-puppets would facilitate dancing and other actions required by these characters. The rest of the group may make stick or bodi-puppets representing lions, bees, serpents, and lightning for the kiva ceremonies.

It is important to plan the flow of movement before involving children in action stories. *Arrow to the Sun* requires an area for each of the kivas, as well as a space representing the home of the boy, the Lord of the Sun, the Corn Planter, the Pot Maker, the Arrow Maker, and the village where the people celebrate the boy's return from his quest by performing the Dance of Life. One solution is to have the boy move in a linear pattern from left to right at the front of the area as he begins his journey. His travel to the sun may be in a diagonal line toward the back of the area. The kivas, then, may be located along the back of the area from right to left. The dance at the conclusion of the story could take place in the middle of the storytelling area. Before the story begins all the children go to the appropriate areas. Children portraying villagers could sit at either side of the playing area until the final dance ceremony. Careful planning will result in a spectacular participatory experience that is orderly as well as enjoyable.

A final type of action participation involves children in small groups using puppets to pantomime a story. Select a story with a number of characters who are all equally involved in the action. *Mr. Gumpy's Outing* by John Burningham, *Mushroom in the Rain* by Mirra Ginsburg, and *Elephant in a Well* by Marie Hall Ets are all good beginning choices. First, tell children the story so they will be familiar with the plot and character actions. Next divide the children into groups with the number necessary to recreate the story.

*Mr. Gumpy's Outing* vividly describes the mayhem that results when Mr. Gumpy goes for a boat ride with his misbehaving animal friends. For this story groups of nine are necessary—Mr. Gumpy, a rabbit, a cat, a dog, a pig, a goat, a cow, and two children. Stick or bodi-puppets, either made by the children or supplied by the storyteller, could be used. These large puppet types are especially suitable since they allow bold movements necessary to the story: hopping, teasing, chasing, falling into the water. A piece of blue paper for the water and a rug for the boat would suggest the setting, as well as provide boundaries for the groups. Begin the action with the characters in each group lined up in the order of their appearance in the story. As you tell the story, pause at appropriate times to allow children to act out their interpretation of the story part.

As with any creative dramatics activity, it is a good idea to establish a definite way of ending the story action. You might suggest that all the puppets "freeze" and form a still picture or tableau when you clap your hands. In this way the storyteller can bring the action and story to an end at the same time, while providing a smooth transition for dismissal, follow-up, or the next activity.

## EXAMPLE OF AN ACTION STORY

The popular story *A Woggle of Witches* can be used to encourage active participation of an entire group of children. The example included here describes an approach in which the children move around the storytelling area in a free manner with puppets. This technique should be viewed as only one of many possible ways of involving children in action participation and should be modified to fit the avoidable physical space, the needs of the children, and the storyteller's purpose and skills.

## A Woggle of Witches

In this Adrienne Adams story, some witches joyously celebrate Halloween night until they are frightened by a parade of monsters.

### Approach
Children move around the playing area and pantomime the actions of the witches and monsters as the leader tells the story.

### Puppets/Props

| Characters/Props | Types/Materials |
| --- | --- |
| Witches | Paper-plate puppets |
| Monsters | |
| Moon | Stick puppet |

### Presentation
#### General procedures
Half the children make witch puppets, the other half make monster puppets to act out the story. Except for the Moon, all props and scenery are imagined.

Children with monster puppets stand to the left at the side of playing space. Children with witch puppets are scattered around the front of playing space which represents the forest.

The Moon, represented by a large stick puppet held by a child or secured to a chair, is at the center of the playing area.

Explain the movement pattern to children—witches will circle the Moon clockwise; monsters will walk across space from left to right; forest is located at front of playing area, cornfield at the back.

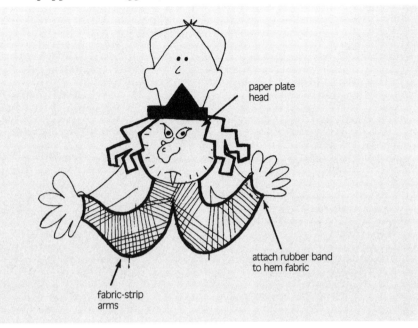

paper plate head

attach rubber band to hem fabric

fabric-strip arms

### Introduction

Discuss the characters that might be seen on Halloween night.

"Did you know that a group of witches is called a woggle of witches? Close your eyes and imagine a woggle of witches at home deep in a dark forest. Look closely and you'll see a witch asleep in the branches of each tree, for the moon is full and it's Halloween night. Open your eyes; it is time for the witches to have some fun."

### Story actions

Witch puppets are asleep as the narrator begins the story.

Witches wake up and have a feast.

Witches jump onto their broomsticks and fly up into the sky.

Witches circle the moon.

Witches return to earth and land in a cornfield.

Witches see monsters approaching so they hide among the cornstalks.

Monsters parade across space.

Witches leap on their brooms and fly home.

Witches go back to sleep among the trees.

### Follow-Up Activities

After naming their witch and monster puppets, children may introduce them to the group. Each character can share his or her favorite Halloween night activity.

The group may design new situations involving witches and monsters for the puppets to enact.

### Construction of Witch and Monster Paper-Plate Bodi-Puppets

#### Materials

One 6″ paper plate

30″ length of fabric strip or ribbon for necktie

Fabric strip 12″ × 26″

Scrap fabric, paper, trim, yarn

Rubber bands

### Procedures

For face, add facial features and hair to the front of the paper plate.

Slit the fabric strip up the center from the bottom edge to 4 inches from the top edge to form two arm sections.

Staple the top of fabric strip to the bottom of plate as shown (on previous page).

Fold over the end of each fabric arm strip and slip a rubber band in each hem. Staple hems to secure rubber bands.

Staple neck ribbon to top of plate.

### Operation

Tie neck ribbon around child's neck and slip rubber bands over wrists. The child then "becomes" the puppet and can freely pantomime the character's actions.

### SUGGESTED TITLES FOR **ACTION STORIES**

Adams, Adrienne. *A Woggle of Witches*; illus. by the author. Macmillan, 1982.

> Witches celebrate Halloween night but are frightened by a parade of monsters.

Agell, Charlotte. *Dancing Feet*; illus. by the author. Harcourt, 1994.

> A celebration of the similarities and differences among people. Children make a body puppet and perform all the actions in the story; waving, digging, baking, skipping, dancing.

Burningham, John. *Mr. Gumpy's Outing*; illus. by the author. Holt, 1976.

> Mr. Gumpy lets guests join him for a boat ride but the guests soon forget their promise to behave. In small groups children participate using puppets and a rug for the boat.

Cannon, Janell. *Stellaluna*; illus. by the author. Harcourt Brace, 1993.

> A baby bat is raised as a bird after she accidentally falls into a bird's nest. Children create bat puppets and pantomime the action of Stellaluna.

Deetlefs, Rene. *Tabu and the Dancing Elephants*; illus. by Lyn Gilbert. Dutton, 1995.

> The elephants carry baby Tabu away and care for him. After a frantic search by his parents, Tabu is returned safely after a moonlight dance. Each child makes an elephant bodi-puppet and joins in the moonlight dance.

Evans, Dilys, comp. *Monster Soup and Other Spooky Poems*; illus. by Jacqueline Rogers. Scholastic, 1992.

> This collection of poems about imagined and mechanical monsters offers delicious opportunities for children to take the role of these spooky characters. In small groups children wearing pin-on pictures pantomime the actions of the monsters as you read the poems. As each group enacts its poem, lower the lights and shine a large spotlight on the group. Poems to dramatize: "The Power Shovel," "Thunder," "Giant," "Ankylosaurus," "Halloween Cats," "HIST WHIST," "From an Old Cornish Litany."

Freeman, Don. *A Rainbow of My Own*; illus. by the author. Viking, 1966.

> A boy creates a fantasy world in which he plays with his own rainbow. Each child makes a rainbow from one-third of a paper plate and colored paper streamers. These puppets can swirl and twirl about the room to specific movement patterns suggested by the story.

Ginsburg, Mirra. *Mushroom in the Rain*; illus. by Jose Aruego and Ariane Dewey. Macmillan, 1987.

An adaptation of a Russian folktale about animals hiding under a mushroom to stay safe and dry.

Grossman, Virginia. *Ten Little Rabbits*; illus. by Sylvia Long. Chronicle, 1991.

Rabbits in Native American costumes act out traditional customs such as rain dances, hunting, and fishing in this original counting book. Wearing pin-on pictures children, in groups of ten, perform the actions.

Kalan, Robert. *Jump, Frog, Jump!*; illus. by Byron Barton. Greenwillow, 1981.

Frog is kept safe by being able to jump away from danger in this cumulative tale.

Lobel, Arnold. *Frog and Toad Together*; illus. by the author. Harper, 1970.

Five adventures of Frog and Toad can be dramatized in pairs. "Anything" puppets with faces attached or pin-on pictures are both appropriate. A Newbery Honor book.

Mayo, Margaret. *Tortoise's Flying Lesson*; illus. by Emily Bolam. Harcourt, 1994.

A collection of folktales from around the world. Before the story "How to Count Crocodiles" is told, each child makes a crocodile stick puppet. The storyteller tells the story using a monkey puppet. When the monkey shouts, "All you crocodiles! Get in a row! Side by side!" the children do just that with their crocodile puppets. The monkey then jumps from crocodile to crocodile and safely crosses the river.

McDermott, Gerald. *Arrow to the Sun*; illus. by the author. Viking, 1974.

A Pueblo Indian tale recounting a boy's journey to the Sun to find his father. A Caldecott Medal book.

Ringgold, Faith. *Tar Beach*; illus. by the author. Crown, 1991.

A young girl dreams of flying away from New York and creating a better life for herself and her family. Children create a simple stick or envelope puppet and pantomime Cassie's adventures. A Coretta Scott King Award and Caldecott Honor book.

Roy, Ron. *Three Ducks Went Wandering*; illus. by Paul Galdone. Seabury, 1979.

Three curious little ducks escape a series of potential disasters while exploring the countryside. Rod puppets or pin-on pictures are suitable for the ducks, as well as the other characters—bull, foxes, hawk, snake, butterflies, and mother duck. Action is pantomimed with puppets as leader narrates the story.

Sendak, Maurice. *Where the Wild Things Are*; illus. by the author. Harper, 1963.

Max, who is sent to bed without his supper for being naughty, visits the land of the Wild Things. Each child can make a bodi-puppet or paper mask and then enter the world of the Wild Things. A Caldecott Medal book.

Stevenson, James. *The Worst Person in the World*; illus. by the author. Greenwillow, 1978.

The kindness of an ugly creature brings out the better nature of a mean man. Half the children use pin-on pictures to portray "Ugly" while the other half play the mean man. Or all the children could draw their version of the worst person in the world, pin it on, and then act out the story.

Wiseman, Bernard. *Morris and Boris*; illus. by the author. Dodd, 1974.

Problems arise when Boris tries to teach Morris how to play games. Half the children use a bear puppet and the rest use a moose puppet to mime the action.

# Chapter 11 — SOUND AND ACTION STORIES

IVING A CHILD the responsibility for supplying the actions or voice of a puppet character, providing sound effects, or imitating scenic elements personalizes the story in a memorable way.

In sound and action participation storytelling, everyone takes part, but not always in the same manner. For one story all the children might use a similar lead character puppet. Acting as a unit, they could respond at appropriate times during the telling with movements and dialogue for that particular puppet. In another story, some children could manipulate specific character puppets while others supply sound effects for characters or even such elements as props or weather.

Stories to select for this technique are those that have sound and action elements built into them. Look for a balance of dialogue and action. *Hand, Hand, Finger, Thumb* by Al Perkins and *Sheep Take a Hike* by Nancy Shaw are both excellent beginning vehicles for sound and action exploration. In addition to equal elements of these qualities, both stories contain one type of character, monkey and sheep, performing the same series of actions.

The antics of a group of lively monkeys in *Hand, Hand, Finger, Thumb* experimenting with drums, requires both large and small movements as children imitate the monkeys and coax sounds from their drums. Each child may make a monkey bodi-puppet and use a table or desk top as a drum to recreate the sound and actions described in the book, followed by simple actions such as picking an apple, playing a fiddle, and shaking hands. The group of sheep taking a hike in the second story offer the puppeteers a series of intriguing actions and sounds to explore. Children wearing sheep bodi-puppets or pin-on pictures can move around the storytelling area as they trot, stomp, bicker, and tramp through the woods.

In some stories, such as *Rosie's Walk* by Pat Hutchins, sound effects woven throughout the action are a satisfactory substitute for dialogue. As Rosie the hen saunters nonchalantly across the barnyard, a fox stalks her. There is no dialogue in this book, but the predicaments faced by the fox, such as falling into a pond, provide a fertile field for developing a series of interesting sound effects.

Often stories with one main character trying to find a solution to a problem can combine sound and action elements successfully. The lead character can ask a question and the other characters give a reply—thus, the sound element. When a suggestion for problem solving is offered by the other characters, the lead character can act on that suggestion—thereby providing the action element. *The Ghost with the Halloween Hiccups* by Stephen Mooser is a case in point. Mr. Penny attempts to rid himself of the hiccups so that he can star in the Halloween play. His call for help elicits a number of interesting responses, all of which he tries—standing on his head, wearing a paper hat, etc. The storyteller can assume the role of the costumed children who finally effect his cure—by frightening him.

Everyone can make a paper-tissue ghost finger puppet as described in chapter 14 under *Georgie's Halloween* to portray Mr. Penny who, of course, must hiccup throughout his quest. Space required is minimal if Mr. Penny is represented by a hand puppet. During the storytelling each child would hold the puppet overhead as the actions and dialogue required by the story were individually interpreted. All responses would be done simultaneously with no attempt made to standardize gestures or vocal quality.

However, if the plot requires space to be covered, such as the walk in *Rosie's Walk*, rod or simple string puppets would be wise choices. Then the children could stand or move around the playing area as the plot dictates.

Another excellent source of material for sound and action participation is the story in which a group of characters attempt to resolve a difficult situation. In Ann McGovern's *Too Much Noise* a farmer is so annoyed by ordinary household sounds that he seeks the advice of a wise man. He follows the wise man's unusual counsel and brings farm animals into the house. The farmer realizes how quiet his house actually is only when the animals have been returned to the barn. Using stick puppets children can explore through sounds and accompanying actions the wide range of animals' feelings when transferred from their own homes into the farmer's house—happy, sad, discontent, angry, satisfied, excited. Before beginning the participation, ask the children to consider: "How does your animal move as it travels from the barn to the house?" "How does your animal act when it is in the house?" "How does it sound?" Designate one section of the playing space as the barn and another as the farmhouse and establish a path which all the animals will follow.

The first part of *Too Much Noise* details all the house noises that annoy the farmer—bed creaks, floor squeaks, tea-kettle whistles, etc. Children not manipulating puppets can form a sound chorus and provide sounds, as indicated, throughout the story. An enriching element is added when rhythm or improvised instruments are employed for these sounds. Or, all the children might vocally supply the sounds. Remember to use a signal, such as a drum beat, to begin and end the sound participation.

## EXAMPLES OF SOUND AND ACTION STORIES

Two examples of sound and action participation follow. In the first example, *Rosie's Walk*, two children using string puppets move around the playing space as other children become scenery or provide sound effects. The second example, *The Little Engine That Could*, employs an even more active participation technique as some children are transformed into trains using pin-on body pictures and others assume the role, without puppets, of toys and presents. All children are involved in supplying sounds. The storyteller should feel free to adapt and change these ideas to tailor them to a particular storytelling situation.

### Rosie's Walk

In this story by Pat Hutchins, Rosie, a hen, goes for a walk in the barnyard, unaware that a wily fox is pursuing her.

#### Approach

Leader tells story as children use puppets to pantomime the action. Other children become the scenery or provide the sound effects, without puppets.

#### Puppets/Props

| Characters/Props | Types/Materials |
| --- | --- |
| Rosie, the hen<br>Fox | Balloon string puppets |
| Haystack<br>Mill<br>Fence<br>Beehives<br>Rake | Children |
| Pond | Blue towel or carpet square |
| Yard | Strip of brown paper |

Fox balloon puppet for *Rosie's Walk*

## Presentation

### General procedures

Arrange seated children in a wide circle in playing space.

With children, decide where in the circle each setting should be; put down carpet square to represent the pond and brown paper for the yard. Children will use their bodies to form other scenery.

Assign two children to play the parts of Rosie and Fox with puppets.

Everyone else will make sound effects: Fox walking into rake, Fox splashing into the pond, Fox landing in haystack, flour spilling, and bees buzzing.

### Introduction

Ask children to close their eyes and imagine that they are taking a walk in the country. Where are they going? What do they see? After they open their eyes, let each child share the imaginary walk with a partner.

Introduce Rosie and tell the children the story of her walk showing pictures from the book.

Ask all the children, in pairs, to try different ways to form a haystack, mill, fence, and beehives with their bodies. (Remind children that Rosie must be able to go over the haystack, through the fence, and under the beehives.) Then select pairs of children to form each scenery element during the storytelling. Pick one child to become the rake lying in the yard. Arrange the children around the inside of the circle in the order that the scenic element they represent appears in the story.

Turn to the pictures in the book that suggest the sound effects needed. Ask the children, "Can anyone think of a sound that would go with this picture?" As children volunteer sounds, ask the whole group to imitate the sound. After trying several suggestions, ask children to pick those sounds to be used as the story is retold. Practice the sounds selected before beginning the sound and action participation.

Invite children to help you tell the story by using puppets and making sound effects.

### Story actions

Begin the story. Rosie, the hen, walks around barnyard area followed by the Fox puppet.

Narrate the story, pausing at each area to give puppeteers time to perform the necessary actions.

Cue the group to make sound effects when appropriate.

## Follow-Up Activities

Create additional adventures for Rosie.

In pairs, pantomime the story with imaginary scenery and no puppets as a creative dramatics activity.

## Construction of Rosie and Fox Balloon String Puppets

### Materials

Large balloons

Oak tag or other stiff paper

Construction paper strips approximately 1½″ wide

Black carpet thread or yarn

### Procedures

Cut out head and tail for Rosie and the Fox from oak tag paper.

Draw on the features.

Accordion pleat (fold) the paper strips to form legs.

Attach head, tail, and legs to balloons with rubber cement. (Put rubber cement on the balloon and the surface to be attached. When rubber cement feels sticky attach features to the balloon.)

Attach one continuous piece of yarn from the head to the tail of each character.

## Operation

Hold string and bounce the puppet along the playing space.

## The Little Engine That Could

A little engine scales the mountain by sheer willpower and positive thinking in this familiar story by Watty Piper.

## Approach

Leader narrates story and uses the Little Blue Engine puppet; children supply dialogue and/or manipulate a puppet.

## Puppets/Props

| Characters/Props | Types/Materials |
| --- | --- |
| Happy Little Train (Red) Shiny New Engine Big Black Engine Rusty Old Engine | Pin-on picture puppets |
| Little Blue Engine | Large paper puppet |
| Toys and gifts | Children |

## Presentation

### General procedures

Have the children sit on the floor near the back of the storytelling area with a large open space in front of them. Be sure to have the Little Blue Engine puppet hidden behind your chair. After the children have been assigned their parts, they will move around the story area acting the parts of different toys, gifts, and trains as the story is told.

### Introduction

Warm-up activities based on the characters and theme of the story will prepare children for sound and action participation.

Ask the children to find their own space in the story-telling area. Then say, "Close your eyes and picture all the special food and presents you'd like to have on your birthday. Open your eyes. What are some of the things you imagined?" Give children an opportunity to share their ideas.

Continue, "When I clap my hands, move as if you were the thing I name. When I say 'Freeze,' stand as still as a statue until I clap my hands again." Use the following toys, as well as toys mentioned by the children, as examples: clown, teddy bear, spinning top, basketball, elephant, sailboat.

"This time when I clap my hands, imagine that you are eating whatever I name. You might want to add sound effects as you eat each item." Examples include: ice cream cone, candy bar, pretzel, glass of milk, birthday cake with lots of frosting.

"Now, imagine that you are a freight train with a long line of boxcars moving along the railroad track. When I clap my hands begin to move around the room as if you were that long freight train. Don't forget to make the sound effects for your train."

"Now the train is very small. It has only an engine and a caboose. How does that train move and sound as it travels along the track?"

When children are seated, introduce the story.

*The Little Engine That Could* is about a Happy Little Train with a cargo of toys and food that is having trouble getting over the mountain. Luckily, a Little Blue Engine passes by that is willing to try to pull the Happy Little Train over the mountain.

**Pattern for Making the Little Engine Cardboard Puppet**

Bring out the pin-on pictures of the trains in the story and select children to be each one: the Happy Little Train, the Shiny New Engine, the Big Black Engine, and the Rusty Old Engine. Pin the picture of the appropriate train directly onto the children's clothing. The Happy Little Train is at the front of the storytelling area, while the other trains sit at the back. Ask the remaining children to be the toys and other good things being carried by the Happy Little Train. Children will move and talk as that toy or present during the storytelling.

### Story actions

Happy Little Train makes chugging sounds as the first part of the story is told.

Happy Little Train comes to a halt. Chugging sounds stop.

Shiny New Engine moves to front. Children (as toys) ask Shiny New Engine to help them get over the mountain.

Shiny New Engine refuses and steams off to the back of the playing area.

Repeat action and dialogue for Big Black Engine and Rusty Old Engine.

Little Blue Engine appears. Toys ask for help getting over the mountain.

Little Blue Engine moves in front of Happy Little Train.

16"

2½"

2½"

18"

12"

*32" long x 18" wide*

With Little Blue Engine the storyteller leads the Happy Little Train and all its toys and presents around the room in a continuous line while saying, "I think I can, I think I can, I think I can!" Toys join in repeating the refrain.

Little Blue Engine circles the room once and then returns to original position saying, "I thought I could. I thought I could. I thought I could."

## Follow-Up Activities

Make up a refrain for each of the other engines to say as it moves around the room.

## Construction of Little Engine Cardboard Puppet

### Materials

Poster board sheet

Paper cup

Paint

### Procedures

Cut outline for top section and bottom section of train from poster board as shown on page 150. Paint these two sections blue.

Cut two strips 2½" wide from red poster board for the mouth. Paint these two pieces red.

Tape mouth pieces together; then tape to engine top and bottom sections. Fold mouth as shown.

Cut two finger holes, two inches apart, in center of top train section to hold puppet.

Tape a cup, open end down, over the holes. The cup serves as a nose and covers the holes.

Paint on features.

### Operation

Slip pointer and index fingers through nose holes. Place thumb under bottom folded mouth section. Move fingers and thumb together and apart to open and close mouth.

## SUGGESTED TITLES FOR SOUND AND ACTION STORIES

Galdone, Paul. *Henny Penny*; illus. by the author. Seabury, 1968.

A group of foolish animals encounter misfortune on their way to tell the King the sky is falling.

Gershator, Phillis. *Tukama Tootles the Flute*; illus. by Synthia St. James. Orchard, 1994.

A tale from the Caribbean about a boy, Tukama, who is captured by a two-headed giant when he disobeys his grandmother. Children wearing large bodi-puppets act out the parts of the giants. A hand puppet can be used for Tukama. The narrator plays the role of grandmother, perhaps wearing a scarf around her head. One group of children is a chorus that chants the nonsense rhyme whenever Tukama plays his flute.

Hutchins, Pat. *Good-Night Owl!*; illus. by the author. Macmillan, 1972.

During the day when Owl tries to sleep, all the other creatures that live in his tree make their usual sounds—bees buzz, crows caw, woodpeckers rat–a–tat–tat. At night while they try to sleep, Owl takes his turn to make noise. All the children use rod or bag puppets to portray the sounds and actions of the animals living in the tree. The storyteller plays the part of Owl.

Hutchins, Pat. *Rosie's Walk*; illus. by the author. Macmillan, 1968.

Rosie, a hen, goes for a walk in the barnyard, unaware that a wily fox is pursuing her.

Jorgensen, Gail. *Crocodile Beat*; illus. by Patricia Mullins. Bradbury, 1988.

The play of animals along a riverbank is interrupted when a hungry crocodile appears. Lion thwarts the crocodile's attempt to dine on any of the creatures. Each child makes an animal puppet to use during the story when the animal is named. Lots of fun sounds and actions for puppets to create.

Kimmel, Eric A. *Anansi and the Moss-Covered Rock*; illus. by Janet Stevens. Holiday, 1988.

Anansi the spider uses a moss-covered rock to trick her animal friends out of their food supply. It takes little Bush Deer to fool Anansi and set things right. Children use stick or bodi-puppets to act out the story. Another group uses drums or their voices to produce the "KPOM!" sound each time an animal faints. A third group of children can say the magic sentence, "Isn't this a strange moss-covered rock?"

Lester, Julius. *John Henry*; illus. by Jerry Pinkney. Dial, 1994.

A retelling of the John Henry legend filled with poetic language. Half the group wearing bodi-puppets acts out John Henry's attempt to out-hammer a machine. The rest of the group can use rhythm instruments to create sound effects. A Caldecott Honor book.

McGovern, Ann. *Too Much Noise*; illus. by Simms Taback. Houghton, 1967.

A man realizes how quiet his home really is only after sharing it with the farm animals.

Mollel, Tololwa M. *Rhinos for Lunch and Elephants for Supper!*; illus. by Barbara Spurll. Clarion, 1991.

Hare's friends, fox, leopard, rhino and elephant, all try to help when a mysterious monster invades her house. But it is frog who saves the day. As children using rod or bodi-puppets act out the story, the remainder of the group blares the chorus, "I'm a monster, a monster! I eat rhinos for lunch and elephants for supper! Come in if you dare!" The caterpillar can be a sock or rod puppet.

Mooser, Stephen. *Ghost with the Halloween Hiccups*; illus. by Tomie de Paola. Watts, 1977.

Mr. Penny's hiccups almost keep him from starring in the Halloween play. Each child makes a ghost puppet from a paper tissue and a rubber band. Small paper cups may be used for the paper hat.

Perkins, Al. *Hand, Hand, Fingers, Thumb*; illus. by Eric Gurney. Random House, 1969.

Lively illustrations and rhyming text explore the many ways monkeys can combine hand and thumb movements with drums.

Piper, Watty. *The Little Engine That Could*; illus. by George and Doris Hauman. Platt & Munk, 1961.

A Happy Little Train has trouble scaling the mountain until a Little Blue Engine comes to its aid.

Sandburg, Carl. "The Wedding Procession of the Rag Doll and the Broom Handle and Who Was in It," in *Rootabaga Stories Part One*; illus. by Michael Hague. Harcourt, 1988.

The Chocolate Chins, Tin Pan Bangers, and the Easy Ticklers are only a few of the guests at the wedding of the Rag Doll and the Broom Handle. Children draw their version of a character to pin to their clothing. Using utensil props, all children participate in the wedding procession. You lead the parade carrying a rag doll and a broom handle.

Seeger, Pete. *Abiyoyo*; illus. by Michael Hays. Macmillan, 1986.

A little boy who plays a ukelele and his father, a magician, save the town from the terrible giant Abiyoyo. Children create Abiyoyo bodi-puppets and dramatize the confrontation between Abiyoyo and the father and son.

Shaw, Nancy. *Sheep Take a Hike*; illus. by Margot Apple. Houghton, 1994.

A hike in the country turns into a riotous adventure when the sheep get lost.

Silverman, Jerry. *Work Songs*; Chelsea House, 1994.

The short, repetitive verses in these songs from the African-American community perfectly capture the hard work being performed. Half the group sings the song as the other half acts it out with bodi-puppets. Songs to try include: "Pick a Bale of Cotton," "Look Over Yonder," "Mule Skinner Blues," and "John Henry." Music is included.

Zemach, Margot. *It Could Always Be Worse*; illus. by the author. Farrar, 1977.

When a man complains that his house is too small, the Rabbi advises him to move the animals into the house. Children wearing bodi-puppets or using stick puppets will enjoy acting out this humorous story and making all the animal sounds. A Caldecott Honor book.

# Part Five

# PRESENTATION FORMATS

**A Red Hen bodi-puppet**

THE MASTERFUL STORY-TELLER details with great foresight all aspects of the dramatic presentation. By combining elements of intrigue, plot revelation, color, and timbre, the storyteller attempts to maximize the impact of the story upon the listener. The teller of tales who wishes to go beyond the conventional domains of narrating or dramatizing stories in informal sessions to introduce the element of visual surprise will enjoy exploring this part of the book on presentation techniques. The ten story format categories included give a wide choice of methods to match with favorite stories.

The traditional form of puppet presentation, i.e., the curtain opening and hand puppet staging, requires special skills and is well documented elsewhere. The intent of chapters 12 through 21 is to develop heretofore unexplored combinations and concepts in establishing settings for puppet presentations. Whether revamped versions of classic forms, such as finger stories, or more recently developed vehicles, such as story aprons or cup and containers theaters, the methods presented here will help broaden the possibilities of storytelling.

Each of the presentation formats is launched with a descriptive introduction that gives clues to pairing stories with method and puppet types. A format or basic idea that appeals to the storyteller may easily be adapted, with a little ingenuity, to older or younger age-level material. A good example is finger stories, commonly associated with young children. Used with more mature material, this technique can appeal to older children as well.

Puppet types are often interchangeable with respect to formats. For example, hand, stick, and finger puppets are quite adaptable to the book theater and open-box theater, providing the puppets are in scale with the components. An open box theater must be large enough in area to include space that will easily accommodate the puppets. One that will be used with hand puppets must be larger than one that will be used with finger puppets.

The size of the audience will help determine a particular format chosen. It is apparent that such small-scale settings as cup and container stories and finger stories will be compatible with small groups, while stories-in-the-round techniques can accommodate larger groups. Overhead shadow puppetry, when projected on a large screen, offers an exciting medium for presentations to very large audiences, as in an auditorium situation.

Availability of space will also influence decisions on which formats to pursue. Book theaters and cup and container theaters naturally require a minimum amount of space, while stories-in-the-round call for expanded playing areas. The very practical factor of storytelling space should, of course, be considered at the outset.

When planning presentation formats for successive sessions, remember that children find a special joy in hearing tales presented in a variety of ways. "Henny Penny," for example, may appear as a miniature version on a straw, conforming to the tiny scale of a cup theater one day; mysteriously emerge from a story apron as a feathery hand puppet on another; then finally make a full-scale appearance in the form of a bodi-puppet for a story-in-the-round interpretation with creative dramatics. Each rendition of this well-loved tale adds a new focus, a fresh outlook to the story. As a didactic tool and as a means of variation, the technique of using multiple story formats has great value in reinforcing the elements of the story.

The format chosen should function solely as a visual enhancement to the basic story; therefore simplicity is the key element. The format should strike a balance between achieving maximal impact upon the viewer and requiring minimal effort in construction and ease of handling for the storyteller. Never should the format overpower the essence of the story or its interpretation. In fact, a surplus of puppet characters, props, and scenery may confuse the story rather than enhance it, and may result in an unmanageable, chaotic presentation. Concentrate, therefore, on creating varied settings which are vivid, clear, and highly effective.

Using the techniques described in these chapters will greatly increase the storyteller's flexibility. Presentation formats not only enhance the story and help focus attention, but also assist the storyteller in dealing with problems of space, mobility, and interest levels.

# Chapter 12    BOOK THEATERS

A BOOK MAKES a natural theater, since the opened book itself can adapt easily as background for a puppet presentation. The top edge of an opened book placed on a tabletop serves as a ledge along which the actions of the story can take place. In essence, the book becomes a miniature stage for enjoyable viewing by small story groups.

Simple scenery or props, such as a cutout hill or circus tent, can be attached to spring-type clothespins and clipped onto the top edge of the book. Small-scale puppets made from paper cutouts secured to drinking straws, tongue depressors, or ice cream sticks can perform the story's actions along the playing area, above the book. Finger puppets, because of their size and ease of use, are also good companions for this technique. Consequently, an alligator in a swamp can slink along, gradually sinking down and then up again, peeking over the book's edge; a car can rumble jerkily or a grasshopper gaily hop along the horizontal length of the book.

The book theater approach allows the storyteller to imbue the children with an appreciation of the storybook itself. Children are usually enthralled with all miniature theaters and are often found imitating this idea at home. Furthermore, this modified technique has added value since the extended physical components of the book are linked with the puppets.

Because the playing space and the scale of the puppets and scenery in this method are limited in size, the story types chosen should be those that demand a minimal amount of intricate actions by the characters themselves. Focus on books and stories that have few characters and that provide sharp visual imagery and simple actions. For example, in *Caleb and Kate* by William Steig, the story's action capitalizes on Caleb's transformation into a dog! This can be accomplished by quickly changing the characters, bringing one puppet down and another up. *The Runaway Bunny* by Margaret Wise Brown elaborates on a similar visual surprise as the main character changes into a number of interesting characters, both animate and inanimate. The same principle, but with changing scenery images on sticks, may be explored in *Frederick* by Leo Lionni, a story about a mouse's search for summer. In this instance segments of scenery, also held up on rods, can appear and disappear along the book's edge illustrating a dreary winter scene, then a colorful summer. The busy mice in this story can be drawn on a single piece of stiff paper, clustered as a unit, and attached to a rod control for ease in handling. The lead character, Frederick, portrayed as a separate rod puppet, busily scampers back and forth along the book's playing space.

Books that contain a collection of stories about real characters, folk heroes, giants, or other creatures make an excellent stage for introducing the characters. *Cut From the Same Cloth,* by Robert San Souci, is a collection of tales about American women of myth, legend, and tall tale. Selected exploits of each woman can be dramatized using stick or hand puppets and simple props on a book theater stage. A group of children working together might each select a favorite exploit of a character to dramatize. In this way, all characters from the book can be introduced with the book itself always visible as an invitation to the listeners to explore each woman in more depth.

If the storyteller knows the story particularly well, the inside of the book might be facing the audience, with the storyteller turning pages in conjunction with the action. In such a way, varied scene changes are easily achieved. Book theaters are highly portable and are a real asset to the storyteller who must move quickly between groups or work in a facility where space is at a premium.

## EXAMPLE OF A BOOK THEATER

 *The Runaway Bunny*

In this Margaret Wise Brown story, a bunny runs away and unsuccessfully tries to hide from his mother by turning into things of fantasy. In each attempt his mother finds him.

### Approach

Opened book stands on table. Leader narrates story from behind book.

Leader assumes role of Mother Bunny without puppet.

### Puppets/Props

**Characters/Props**
Bunny
Fish
Bird
Trapeze Bunny
Boy Bunny
Crocus
Sailboat
Rock
Carrot

**Types/Materials**
Paper stick puppets

### Presentation

**General procedures**
Stand opened book on tabletop with covers facing audience. Arrange puppets and props behind book in order of appearance.

### Introduction

Let the children fantasize about the things they'd like to be.

Ask them, "If you could change into anything in the world, what would you like to be? Why?"

Then say, "I know a story about a bunny who wanted to change into many things because he wanted to hide from his mother."

### Story actions

Begin story.

Show bunny puppet.

Fish swims across stage (top edge of book).

Remaining puppets and props appear in sequence:

   Rock

   Crocus

   Bird

   Sailboat

   Wind (blow over top of action area)

   Trapeze Bunny (walks over edge of book, balancing)

   Boy Bunny (catch him in your arms)

   Carrot

### Follow-Up Activities

Have children make a stick puppet of something they wish to become. Children may draw freestyle or search through old magazines to find pictures that can be cut and glued to tagboard to make puppets.

Ask children to share with the group why they want to change into their newly chosen character; what feats they could accomplish, etc.

Stick puppet for *The Runaway Bunny*

**Stick Puppet Patterns for Presenting The Runaway Bunny**

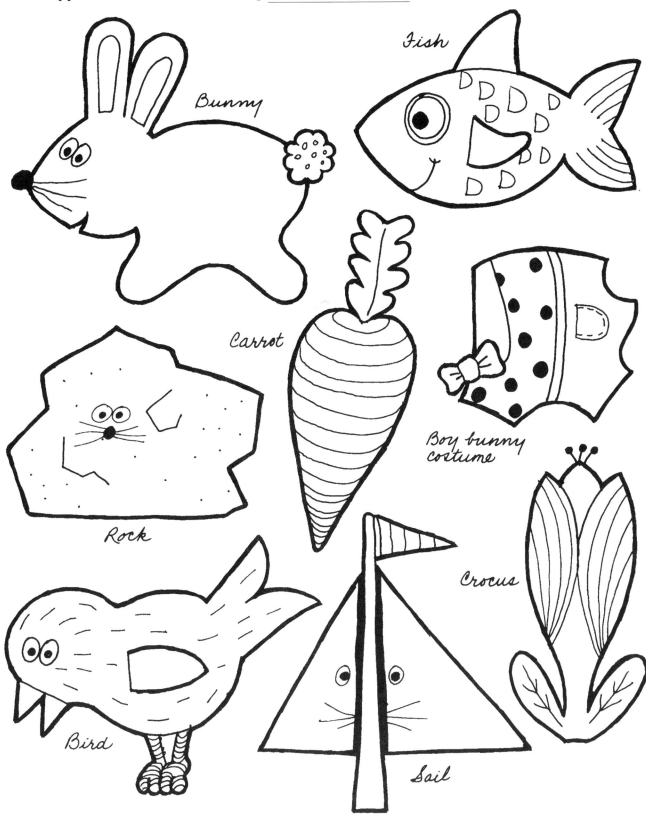

Bunny

Fish

Carrot

Boy bunny costume

Rock

Crocus

Bird

Sail

## Construction of Book Theater Puppets

### Materials

Tagboard or construction paper

Drinking straw, tongue depressors, or popsicle sticks

Spring-type clothespins

Clear plastic or adhesive-backed material such as
Contact (optional)

### Procedures

Cut out story characters from tagboard or construction
paper.

Color with felt-tip marking pens or crayons and tape
characters to end of straw or other stick rod.

Cut out scenery and props (table, boat, island, tree,
etc.) and glue to flat side of clothespin.

Laminate with clear Contact or other adhesive-backed
plastic.

### Operation

Scenery and props can be clipped onto upper edge of
book while puppets are maneuvered along top edge
from behind book.

### SUGGESTED TITLES FOR BOOK THEATERS

Allard, Harry. *I Will Not Go to Market Today*; illus. by
James Marshall. Dial, 1979.

> One calamity after another interferes with Feni-
> more's plans to go to market. Incorporate props such
> as a toothbrush, thermometer, and toy paper um-
> brella into the telling.

Bear, John. *The Frog and the Princess*; illus. by Charlie
Powell. Tricycle, 1994.

> A new twist has been added to the well-known
> story of a frog who turns into a prince when a prin-
> cess kisses him. In this version the kiss changes both
> characters. The transformation of the characters is
> easily and quickly done using a book theater format.
> Ask students to create the thunder's roar and attach
> a lightning bolt cut from gold foil to a straw.

Brown, Margaret Wise. *The Runaway Bunny*; illus. by
Clement Hurd. Harper, 1942.

> The love of his mother keeps a bunny from run-
> ning away.

Getz, Arthur. *Humphrey, the Dancing Pig*; illus. by the
author. Dial, 1980.

> Humphrey discovers that dancing makes him
> thinner but not necessarily happier. A stick puppet
> of Humphrey in each of his costumes may dance
> along the top edge of the book.

Kherdian, David. *Feathers and Tail*; illus. by Nonny
Hogrogian. Philomel, 1992.

> A collection of animal fables from around the
> world. Several titles are adaptable to book theater
> presentations, including "Heron Woos Crane," "Pig
> and Bear," "The Lemming and the Owl," and "The
> Incautious Fox and the Foolish Wolf."

Knutson, Barbara. *How the Guinea Fowl Got Her
Spots*; illus. by the author. Carolrhoda, 1990.

> This Swahili tale of friendship explains how cow
> gave guinea fowl the protective coloration that pro-
> tects her from enemies. Make two stick puppets of
> guinea fowl; one all black, the other black with
> white spots. Add clip-on scenery to represent the
> river and cow's home.

Lionni, Leo. *Frederick*; illus. by the author. Pantheon,
1967.

> A mouse shares his talent with words to recreate
> summer during the cold, dreary winter. Clip Fred-
> erick to the book when you manipulate the other
> mice busily gathering food. A Caldecott Honor book.

McFarland, John. *The Exploding Frog*; illus. by James Marshall. Little, 1981.

This is a collection of fables that contains several titles especially adaptable to book theater presentations. Among these are: "The Crab and Her Son," "The Mouse and the Bull," "The Hound and the Hare," and "The Mole and Her Mother."

Ringgold, Faith. *Dinner at Aunt Connie's House*; illus. by the author. Hyperion, 1993.

The accomplishments of twelve famous African-American women are shared at a dinner party. The book can serve as the stage for puppet characters of the women to share their achievements.

San Souci, Robert D. *Cut from the Same Cloth*; illus. by Brian Pinkney. Philomel, 1993.

Fifteen tales spotlighting American women from folklore. Includes women from across the country including Bess Call, a wrestler who took on all challengers; Annie Christmas, the strongest keel-boat captain on the Mississippi, and Hiiaka, the calm and creative sister of Pele, the Hawaiian fire goddess.

Steig, William. *Caleb and Kate*; illus. by the author. Farrar, 1977.

A witch casts a magic spell on a quarreling husband and turns him into a dog. The husband learns of his wife's kindness and grief when she shares her feelings with the dog. Make the switch from man to dog with simple stick puppets.

Yolen, Jane. *Dinosaur Dances*; illus. by Bruce Degen. Putnam, 1990.

Amusing poems about dancing dinosaurs. As each poem is read the appropriate dinosaur characters can prance across the top of the book.

# Chapter 13  CUP AND CONTAINER THEATERS

NDIVIDUALIZED THEATERS MADE from cups, small boxes, or other containers bring storytelling down to miniature proportions, dimensions that young children find particularly inviting. These small theaters are quick to assemble and provide an impromptu tool to help children visualize and remember tales. They also make excellent companions to nursery rhymes, poems, and songs, as well as to stories with simple plots. Best of all, their portability makes them convenient to carry about when visiting various story groups or classrooms. Children can also make their own portable and personalized theaters as a reminder of the tale to take home with them after the story hour.

Paper cups with fold-out handles (for hot liquids) provide a convenient grip when presenting stories. However, other types of cups without handles may be more readily available and serve equally well. Cups decorated with flowers or other designs may be used with specific stories that have related themes. The small area of the cup container will comfortably accommodate three to four images; if a presentation requires more than four images, consider exploring such elongated containers as a cut-down cereal box or even a long

**Cup theater for "Old Mother Hubbard"**

wax-paper or sandwich-wrap box. These elongated boxes make better choices when a row of characters is to be viewed from the front, for example, the five jack-o-lanterns in "Jack-O-Lantern" or the pretty maids in a row in "Mary, Mary, Quite Contrary." Wax-paper and sandwich-wrap boxes also have stand-up lids that can be used for scenic backgrounds. Larger versions of the cup theater can be created from paper paint buckets, using larger puppets for viewing by sizeable story groups.

Scenery possibilities for these theaters are endless and can be achieved in short order. Taping paper cutouts of water ripples, grassy patches, or a toadstool to the front of the container gives enchanting foreground enrichment to sets. Background scenery can be secured to the back rim of the container to provide such details as an African hut, a volcano, the rising sun, or a floating cloud required by a story. The container itself can be cleverly decorated to match a theme. For example, a box container may be the perfect vehicle for Vachel Lindsay's poem "The Little Turtle" (a turtle who actually lives in a box), or a brick wall for "Humpty Dumpty."

Puppet characters should be in proportion to the scale of the chosen container theater. Magazine pictures, greeting cards, drawings, and even family photographs make excellent sources for characters to convert into cast members when taped to the end of a drinking straw and slipped through holes punched into the bottom of the container. The puppets are operated from beneath the container and can hide inside and pop up at will. Because of the popping up and down actions in this puppet approach, it is ideally suited to stories that can be enhanced by this element of surprise. Themes that focus around growing things, such as Ruth Krauss's *The Carrot Seed* or the folktale "The Enormous Turnip," can be presented with plants that "grow." The Mother Goose rhyme "Two Little Blackbirds" is another good example in which each of the blackbirds can "fly away" by disappearing into the container and reappear by popping up again. For Mercer Mayer's *There's a Nightmare in My Closet*, a cup theater can be used effectively to hold an audience in suspense as the terrible Nightmare slowly creeps up into full view over the cup's rim.

Scenic panels can be changed in a cup or box theater by using several small paper plates held together with a paper clip. Each paper plate can depict a different background, and the plate scenes can be removed one by one to correspond with the story's sequencing. Be sure to secure the last plate scene to the back rim of the cup to serve as a support for stacking the other plates together before the presentation. *Henry Finds a Home* by Wendy St. Pierre would be fun to present with this method. Henry, a turtle stick puppet, can search for each home as it is revealed on the plate scene of a paper cup theater. A beehive, a cave, an underwater home, and other dwelling places are revealed in succession as each plate scene is removed, until he finally discovers his own home is right on his back!

Although they are small in size, the cup and container theaters are very versatile and seem to have particular appeal to the young child. The storyteller can enhance the elements of suspense and surprise and keep the audience captivated with these creations.

## NURSERY RHYMES

 ### "Old Mother Hubbard"

An old woman discovers she has no bone in her cupboard for her dog. This version includes her many attempts to please her dog by going on shopping expeditions for various items and foodstuffs.

### Approach

Leader narrates story while using a cup theater. Two children provide sound effects.

### Puppets/Props

| Characters/Props | Types/Materials |
|---|---|
| Old Mother Hubbard Dog Upside-down dog | Paper stick puppets |
| Newspaper | Piece of newspaper attached to stick |
| Cupboard | Paper cutout attached to back of cup |
| Noisemaker Flute | Toy or real |

### Presentation

#### General procedures

Assign one child to play the noisemaker (for jig) and one the flute and cue them when to provide sounds.

Hide all puppets and newspaper prop inside cup.

#### Introduction

Involve the children in a discussion about a shopping trip for food for a hungry dog by asking the following questions:

"If you were a hungry dog, what would be your favorite thing to eat?"

"If you were to fill up your cupboard with foods for your dog to eat, what would you buy? Where would you go to buy these items?"

"I know a poem about an old lady who went shopping for food for her hungry dog."

## Story actions

Begin narrating poem.

Bring up Old Mother Hubbard and Dog.

When she goes to Baker, pop Dog down and weep.

When she goes to Undertaker, bring Dog up and make him laugh.

When she goes to Tavern, pop Dog down and bring upside-down dog up and laugh again.

When she goes to Barber, switch dogs again and let Dog dance a jig (sound provided by child).

After she come backs from Fruiterer, pop Dog up again and show Old Mother Hubbard listening to flute by putting your hand to your ear (sound provided by child).

When she goes to Cobbler, bring up newspaper.

Let Old Mother Hubbard make a curtsy and the Dog a bow.

### Old Mother Hubbard

*Old Mother Hubbard went to the cupboard, to give her poor dog a bone.*
*But when she got there, the cupboard was bare and so the poor dog had none [boo–hoo, boo–hoo, boo–hoo].*
*She went to the baker's to buy him some bread,*
*When she came back the poor dog was dead [boo–hoo, boo–hoo, boo–hoo].*
*She went to the undertaker's to buy him a coffin,*
*When she came back, the dog was laughing [ha, ha, ha].*

*She went to the tavern for white wine and red,*
*When she came back, the dog stood on his head [ho, ho, ho, ho].*
*She went to the barber's to buy him a wig,*
*When she came back he was dancing a jig [music].*
*She went to the fruiterer's to buy him some fruit,*
*When she came back he was playing the flute [music].*
*She went to the cobbler's to buy him some shoes,*
*When she came back he was reading the news.*
*The dame made a curtsy, the dog made a bow,*
*The dame said, Your servant,*
*The dog said—Bow–wow, bow–wow, wow, wow, wow, WOW!*

## Follow-Up Activities

Let the children play the parts of the lead characters and merchants and replay the rhyme through creative dramatics. Various parts of the room can be set up as stores with related merchandise proper. Bodi-puppets may be used for the merchants.

Ask the children to make their own paper cup theater, using a nursery rhyme of their choice to present to the group.

## Construction of Cup Theater and Puppets for "Old Mother Hubbard"

### Materials

Copies of patterns

Clear adhesive-backed shelving paper or a laminating plastic (optional)

Yarn

4 drinking straws

1″ newspaper square

Paper cup

## Procedures

Cut out and color copies of patterns with felt-tip marking pens or crayons.

Cover with clear adhesive-backed paper or laminate in plastic for permanency, if desired.

Attach each character to end of drinking straw rod and insert free end in hole punched in bottom of cup.

To make cupboard, color copy of pattern and reinforce with stiff paper. Attach to upper back edge of cup.

To make newspaper, cut out a small piece of real newspaper, make a center crease, and attach to end of drinking straw rod; insert free end in hole punched in bottom of cup.

## Operation

Push rod controls up and down from beneath the container.

Old Mother Hubbard

Dog

Add yarn tail

Upside-down dog

Cupboard
Tape to back of cup

Piece of real newspaper attached to drinking straw

**Puppet Patterns for Presenting "Old Mother Hubbard"**

A cut-down cereal box decorated to look like a fence and used as a theater for "Jack-O-Lantern"

## More Nursery Rhymes

### Jack-O-Lantern

*Five little Jack-O-Lanterns sitting on*
*a gate,*
*The first one said, "My, it's getting*
*late!"*
*The second one said, "Let's have*
*some fun."*
*The third one said, "Let's run, run,*
*run."*
*The fourth one said, "Let's dance, let's prance."*
*The fifth one said, "Now is our chance."*
*When "Whooo," went the wind and out went the light,*
*And away rode the witch on Halloween night.*

### Two Little Blackbirds

*Two little blackbirds*
*Sitting on a hill.*
*One named Jack;*
*One named Jill.*
*Fly away, Jack;*
*Fly away, Jill.*
*Come back, Jack;*
*Come back, Jill.*

### Mary, Mary, Quite Contrary

*Mary, Mary quite contrary,*
*How does your garden grow?*
*Silver bells and cockle-shells,*
*And pretty maids all in a row.*

### Humpty Dumpty

*Humpty Dumpty sat on a wall,*
*Humpty Dumpty had a great fall;*
*All the King's horses, and all the King's men,*
*Couldn't put Humpty Dumpty together again.*

"Two Little Blackbirds" cup theater (left); sandwich-wrap box with lid converted to theater for "Mary, Mary, Quite Contrary" (center); "Humpty Dumpty" container theater, with box decorated to look like a brick wall (right).

Durell, Ann. "Wait Till Martin Comes," in *The Diane Goode Book of American Folk Tales & Songs*; illus. by Diane Goode. Dutton, 1989.

> A man who takes shelter in a haunted house meets three large cats who plan to wait till Martin comes before deciding what to do with him. The visitor wisely decides not to wait for Martin. Decorate a box container to look like the foundation of a house.

Field, Eugene. *Wynken, Blynken, and Nod*; illus. by Susan Jeffers. Dutton, 1982.

> A version of the familiar rhyme illustrated by a popular artist. Glue a wooden-shoe paper image onto front of the box or other container.

Heine, Helme. *King Bounce the First*; illus. by the author. Alphabet, 1976.

> A king finds relief from his problems by bouncing on his bed. When the Royal Council outlaws such undignified behavior, the king almost dies until the ruling is reversed. A box decorated as a bed is an ideal setting for the king's bouncing actions.

Krauss, Ruth. *The Carrot Seed*; illus. by Crockett Johnson. Harper, 1945.

> Even though everyone in his family doesn't believe the seeds he plants will grow, a little boy is sure they are wrong.

Mayer, Mercer. *There's a Nightmare in My Closet*; illus. by the author. Dial, 1968.

> Apprehension changes to affection when a boy meets the Nightmare in his closet.

Nash, Ogden. "The Tale of Custard the Dragon," in *Custard and Company* by Ogden Nash; illus. by Quentin Blake. Little, 1980. Pp. 42–46.

> Custard, who was a coward, saves the day in this delightful poem. Decorate container to represent Belinda's white house and red wagon.

*Old Mother Hubbard and Her Wonderful Dog*; illus. by James Marshall. Farrar, Straus & Girous, 1991.

> A bulldog with a taste for hats make this a humorous single edition of the Mother Goose rhyme.

Prelutsky, Jack. *Monday's Troll*; illus. by Peter Sis. Greenwillow, 1996.

> A collection of poems about wizards, trolls, giants, ogres, and witches by a poet popular with children. "Monday's Troll," "Five Giants," and "We're Seven Grubby Goblins" all are suitable for container theaters.

Retan, Walter. *Piggies, Piggies, Piggies*; illus. by S. D. Schindler and others. Simon & Schuster, 1993.

> A collection of stories, songs, and rhymes all about pigs. Many of the selections, such as "A Pig Tale," are ideal for the cup theater technique.

Schwartz, Alvin. *And the Green Grass Grew All Around*; illus. by Sue Truesdell. HarperCollins, 1992.

> A delightful collection of folk poetry including autograph and street rhymes, story poems and love poems. Many of the selections are well suited to the cup theater technique.

"Sweet Betsy from Pike" in *From Sea to Shining Sea*, comp. by Amy L. Cohn; illus. by eleven Caldecott Medal and four Caldecott Honor book artists. Scholastic, 1993. Pp. 186–87.

> The traditional song about Betsy and her husband, Ike, who travel to California during the gold rush. Decorate a plastic-wrap box to look like a Conestoga wagon.

Tripp, Wallace. *Granfa' Grig Had a Pig and Other Rhymes Without Reason from Mother Goose*; illus. by the author. Little, 1976.

> Popular Mother Goose rhymes with humorously illustrated animal characters. A wonderful resource when designing container theaters.

# Chapter 14   FINGER STORIES

ONE OF THE most appealing and manageable forms of puppetry for young children is the concept of glove and finger puppets. The tiny size and easy manipulation make finger puppets a natural choice for young children. Furthermore, they are ideally suited to an unlimited range of nursery rhymes, poems, stories, and finger plays. Counting rhymes that center around the concept of "Five Little ____" and fairy tales such as "The Three Little Pigs" provide stock material for hand casting. Although universally used with younger children, there is no reason finger puppets cannot be imaginatively adapted to more mature material and enjoyed by older children as well. The poem, "Backward Bell" in *A Light in the Attic* by Shel Silverstein could be humorously conveyed with a series of characters worn backwards.

Basically unexplored, but very natural for glove and finger puppets, is the use of contemporary fiction. Such modern classics as Arnold Lobel's *Frog and Toad* and James Marshall's *George and Martha* are but two of the many stories suitable for glove and finger puppet dramatizations. Stories that include up to ten cast members can be comfortably displayed on both hands, as in depicting Beatrice Schenk de Regniers's *May I Bring a Friend?*

In general, cumulative stories and songs seem well suited to this technique. Two handsful of barnyard animals for "The Farmer in the Dell" make delightful imagery as each animal pops up to cue the singing. Of course, stories in which the main character is diminutive, such as "Tom Thumb," *The Teeny Tiny Woman* by Barbara Seuling, and *Inch by Inch* by Leo Lionni are obvious choices for the small scale of finger play.

Glove and finger puppets come in many forms and varieties. A typical finger puppet is a small sewn shape that covers the entire finger. Or, an instant finger puppet can be made from a cutout greeting card, drawing, magazine picture, or family photograph secured to the finger tip with double-stick tape. It is helpful to cover these paper characters with plastic or with clear adhesive-backed laminating material for permanency. Add a glove to create a unified "stage," with puppets attached to fingertips. Also, any type of felt, paper, or pom-pom characters can be fastened to the tips of a glove with double-stick tape or Velcro. While a rubber household glove provides a smooth surface for sticking and a neutral background, other gloves may reflect a particular setting, such as a bright gingham checkered or denim glove for a barnyard scene, a glittery glove for a magical theme, or a red and green glove as a background for Christmas stories.

For greater versatility, you may wish to make your own glove with the pattern included in this chapter. Gloves made from heavy-weight nonwoven interfacing material, such as Pellon, allow designs—the North Pole, a rainbow, a desert, or other scenic reference—to be colored on the surface with colored marker pens. Another feature that can be added to the basic glove is a button in the palm area for attaching props such as a clock

**Glove with interchangeable button scenery; mouse is paper or felt**

for "Hickory Dickory Dock" or a candlestick for "Jack Be Nimble."

Small props can enrich finger stories. Use miniature doll furniture, such as tables and beds, for "Goldilocks and the Three Bears," a toy or cardboard box house with peek-through windows for *The Teeny Tiny Woman*, and a small plant for *Inch by Inch*. A cardboard sled with jingling bells attached can be held up for Santa's sled in "Rudolph the Red-Nosed Reindeer."

A unique feature to use with finger puppets is a peek-through panel. A peek-through panel consists of a cardboard rectangle with scenery images drawn on it and containing holes into which the puppets can be inserted as the panel is held over the lap. Young children are entranced by the surprise element of characters popping in and out of the scenery. The peek-through panel is particularly suited to stories with limited scene changes and action that remains somewhat static. *Georgie's Halloween* by Robert Bright is an apt example since the actions take place in only two locations, an attic and a park, both of which can be cleverly incorporated into a single turn-around panel. Another excellent story for a similar interpretation is "Pooh Goes Visiting" by A. A. Milne in *Winnie the Pooh*. This panel could show a forest on one side and the interior of Rabbit's hole on the other. The children will be ecstatic at seeing Pooh get stuck in the tree's hole.

In addition, interest can be created by choosing intriguing locations for peek holes. A squirrel can drop nuts through a hole in a tree, a princess peek out a tower window, a captain scan the ocean through portholes on a ship, or a character pop in and out of holes of geometric shapes—circle, triangle, and square—for teaching concept words. Scenes might also take on a

dual image focus. An under- and above-ground set could include holes at the lower level for burrowing animals to peek through, then scamper to the surface level for extended activity. Land-sky and upstairs-downstairs are other ideas to explore.

The peek-through panel can take on various dimensions. A long horizontal panel can accommodate a series of zoo dwellings for *Sam Who Never Forgets* by Eve Rice, permitting a variety of zoo animals to appear in order along the strip. A train or panoramic landscape of a native village, modern city, or other site could also be ideally adapted. A circle panel would be fun to try. It is especially appropriate for a round blue pond with an aerial view showing floating lily pads among which frogs and fish sneakily appear.

Finger and glove puppets are lively and diverse. They provide movement, surprises, and cues to carry the action along and keep the children involved. This style of puppetry is a simple but important addition to the storyteller's repertoire.

## EXAMPLES OF FINGER STORIES

 *The Teeny Tiny Woman*

In this English folktale the teeny tiny woman finds a teeny tiny bone in a graveyard. When the owner spookily asks for the return of the bone, he gets a surprising answer.

### Approach

Leader flips scenery background worn on body while narrating story with finger puppets in foreground.

## Puppets/Props

| Characters/Props | Types/Materials |
|---|---|
| Teeny Tiny Woman | Paper finger puppet |
| Purse | Paper cutouts |
| Bonnet | |
| Bone | |
| House (Panel 1) | Scenery made from paper or |
| Fence with gate (Panel 2) | construction paper in the |
| Churchyard (Panel 3) | form of flip-over scenery |
| Bedroom (Panel 4) | panels held together by a |
| | large paper clip. Wear |
| | around the neck. |

## Presentation

### General procedures

Conceal puppet, bonnet, and purse in story apron pockets or tote.

Tie scenery panels around neck in order of appearance.

Attach bone to churchyard scene with double-stick tape.

### Introduction

Ask the children, "How small do you think 'teeny tiny' is?"

"What things can you think of that are teeny tiny?"

Then say, "I have a story to tell about someone I know who is teeny tiny."

### Story actions

Put Teeny Tiny Woman on finger and begin story with Panel 1 (house).

Put bonnet on woman.

Flip to Panel 2 (fence and gate scenery).

Open gate of fence and walk woman through. (Swing open section in paper scene.)

Flip to Panel 3 (churchyard scene).

Slip chicken bone into woman's purse.

Flip to Panel 4 (bedroom scene).

Put bone in cupboard and woman in bed.

Exaggerate "Take it!" at end.

### Follow-Up Activities

Let children construct their own teeny tiny characters. Some may also wish to draw scenery panels to wear for the stories they create to present to the group.

Paper finger puppets and scenery panels for *The Teeny Tiny Woman* (Photo of Jeanne Beuoy by Michelle Owen)

## Paper Patterns for The Teeny Tiny Woman

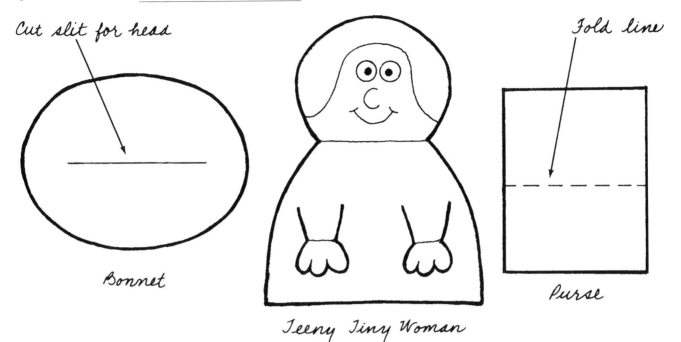

*Cut slit for head*

*Bonnet*

*Teeny Tiny Woman*

*Fold line*

*Purse*

## Construction of Puppet and Scenery Panels for The Teeny Tiny Woman

### Materials

Copies of patterns

Small rubber band

Tagboard or poster board (four 12″ × 12″ sheets)

Large paper clip

2½″ neck ribbon

### Procedures

To make a woman, cut out character and glue to stiff paper for reinforcement; staple rubber band in back for finger, as shown.

To make bonnet, fold oval of paper in half and crease along dotted line. Cut slit along solid line and slip over top of woman's head.

To make purse, fold and crease along dotted line of rectangle. Glue ends down, and attach to woman's

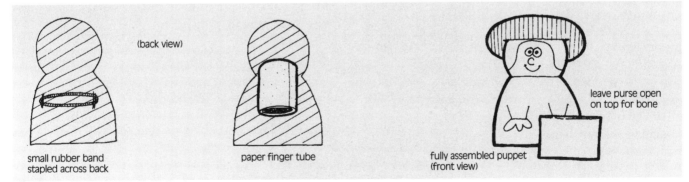

(back view)

small rubber band
stapled across back

paper finger tube

leave purse open
on top for bone

fully assembled puppet
(front view)

Puppet construction for *The Teeny Tiny Woman*; two back views (left and center) show two methods of control

body, leaving top part of purse open for bone.

To make flip-down scenery panels, cut out four 12″ × 12″ panels from tagboard or stiff paper. Draw a scene on each panel and arrange panels in sequential order. Tape together bottoms of panels and use a large paper clip to hold tops together. Attach a neck ribbon to back of panel and tie to neck.

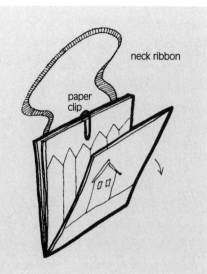

Scenery panel unit for *The Teeny Tiny Woman*

neck ribbon

paper clip

## Operation

Flip each panel downward as it is required.

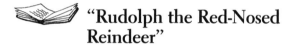

## "Rudolph the Red-Nosed Reindeer"

This popular song demonstrates the benefits of teamwork in utilizing our special resources.

## Approach

A glove made of white interfacing fabric and decorated (using colored marker pens) with a scene of the North Pole serves as scenic background to which each character is added, one by one, to correspond with the song.

## Puppets/Props

| Characters/Props | Types/Materials |
| --- | --- |
| Rudolph | Paper finger puppets |
| Three reindeer | |
| Santa Claus | |
| Sled | Cardboard cutout with real bells attached. |

## Presentation

### General procedures

Put Rudolph on little finger of glove and hide remaining puppets and characters.

### Introduction

Ask the children who their favorite reindeer is.

Then ask, "What makes Rudolph special or different from all other reindeer?"

"What are some games or activities reindeer would enjoy?"

### Story actions

Begin story with fingers in upright position.

Put on each reindeer.

Put on Santa Claus (ho, ho, ho!)

Hold up sled and glide it merrily along.

## Follow-Up Activities

Have children think of other creatures with peculiar features that could possibly help lead Santa's sled—a blue-nosed alligator, a green-eared bunny, or a red-eyed cat. Sing the song again substituting the new characters.

## Construction of Finger Puppets for "Rudolph the Red-Nosed Reindeer"

### Materials

Copies of patterns (page 173)

Oak tag or stiff paper

Glove (rubber household or other)

Double-stick tape

Clear adhesive-backed laminating material (optional)

**Finger Puppet Patterns for
"Rudolph the Red-Nosed Reindeer"**

## Procedures

Cut out and color copies of patterns with felt-tip marking pens or crayons.

Reinforce characters by gluing them to stiff paper. Cover with adhesive-backed laminating material such as Contact for permanency, if desired. Attach a piece of double-stick tape to back of each character and stick to glove tips.

To make sled, decorate a piece of cardboard like a sled. Add bells and small presents.

## Construction of Basic Glove for Finger Stories

### Materials

Heavyweight muslin

Interfacing fabric, such as Pellon

Felt

Cotton

### Procedures

Following the pattern (page 174), cut out two opposite glove pieces.

Sew with right sides together; turn right side out and hem bottom edge.

**Basic Glove Pattern**

## Georgie's Halloween

In this Georgie story by Robert Bright, the amiable ghost attends a Halloween party with his all-time familiar costume. His shyness prevents him from receiving a prize; instead, he earns a special prize from his friends who dwell in the attic and is highly commended.

### Approach

Leader narrates the story while maneuvering puppets and peek-through panel over lap.

### Puppets/Props

| Characters/Props | Types/Materials |
| --- | --- |
| Attic scene | Cardboard turn-around panel |
| Park scene | |
| Georgie | Paper-tissue finger puppet |
| Mouse | Finger puppet |
| Pumpkin | Real or plastic with candle |
| Ribbon prize | Real |
| Noisemakers | Pots and pans or toy instruments |

### Presentation

#### General procedures

Give children noisemakers and cue them when it is time to make noises, during the trick-or-treat scene.

Instruct children when to shout "It's Georgie! It's Georgie!"

Hide puppets, props, and theater panel in a box or tote.

#### Introduction

Ask the children to describe their favorite Halloween costumes.

Bring out pumpkin and display on tabletop. Light candle in pumpkin, if desired, to signify beginning of story.

Then tell children, "I have a story to tell you about a little ghost named Georgie and his favorite costume."

#### Story actions

Begin story while holding up panel displaying the attic scene.

Pop Georgie and Mouse through holes.

Turn panel around for park scene.

Let Georgie peek through hole, then out again.

Have children shout, "It's Georgie! It's Georgie!"

Put scene down and pretend Georgie runs home.

Turn panel back around to show attic scene.

Have Mouse present Georgie with ribbon prize.

Have Georgie blow out candle inside pumpkin (with your help).

### Follow-Up Activities

Let all the children make Georgie puppets from paper tissues and have them cut out and decorate a peek-through panel of their own. Round paper plates also make excellent impromptu peek-through theaters.

Ask children to create short stories with a different theme focus, either orally or in written form, about:

"Georgie's Thanksgiving"

"Georgie's Favorite Summer Day"

"Georgie's Good Deed"

and any other themes you may have in mind.

Display other books about ghosts:

Carter, David H. *In a Dark, Dark Wood*; illus. by the author. Simon & Schuster, 1991.

Benchley, Nathaniel. *Ghost Named Fred*; illus. by Ben Shecter. Harper, 1968.

San Souci, Robert. *Boy and the Ghost*; illus. by Brian Pinkney. Simon & Schuster, 1989.

## Construction of Georgie the Ghost Puppet

### Materials

Paper-tissue hanky

Small rubber band

Extra tissue or cotton

### Procedures

Stuff center of tissue square with
wadded tissue or cotton to form
a head.

Slip stuffed tissue over index finger,
as shown.

Wrap rubber band around neck.

Draw features with felt-tip marking pens.

### SUGGESTED TITLES FOR FINGER STORIES

Bennet, Jill. *Teeny Tiny*; illus. by Tomie de Paola.
Putnam, 1985.

Picture book about the teeny tiny woman who
finds a bone in a graveyard.

Briggs, Raymond. *The Mother Goose Treasury*; illus. by
the author. Coward, 1966.

A collection of over four hundred illustrated
rhymes, which is an excellent resource since it includes the popular rhymes as well as many that are
less familiar.

Bright, Robert. *Georgie's Halloween*; illus. by the author. Doubleday, 1971.

Georgie, an amiable but shy ghost, is given a special prize by his attic friends after attending a
Halloween party. A suitable finger story for peek-
through panel presentation.

**A paper-tissue ghost puppet for**
*Georgie's Halloween*

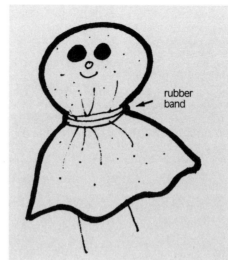
rubber band

Cohlene, Terri. *Little Firefly*; illus.
by Charles Reasoner. Rourke, 1990.

An Algonquian legend, similar to "Cinderella," about a
young girl who becomes the
wife of Invisible One, the great
hunter. Create scenery panels
incorporating Indian motifs to
use as background for the storytelling with finger puppets.

de Angeli, Marguerite. "Who
Killed Cock Robin?" in *Book of
Nursery and Mother Goose Rhymes*;
illus. by the author. Doubleday, 1954. Pp. 140–41.

This version of the rhyme about Cock Robin has
ten verses. Use both hands.

de Regniers, Beatrice Schenk. *May I Bring a Friend?*
illus. by Beni Montresor. Atheneum, 1964.

The king and queen's tea party is attended by a
colorful menagerie. Leader assumes role of "Me" or
first-person character, without a puppet. A Caldecott
Medal book.

Hopkins, Lee Bennett. *Side by Side*; illus. by Hilary
Knight. Simon & Schuster, 1988.

A collection of poems for the young child. Try
sharing "Five Little Chickens," "The Mouse, the
Frog, and the Little Red Hen," "Seven Little
Rabbits," "Five Little Monkeys," and "The Three
Little Kittens" with finger puppets.

Hughes, Monica. *Little Fingerling*; illus. by Brenda
Clark. Ideals, 1992.

A boy, only as long as a finger, proves himself to
be brave and valiant, winning the hand of a princess
as well as being transformed into a samurai warrior.
Scenery panels of the Japanese settings will enhance
the telling of this tale.

Lester, Julius. *The Knee-High Man*; illus. by Ralph Pinto. Dial, 1972.

In this African-American folktale, a knee-high man learns that his size doesn't really limit him. Put the knee-high man puppet on one hand and the animals he encounters on the other hand.

Lionni, Leo. *Inch by Inch*; illus. by the author. Astor-Honor, 1962.

A clever worm uses his natural abilities to outsmart a bird. Finger puppet can measure a real plant. A Caldecott Honor book.

Lobel, Arnold. *Frog and Toad All Year*; illus. by the author. Harper, 1976.

Five short stories relate the adventures and comradeship of Frog and Toad during each season of the year.

Marshall, James. *George and Martha One Fine Day*; illus. by the author. Houghton, 1980.

Hilarity in the problems of friendship is the primary focus of this series of humorous stories.

McCord, David. *All Small*; illus. by Madelaine Gill Linden. Little, 1986.

A selection of short poems by David McCord. A great collection to share with finger puppets. Includes "I Want You to Meet . . ." a poem about a family of ladybugs, "Snowman," "Glowworm," and "Snail."

Petersham, Maud, and Miska Petersham. *The Rooster Crows*; illus. by the authors. Macmillan, 1945.

A collection of American rhymes and jingles whose humor will appeal to older boys and girls. A Caldecott Medal book.

Prelutsky, Jack. "The Gribble" in *The Snopp on the Sidewalk and Other Poems* by Jack Prelutsky; illus. by Byron Barton. Greenwillow, 1977.

An amusing poem about the gribble who frowns at all who pass but is too small to do much harm. A finger puppet can gently nibble each child after the poem is recited.

Rosen, Michael. *Itsy-bitsy Beasties*; illus. by Alan Baker. Carolrhoda, 1992.

Finger puppets are a natural companion to these poems from around the world that feature spiders, fleas, flies, and other small creatures. Cut out pictures of the insects and turn them into instant puppets by taping them to your fingers.

Silverstein, Shel. A *Light in the Attic*; illus. by the author. Harper, 1981.

A collection of humorous and nonsense poems that provide imaginative and mature material to combine with finger play for older children.

Van Laan, Nancy. *The Tiny, Tiny Boy and the Big, Big Cow*; illus. by Marjorie Priceman. Knopf, 1993.

An adaptation of a Scottish folktale about a small boy determined to milk a large cow that will not stand still. The storyteller plays the part of mother as well as using a boy finger puppet. Ask a child to use a large stick puppet cow to act out the story.

# Chapter 15 — OPEN-BOX THEATERS

SIMPLE PUPPETS COMBINED with a box theater equal a versatile approach to storytelling. An open box, transformed into a diminutive stage, becomes a portable and compact theater that can be comfortably arranged on the seated narrator's lap or hung from a neck strap for story presentation while standing. An outstanding feature of this type of theater is the wide strip of double-stick carpeting tape that is affixed to the inside upper edge of the box. Paper images, such as pictures from greeting cards, magazines, and drawings, can be secured to drinking straws and quickly attached to the sticky surface of the strip. This technique enables the storyteller to display and mobilize several characters at one time, rather than just a few, as in other presentation formats. Thus, a wide range of stories can be presented with the box theater, ranging from those with simple casting to the more complex. "The Big, Big, Turnip," a folktale, and *Seven Chinese Brothers* by Margaret Mahy are examples suited to multicast presentation. After appearing onstage, characters can be secured to the strip and left while the action continues. Another worthwhile feature of this stage is that the inside of the box provides an ideal place in which to conceal puppets and text material while reading.

Stories with travel sequences, such as Bill Peet's *Cyrus the Unsinkable Sea Serpent* and William Steig's popular stories

*Amos and Boris* and *Farmer Palmer's Wagon Ride*, also may be dramatized effectively along the front length of the box. Cyrus or Amos in a boat can slowly bob up and down along a make-believe ocean setting, or Farmer Palmer's wagon can ramble along the top edge of the box, from one end to the other. Include a variety of actions during the course of the story. Short hops, skips, glides, and other movements can be expressed as puppets travel along the box's length. Also, plan the puppets' entrance and exit points. For example, puppets in "Goldilocks and the Three Bears" may enter from the right and exit to the left in a consistent pattern. Remember to decorate both sides of the puppet if it is to be shown in both profile views during the performance.

The addition of "quick-change" scenery or prop components adds to the versatility of this theater. Paper

An open-box theater for "The Big, Big Turnip" (Photo of Nancy Renfro by Bill Boulton)

ocean waves or a garden patch can be taped to the front upper edge of the box. Other scenery or props can be attached to drinking straws and applied to the carpeting tape strip in the same manner as the puppets. A ship for oceanfaring themes or a leafy green turnip top that slowly "grows" to reveal a turnip are interesting examples. Visuals should be kept to a minimum, however, so as not to obstruct the playing space of the theater. Also keep puppets and props small in scale in order to utilize the limited space of the box most efficiently.

The outside of the box can be decorated according to personal preference. The box itself can be painted or covered with colorful adhesive-backed shelving paper, gift wrapping paper, or wallpaper. Drapery pom-poms, rickrack, and other trims add a festive touch. Metallic trims, sequins, glitter, and signs with the performer's name "up in lights" will create an exciting on-Broadway effect.

Another variation of the open-box theater is to use all four sides of the box in conjunction with clothespin puppets rather than stick. Those stories that require a number of characters to appear at one time can be comfortably managed with clothespin puppets by clipping them along the edges of the box when used for intimate group presentations. Spring-type clothespins attached to paper characters make puppet creation affordable as well as easy. A rich supply of characters can be found in children's drawings, greeting cards, coloring books, and magazines.

Children will be attracted to the quadruple playing spaces that this miniature theater offers. The four-sided rim of the box gives great flexibility because puppets and scenery are easily maneuvered to any playing side, along the box's edge; the four sides can provide foreground or background as well. The box can be placed on the storyteller's lap for easy viewing by children sitting on the floor in front of it, or it can be arranged on a tabletop so that children standing around the table's

perimeter can experience a theater-in-the-round effect. The interior space of the box provides a convenient resting place for three-dimensional props. Consider using miniature toys such as boats, farm animals, or doll furniture to enlarge the sets.

Ludwig Bemelmans's *Madeline*, a story about twelve little girls who live in a Paris boarding school, is a noteworthy example for managing a multiple cast with clothespin box presentation. The twelve little girls can be made to stand up in two parallel rows along the long edges of a shoe box. The box cleverly takes on a double image as each little girl is laid down inside the box "bedroom" during the story's nighttime scenes.

Because of its versatility and potential for innovation, the storyteller will find the open-box theater a popular item in any puppet collection. Children will take great delight in using this lightweight theater for play and informal performances.

## EXAMPLES OF OPEN-BOX THEATERS

 ### "The Big, Big Turnip"

In this folktale a farmer plants a turnip seed which grows so big that it requires the aid of the entire barnyard to pull it out. Through the efforts of group cooperation they achieve their task.

### Approach
Leader narrates story using open-box theater and stick puppets on lap or tabletop.

### Puppets/Props

| Characters/Props | Types/Materials |
| --- | --- |
| Seed | Real |
| Turnip | Paper cutout |

Farmer
Wife
Daughter
Dog
Cat
Mouse

Paper stick puppets

## Presentation

### General procedures

Arrange characters in order of appearance, upside down, inside box. Also place inside box the book to be read.

Recite refrain with children and ask them to join in story when cued:

*Fe, fi, fo, fout,*
*We pulled the turnip*
*But it wouldn't come out!*

### Introduction

Bring in a real turnip to show the children. Begin a discussion about turnips with the children.

Ask, "Has anyone here ever tasted a turnip? Can you tell us what it tastes like?"

"I know a story about a farmer who loved to grow turnips. He had only one problem—they grew too big!"

### Story actions

Pretend to plant a turnip seed.

Make turnip rise, exposing green top only.

Bring out each character in order of appearance and attach to front edge of stage. Arrange in a neat row across entire edge and point to each character when mentioned.

Cue children to recite refrain at appropriate times.

Pull up the entire turnip with a quick jerk.

Hold up the mouse and say with a squeak, "I told you so!"

## Follow-Up Activities

Let children create their own paper stick puppets (or other type puppet) and repeat the story in an open space using creative dramatics methods. Plant turnip seed in a flower pot, which has a turnip hidden in the soil. Have the characters line up behind pot, each holding on to the preceding character's back, as they pull together and recite refrain. They may wish to add more animal types to the procession.

Ask children to draw a picture of another vegetable, fruit, or other plant that could be pulled out by characters. What food did they select? What characters did they choose?

Explore such other themes as sea life pulling at an immense tangle of seaweed, jungle animals pulling a tropical vine, etc.

## Construction of a Basic Open-Box Theater

### Materials

A grocery carton (at least 18″ wide)

Adhesive-backed shelving paper, wallpaper, paint, and trim for covering and decorating box

Double-stick masking or carpeting tape (obtained from local hardware store)

### Procedures

Cut off top and back of box.

Cut box down to the desired height. Box should be approximately 12″ high so face of performer can be seen. A higher box may be preferred if the performer wishes to be hidden.

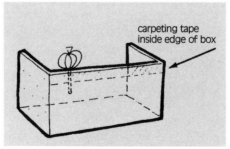

carpeting tape inside edge of box

Construction of a basic open-box theater

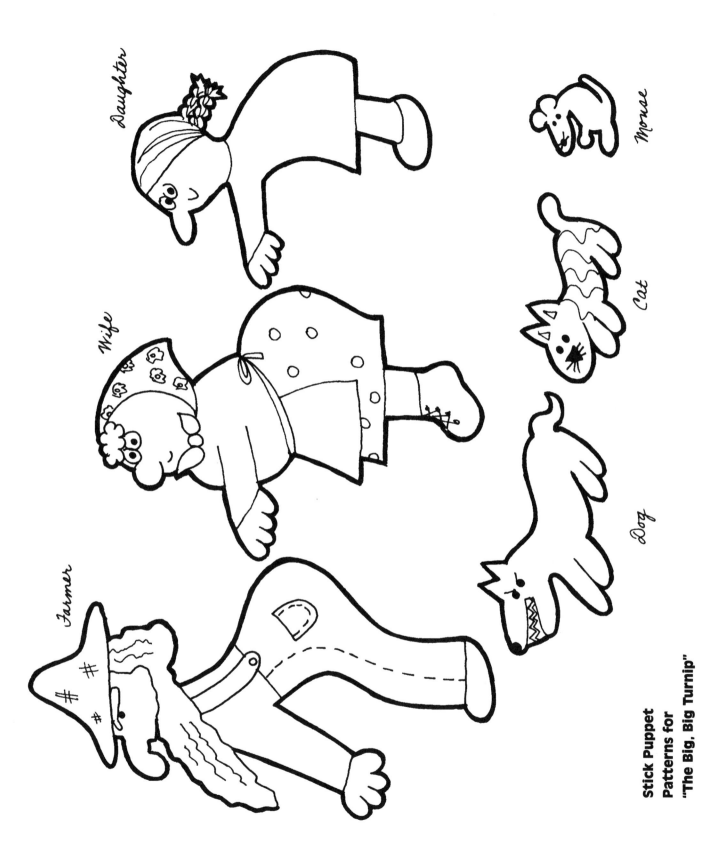

Daughter

Mouse

Wife

Cat

Farmer

Dog

**Stick Puppet
Patterns for
"The Big, Big Turnip"**

Decorate box with paint, paper, and trim. It can be either simply covered or gaily decorated with fringes, patterns, glitter, or other decorations, if desired.

Leave protective paper backing attached to one side of double-stick carpeting tape (when not in use) and stick other side to inside front edge of the box.

## Operation

Stick puppet rod to tacky surface of tape when positioning puppets.

## Construction of Stick Puppets for Box Theaters

### Materials

Drawing or picture from coloring book, greeting card, or magazine

Drinking straw

Stiff paper

Tape

### Procedures

Mount picture on stiff paper for reinforcement, if desired.

Attach picture to straw with tape.

 *Madeline*

In this first of the Madeline books by Ludwig Bemelmans, Madeline is the only one of twelve French girls in two straight lines who must go to the hospital. The crisis is shared by all the girls, who, in caring for her, find an envious moment in all the special attention she receives.

## Approach

Leader narrates story holding shoe box stage with clothespin puppets clipped to edges while children sit on floor in story area.

## Puppets/Props

| Characters/Props | Types/Materials |
|---|---|
| Madeline, smallest child<br>Eleven other little girls<br>Miss Clavel | Spring-type clothespin puppets |
| Girls' bedroom | Shoe box |
| Toothbrush | Real |
| Rain | Silver tinsel on stick |
| Sun | Yellow paper on stick |
| Blanket | Fabric square |
| Hospital room | Another box |
| Flowers | Paper or real cut flowers |
| Visitors' sign, "From 2 to 4" | Paper |

Shoe-box theater for *Madeline* (Photo of Misang Han by Michelle Owen)

## Presentation

### General procedures

Arrange the puppets, Madeline and the eleven other little girls in two rows along long edges of box (six on each side), with Miss Clavel at one end.

Put the hospital room box on a tabletop.

Hide the remaining props in a story apron or tote.

## Introduction

Discuss with the children their illnesses or ask if any of them have ever been to a hospital. Ask them, "Have you ever been kind to someone who was sick? What would be a nice thing to do to cheer up someone who is in the hospital?"

## Story actions

Begin narrating story. Each time the phrase "Twelve little girls in two straight lines" appears, point to girls on edge of shoe box.

Brush all their teeth with toothbrush.

Put them to bed, laying each one down in the box as you count to twelve.

Madeline

Miss Clavel

11 little girls

**Clothespin Puppet Patterns
for <u>Madeline</u>**

Smile widely (when they smile at the good happenings).

Frown deeply (when they are sad).

Clip the girls back onto the sides of the box as you count to twelve.

Hold up the rain wand, then the sun wand.

Hold up Madeline to show the group that she is the smallest one.

Put the girls back to bed inside the box as you count to twelve again.

Set Madeline on the edge of the box, then wrap her in a blanket.

Place Madeline in the hospital box.

Bring Miss Clavel and eleven little girls (clip back on shoe box) to visit Madeline in the hospital (entire shoe box can be carried to hospital box).

Place flowers in hospital box.

Hold up visitors' sign, "From 2 to 4."

Show group Madeline's scar (painted on clothespin, under clothing).

Bring out rain wand.

Brush the girls' teeth again and put them back to bed as you count to eleven.

Move Miss Clavel as she frantically runs about, checks on the girls, and then quietly leaves.

## Follow-Up Activities

Have each child make a Madeline clothespin puppet to take home.

Have each child get a shoe box and make up a story about Madeline to present, using the clothespin puppet and his or her own cast members.

Let the children dramatize the story in a creative dramatics activity by playing the parts of the twelve little girls with the leader playing the nun. Madeline can wear a yellow hat to distinguish her.

## Construction of Clothespin Puppets for <u>Madeline</u>

### Materials

13 spring-type clothespins

Copies of patterns

### Procedures

Cut out and color copies of patterns for eleven little girls, Madeline, and Miss Clavel.

Glue to flat side of clothespins.

For Madeline, glue down head section only and leave lower section loose so it can be lifted to show scar. Draw scar with a dark marking pen on clothespin under lower section.

### Operation

Simply attach puppets by clipping clothespins to box stage.

## SUGGESTED TITLES FOR <u>OPEN-BOX THEATERS</u>

Bemelmans, Ludwig. *Madeline*; illus. by the author. Viking, 1960 (1939).

Madeline's eleven boarding school friends share the adventure of her first hospital stay. A Caldecott Honor book.

Grimm, Jacob. "The Golden Goose," in *About Wise Men and Simpletons*; trans. by Elizabeth Shub; illus. by Nonny Hogrogian. Macmillan, 1986. Pp. 47–51.

The parade of characters stuck fast to a goose is effectively displayed on an open-box theater.

Kimmel, Eric A. *Anansi and the Talking Melon*; illus. by Janet Stevens. Holiday House, 1994.

Anansi tricks Elephant and his friends into thinking that a melon can talk. Arrange the animals along the side of the box as they journey to see the king. When the melon breaks, exchange the melon for a banana tree.

Lottridge, Celia Barker. *The Name of the Tree*; illus. by Ian Wallace. Macmillan, 1989.

The animals must search for food when a drought spreads through the land. When they reach a tree with delicious fruit on its branches they discover they must learn the name of the tree before the fruit can be eaten. In this Bantu folktale it is not the animals with the greatest talents that succeed but the animal that tries the hardest. Clip the tree onto the short end of a box theater. Move spring-type clothespin puppets along one side of the box as they search for the tree. Use the other side of the box for the journey to the home of the lion.

Mahy, Margaret. *The Seven Chinese Brothers*; illus. by Jean and Mou-sien Tseng. Scholastic, 1990.

Each brother possesses an exceptional ability which saves him from harm. Line the seven brothers up on the front edge of the box. Back edge of box can be used for scenes involving the Celestial Emperor's army.

Morgan, Pierr. *The Turnip*; illus. by the author. Philomel, 1990.

The attempts of an old man, his wife, and several animals to pull up a turnip are unsuccessful until help is offered from a most unlikely source.

Peet, Bill. *Cyrus the Unsinkable Sea Serpent*; illus. by the author. Houghton, 1975.

Cyrus, a sea serpent tired of wandering, goes in search of something exciting to do and decides to accompany a ship. Cyrus takes personal charge of its safety when the ship runs into unexpected trouble.

Preston, Edna Mitchell. *Squawk to the Moon, Little Goose*; illus. by Barbara Cooney. Viking, 1985.

Little Goose, who believes that the Moon has fallen into the pond, channels her fear and outwits a fox who catches her. Use two sides of the box—one showing the pond, the other the house.

Reddix, Valerie. *Millie and the Mud Hole*; illus. by Thor Wickstrom. Lothrop, 1992.

Millie, a pig, disregards her animal friends when they warn her that the mud hole is too deep. When she gets stuck, it takes the combined efforts of all the animals and the pig keeper to pull her out. The open box should look like a large mud puddle.

Steig, William. *Amos and Boris*; illus. by the author. Farrar, 1971.

A mouse saves the life of his friend, a whale.

Steig, William. *Farmer Palmer's Wagon Ride*; illus. by the author. Farrar, 1974.

Farmer Palmer and his hired hand use ingenuity to get safely home from the market.

Steptoe, John. *The Story of Jumping Mouse*; illus. by the author. Lothrop, 1984.

A Native American legend of Jumping Mouse who is aided on his journey to the Far-Off Land by Magic Frog. Keep the spring-type clothespin puppets for Jumping Mouse and the animals he meets in the box until they appear in the story. Decorate sides of the box as the river, grassy plain, and the mountain. Turn the box when Jumping Mouse enters a new environment. A Caldecott Honor book.

Wood, Audrey. *The Napping House*; illus. by Don Wood. Harcourt, 1984.

A flea disturbs all the sleeping inhabitants of a house in this humorous cumulative tale. Decorate the box as a bed. Add each character to the bed during the first half of the story and remove the characters during the second half of the tale.

# Chapter 16

# OVERHEAD SHADOW STORIES

THE OVERHEAD PROJECTOR is perhaps one of the most challenging tools at the disposal of the storyteller even though its intrinsic potential has been virtually untapped for conveying complex images and plots to the screen. With it both black-and-white and color imagery can be explored. One of the major benefits of this technique is that it requires minimal effort and skills, both in construction and manipulation. Shadow presentations usually work most efficiently through teamwork of some sort, unless the storyteller can relate the story from memory. With the overhead projector one person acts as narrator, while others manipulate the puppets. One or two puppeteers may serve to operate the entire cast, or larger groups may wish to share in the casting, one puppet per child. The overhead projector is a tool well suited to students of all ages because of its ease of operation and dramatic effects. Even high schoolers will discover a special challenge in the mechanical aspects of shadow animation. Suggestions on choosing stories and creating puppets and special effects for this method are fully covered in Part Two, chapter 3.

Cumulative tales, such as "The House That Jack Built" and "The Old Lady Who Swallowed a Fly," are particularly suited to shadow presentations with the overhead projector. Cumulative tales involve a collection of characters in simple, repetitive actions. A series of characters moving across the screen in pursuit of a runaway Gingerbread Boy can easily and effectively be brought to life with the overhead projector and a few "group" puppets. A group puppet is made by cutting out three or four characters from a single piece of oaktag and attaching one drinking straw or wire control to the formation.

While many modern and classic texts may be adapted to the overhead shadow technique, folktales offer a particularly rich reservoir of source material. Because of the graphic nature of the images themselves, qualities reflecting the style of ethnic or cultural backgrounds in folktales can predominate, thus enhancing the mood of the story. For example, the bold geometric style of Gerald McDermott's *The Stonecutter* can be evoked by the use of bright primary colors and angular geometric shapes in the set. Likewise, McDermott's bold rendition of the Anansi tales lends itself to similar overhead dramatization.

The overhead shadow technique has the potential for "quick-change" from one character to another. Take advantage of this trick and use overhead projector techniques for fairy tales such as "The Frog Prince," "Cinderella," or "Beauty and the Beast" in which a character is suddenly transformed into another character.

Another useful format to explore is "see-through" or cutaway views in characters or sets. For example, an underground tunnel may be exposed to show animal life not normally visible, as in "The Ants and the Grasshopper" or Norman's studio in Don Freeman's *Norman the Door-*

**Group puppet for "The Gingerbread Boy"**

man; or a see-through stomach in "The Old Lady Who Swallowed a Fly" could show the accumulation of animals the old lady swallowed; or a trap animals fall into as in "Tortoise and the Leopard" from *African Animal Tales*.

Still another dimension to explore with overhead shadow puppets is the ability of objects or characters to appear and disappear suddenly, such as the objects from the stomach of the central character in *Mother, Mother I Feel Sick* by Remy Charlip and Burton Supree. In *Two of Everything*, Lily Toy Hong's retelling of a Chinese folktale, objects popping out of the pot can be projected onto the screen.

Exciting backgrounds can be created with overlays of colored acetate. Use clear acetate as a base for creating the background. Cut out scenic shapes—a yellow sun, a red house, blue ocean waves, or green grass. Adhere them to clear background with double-stick tape. Additional images, such as sun rays, flowers, or fish, can be added with contrasting colored acetate. Marker pens can be used to draw in finer details, such as leaves, fish

scales, and stars. Also consider using a roll of clear acetate (found in most media departments) and designing a moving scenic background. When the storyteller pulls the full-length scenic acetate along the glass, a character can actually appear to take a stroll through a city or woods.

When planning overhead shadow presentations, map out the story in terms of scenes to include and scenes to omit. Since it is predominantly the outline of the puppet or prop that is seen through the overhead projector technique, all shapes must be clear and well defined. Analyzing stories with these facts in mind will help assess those best suited for the shadow technique and those best left to another method. Overhead shadow puppet construction and techniques are fully covered in Part Two, chapter 3.

**Underground scene for "The Ants and the Grasshopper"**

## EXAMPLE OF AN OVERHEAD SHADOW STORY

 *The Stonecutter*

This Japanese folktale, retold and illustrated by Gerald McDermott, is about a stonecutter who believes wealth and power will bring him greater happiness. He realizes the folly of his belief after his wish is fulfilled.

### Approach

Leader narrates story while children operate puppets using overhead projector. Children create sound effects.

The Mountain and Stonecutter shadow puppets for *The Stonecutter*

## Puppets/Props

| Characters/Props | Types/Materials |
| --- | --- |
| Stonecutter | Paper shadow puppets |
| Prince | |
| Spirit | |
| Mountain | |
| Hut | |
| Sun | |
| Cloud | |
| Lightning bolts | Red acetate |
| Water | Blue acetate |

## Presentation

### General procedures

Assign all the parts to children, line them up in order of appearance, and brief them on the action and sequencing of story. Give them an opportunity to practice manipulation of puppets, providing assistance when necessary.

Assign a child to produce stonecutter's sound effect by hitting two stones together.

### Introduction

Have the children discuss the things they would like to be.

Ask, "Did you ever wish that you were something you were not? What are some of the things you wished to be? Why?"

"Do you think you would be happy forever being what you wished to be? What kind of problems might you have?"

"I have a story that takes place in Japan about someone who wished he was many things, but was never satisfied. Here is what happens to him."

## Story actions

Place mountain on projector glass, turn on projector light, and start narrating story.

Stonecutter chips away at Mountain.

Prince walks by Stonecutter.

Remove Mountain and replace with Hut.

Remove Hut and replace with Palace.

Replace Stonecutter with Prince.

Spirit appears and transforms Prince into Sun.
(Bring Prince *down* and Sun *up*.)

Spirit appears and transforms Sun into Cloud.
(Bring Sun *down* and Cloud *up*.)

Thunderstorm occurs.
(Streak lightning bolts down over Cloud.)

Run Water across scene.

Spirit appears and transforms Cloud into Mountain.
(Bring Cloud *down* and Mountain *up*.)

Stonecutter chips away at Mountain.

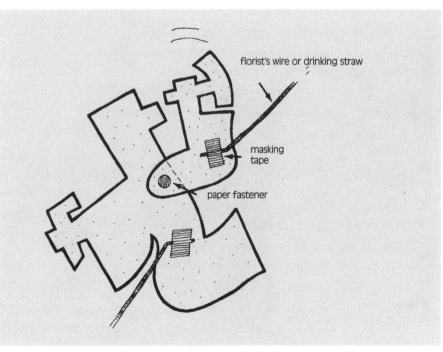

Overhead shadow puppet construction for *The Stonecutter*

### Follow-Up Activities

Ask children, individually or in small groups, to write their own version of the Stonecutter tale, using a lead character of another profession, for example: a weaver, candle maker, doctor, or construction worker. Encourage them to set stories in either modern or historic times.

Have children create puppets and present their stories to the group.

### SUGGESTED TITLES FOR <u>OVERHEAD SHADOW STORIES</u>

Barbosa, Rogerio Andrade. "The Tortoise and the Leopard," in *African Animal Tales*; illus. by Cica Fittipaldi. Volcano, 1993.

A clever tortoise tricks a leopard into throwing her out of a trap. The overhead technique is very effective for showing the animals in the trap. Another tale in this collection, "The Considerate Fly," a cumulative story about a series of misfortunes initiated by a fly, also lends itself well to the overhead technique.

Charlip, Remy, and Burton Supree. *Mother, Mother I Feel Sick, Send for the Doctor Quick, Quick, Quick*; illus. by Remy Charlip. Parents, 1966.

A doctor removes a most unusual assortment of objects from a boy's stomach. For maximum effect, pull each item slowly from the boy's stomach.

Croll, Carolyn. *The Three Brothers*; illus. by the author. Putnam, 1991.

A father tells his three sons that whoever fills the barn in one day will inherit the farm in this German folktale. The youngest brother fills the barn with light to the astonishment of his family. Convincingly told by creating a silhouette of the barn on the screen, which each brother fills. Colored transparency film is effective for the light.

Demi. *The Magic Tapestry*; illus. by the author. Holt, 1994.

A Chinese folktale about a mother who spends years weaving a beautiful tapestry which is lost because of her sons' greed. The youngest son's quest to find the tapestry carries him to exotic locations that can be vividly depicted on an overhead stage.

Dunphy, Madeline. *Here Is the Arctic Winter*; illus. by Alan James Robinson. Hyerion, 1993.

In a format similar to "The House That Jack Built," the animals struggling to survive the Arctic winter are introduced. As the story is told, present a silhouette of each animal on a barren, snow-covered overhead background.

Freeman, Don. *Norman the Doorman*; illus. by the author. Viking, 1959.

Norman, doorman of the basement entrance to the art museum, enters his sculpture in an exhibit. Use cutaway scenery to expose Norman's studio.

Gordon, Ruth, comp. *Peeling the Onion*. HarperCollins, 1993.

An anthology of poems from different cultures. These poems will be effectively shared using simple puppets and economical backgrounds. Be sure to let your audience know when and where each poem was written.

Grimm, Jacob. *The Frog Prince*, retold by Edith H. Tarlov; illus. by James Marshall. Four Winds, 1974.

Traditional tale of the frog who turns into a handsome prince. Transformation of the character is most effective when done on the overhead.

Hong, Lily Toy. *Two of Everything*; illus. by the author. Whitman, 1993.

Mr. Hak-Tak discovered the old brass pot in his garden yields a duplicate of everything placed inside it. Problems arise when his wife slips into the pot and a second Mrs. Hak-Tak appears. Place the pot cutout in the center of the projector screen as objects are lifted from it.

Johnston, Tony. *The Badger and the Magic Fan*; illus. by Tomie de Paola. Putnam, 1990.

A Japanese folktale filled with wonderful characters: a shape-changing badger, tengus (also known as goblins), the thinkers of Japan, and heavenly workers. Badger first steals a magical fan, which makes noses grow, from the tengu children and then continues to cause mischief. Attach a strip of oaktag to the faces of the tengus, girl, and badger that can move in and out as noses grow and shrink. Group puppets should be used for the thinkers, doctors, and heavenly workers.

McDermott, Gerald. *Anansi, the Spider, a Tale from the Ashanti*; illus. by the author. Holt, 1972.

Two adventures of Anansi and his six sons. Incorporate African design elements into the overhead staging. A Caldecott Honor book.

McDermott, Gerald. *The Stonecutter*; illus. by the author. Viking, 1975.

Japanese folktale about a stonecutter who believes wealth and power will bring him greater happiness. He realizes the folly of his thinking after his wish is granted. A Caldecott Honor book.

Prelutsky, Jack. "The Vampire," in *Nightmares: Poems to Trouble Your Sleep*; illus. by Arnold Lobel. Greenwillow, 1976.

The gruesome nightly foray of a vampire is described with appropriately chilling images. Red acetate for teeth and yellow for the eyes will create a vampire upper elementary-age children will love.

Silverman, Jerry. *Slave Songs*. Chelsea House, 1994.

This collection includes spirituals, hymns, work chants, ballads, humorous ditties, protest songs, and minstrel songs sung in the South before the Civil War. Music is included for each title. Songs to share with overhead shadows: "Go Down, Moses," "Blue-Tail Fly," "All the Pretty Little Horses," "Michael, Row the Boat Ashore," "I Am Sold and Going to Georgia," and "Follow the Drinking Gourd." Shadows produced by the overhead format are a dramatic complement to these songs.

Whipple, Laura, comp. *Eric Carle's Dragons, Dragons & Other Creatures That Never Were*; illus. by Eric Carle. Philomel, 1991.

Over thirty poems introducing kids to marvelous, mystical characters. The Basilisk, Leviathan, Amphisbaena, Manticore, Cerberus, and a variety of dragons are some of the creatures presented. Carle's luminous, tissue-paper illustrations can inspire young puppeteers to create overhead presentations for these creatures using bright colored puppets and backgrounds.

# Chapter 17  PANEL THEATERS

A VERSATILE THEATER can be created by taping together several cardboard panels of the same size, with a different scene per panel, and opening them out on a tabletop. This series of stand-up panels, either horizontal or vertical, is an ingenious means of linking various elements of a narrative together so that children can easily perceive the story as a unified whole. By securing a narrow cardboard strip to the bottom edge of the panels, two-dimensional characters can easily be moved along the base of the set from one scene panel to another.

In choosing stories to accompany this technique, search out those that required scenic focus. In panel theaters the scenery predominates, as opposed to some other methods in which the puppets are generally all-important. A panel theater presentation of Clement Moore's *The Night before Christmas* could depict charming home interior scenes lavish with such details as a fireplace, rocking chairs, rugs, windows, and other items of interest.

Three Billy Goats Gruff" by a bridge segment provides a clear division between the two areas, as well as a visual connection between the two. Other scenes well suited to this format include the following: the universe, from earth's surface to outer space; a seaside, from sandy beach surface to underwater terrain; a circus, including three rings and entrance; and two villages, linked together with various roads and waterways. The storyteller must be aware that performances by puppets in this technique are extremely limited. The simple cardboard shapes, having little means for control, are basically maneuvered across the base strip or up or down. Their movements are directional rather than expressive.

Therefore, travel sequence seems to be particularly compatible to a horizontal panel setting. In maneuvering the characters, take advantage of the entire length of the panels to be most effective. For instance, in Wanda Gág's *Millions of Cats*, the story begins with the house scene; then the Old Man can wander across and over the hills of the central panel and finally reach the cats at the opposite end. *Benjamin and Tulip* by

## TYPES OF PANEL THEATERS

Using a trio of horizontal panels is especially advantageous, since the middle panel serves as a transitional scene that connects the beginning and ending scenes of the story. This three-panel format has many applications. For example, linking together the two grassy areas in "The

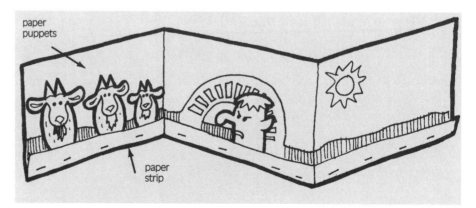

Horizontal panel theater for "The Three Billy Goats Gruff"

**Vertical panel theater for "Jack and the Beanstalk"**

paper puppets

paper strip

Rosemary Wells capitalizes on travel segments as Benjamin makes repeated trips to the grocery store from his house. The central panel illustrates the tree in which Tulip is hiding. As Benjamin passes by, he is bombarded as Tulip mischievously drops things down on him.

Consider increasing the number of panels to make an extra-long travel set. Children will particularly enjoy playing with such a set and manipulating the characters along its base. In the story "Hansel and Gretel," the forest may take on elaborate details with dark, brooding trees and undergrowth, hidden eyes, and foreboding creatures. Extended panels would also be interesting for exploring panoramic views of an entire city, countryside, or even an ocean!

A variation of the panel theater concept is to create a vertical standing panel. There are many examples that can be explored in this formation. A standing vertical two-level set for "Jack and the Beanstalk" could show the Giant's living quarters at the upper level of the panels with Jack's home at the bottom and a leafy beanstalk connecting the two. Another obvious setting is a cutaway view of a house in which the upstairs and downstairs scenes are illustrated. *Fourteen Rats and a Rat-Catcher* by James Cressy is a delightful example in which a family of rats and an old lady share a house. The woman's parlor is at an upper level while the rats live underground. When using more than one panel for the vertical method, simply add additional base strips at each playing level to accommodate puppets.

A novel panel setting is the combination exterior-interior design, a set that exposes both interior and exterior views by means of panels that open and close. Such a set may be used for stories that take place inside a cave, for instance. In the *Arabian Nights*, the doors that open on cue to passwords, such as "Open Sesame," can expose magnificent treasures inside. A pyramid, tomb (for a horror story), or dirt wall to an underground burrow can all be handled in this manner. Children will enjoy the surprise of anticipating what is inside the panel.

Undoubtedly the storyteller will find new ways to link and arrange the panels to best amplify certain stories. After the story is over, panels can be folded for easy storage, requiring minimal space. Consider covering panels with clear adhesive-backed laminating materials to protect them from extra wear and tear by children.

## EXAMPLE OF A PANEL THEATER

 *Millions of Cats*

In this popular story by Wanda Gág, an Old Man goes in search of a cat to bring back for his wife to ease her loneliness. Due to his acute indecisiveness he ends up with not one but millions of cats!

### Approach

Leader narrates the story while using the puppets with panel theater arranged on tabletop.

## Puppets/Props

| Characters/Props | Types/Materials |
|---|---|
| Old Man | Stiff paper cutouts |
| Old Woman | |
| White, grey, yellow, and black cats | |
| Kitten | |
| Pond, grassy hill with millions of cats | Movable cardboard scenic cutouts |
| Brush | Real |
| Saucer of milk | |
| Three scene panels | Cardboard panels linked together |

## Presentation

### General procedures

Arrange house in base strip of first panel, pond and grassy hill in middle panel, and hill with millions of cats in third panel. Fold up panels and place on lap.

Hide puppet characters and remaining props in a box.

Instruct children to join in the refrain:

*Cats here, cats there,*
*Cats and kittens everywhere.*
*Hundreds of cats,*
*Thousands of cats,*
*Millions and billions and trillions of cats!** 

### Introduction

Discuss with the children their power to make choices.

Ask them, "Did you ever have difficulty making a choice about something? What was it?"

"Which choice did you make? Why?"

"I know a story about an Old Man who went to look for a cat. He saw so many beautiful ones, he couldn't

*From *Millions of Cats* by Wanda Gág, copyright 1928 by Coward-McCann, Inc., copyright renewed © 1956 by Robert Janssen. Reprinted by permission of Coward-McCann, Inc.

make up his mind which to choose. Here is the house where he lives." (Place panel on tabletop facing children, open to display house, and put Old Man in panel strip.) "And here is his wife." (Place Old Woman in panel strip as well.)

### Story actions

Begin story at first panel with description of Old Man and Old Woman.

Move Old Man over the hills (middle panel) until he reaches the third panel with cutouts of millions of cats.

Cue children as to when to join in the refrain.

Place white, grey, black, and yellow cats in the panel strips in order of appearance.

Pick up all the cats, hill with cats, and the Old Man and have them march to the pond in the middle panel. Remove the pond from view after the cats drink it dry.

Repeat action with the grassy hill.

Bring the cats and the Old Man home to the Old Woman, at the first panel.

Shake the cats around when they quarrel and remove them.

Place tiny kitten in first panel strip and brush its fur.

Put saucer of milk on tabletop.

## Follow-Up Activities

Let children create their own cats from construction paper. They may be decorated in bright colors and cut out. On wall arrange cats on a very large picture of a grassy hill and display with other books about cats.

Vary the theme and let the children think of other animals they would like to see by the millions, such as millions of frogs in a pond, millions of lions in a den, millions of space creatures in a universe, millions of butterflies in a garden, etc.

## Construction of a Basic Horizontal Panel Theater

### Materials

Three cardboard or poster board panels 12″ × 10″ high

Three cardboard or poster board strip 12″ × 1½″ high

Masking tape

Stiff paper

### Procedures

Tape the three horizontal panels together on one side with masking tape, to link them together.

Secure a strip to bottom of each panel by stapling it to panel along lower edge only. Leave upper section of strip free for inserting paper figures and props.

Color a scene on each panel with felt-tip marking pens, crayons, or another coloring medium.

Create a simple puppet cast by cutting out images from stiff paper. Vehicles such as a car or boat, other props and removable scenic pieces such as a tree or house can also be made from stiff paper. Insert these items in base strip for standing up.

**SUGGESTED TITLES FOR <u>PANEL THEATERS</u>**

*Arabian Nights*; ed. by Kate Douglas Wiggin and Nora A. Smith; illus. by Maxfield Parrish. Scribner's, 1994.

An exciting introduction to the world of Ali Baba and Aladdin.

Bruchac, Joseph. *Native American Animal Stories*; illus. by John Kahionhes Fadden and David Kanietakeron Fadden. Fulcrum, 1992.

Open-out panel theater for *Arabian Nights*

A collection of stories used by Native American parents to teach their children basic concepts. Stories deal with survival, creation, and celebration. When telling "How the Spider Symbol Came to the People" emphasize the forest setting on the panel. A bayou becomes the background for "How Poison Came into the World." A pond is the setting for "Turtle Races with Beaver."

Cowen-Fletcher, Jane. *It Takes a Village*; illus. by the author. Scholastic, 1994.

When Yemi takes her brother to the market she learns the meaning of the saying, "It takes a village to raise a child." On one side panel act out Yemi's actions; on the other side panel show what is happening to Kokou as various market vendors care for him. The center panel can show the various stalls in the marketplace.

Cressy, James. *Fourteen Rats and a Rat-Catcher*; illus. by Tamasin Cole. Prentice-Hall, 1977.

A handsome rat-catcher satisfactorily solves the problem of a family of rats and an old lady who share a house. The perspective from the woman's parlor and the rat's home beneath the floor are well illustrated by a panel theater that opens and closes or by means of a vertical panel.

Dee, Ruby. *Tower to Heaven*; illus. by Jennifer Brett. Holt, 1991.

The sky god is forced away from earth when Yaa constantly hits him with her pestle. The only way for the people to talk to him is to build a tower to the sky. But try as they might they are always one mortar too short. This popular West African story can be told using a vertical panel theater with a level for the earth and the top levels for the sky. Paper puppets of Yaa and the sky god can easily show the movement between earth and sky. Use stiff paper for the single first mortar and a strip of mortars which reach almost to the top level. Insert these items in the base strip as the story is told.

de Paola, Tomie. *Strega Nona*; illus. by the author. Prentice-Hall, 1975.

In this humorous retelling of an old folktale, a witch, her magic pasta pot, and a bumbling village lad create bedlam! When Big Anthony attempts to show off the magic pasta pot to the village people, the magic backfires and the fun begins. Thread a continuous piece of yarn through a hole in the panel behind pot and pull out the spaghetti from it. A Caldecott Honor book.

Gág, Wanda. *Millions of Cats*; illus. by the author. Coward, 1977, 1928.

A childless couple wants a cat but almost gets more than they can handle. Arrange house in base strip of first panel, pond and grassy hill in middle panel, and hill with millions of cats in third panel. A Newbery Honor book.

Gramatky, Hardie. *Hercules*; illus. by the author. Putnam, 1940.

Hercules, an old horse-drawn fire engine, succeeds in saving city hall when the newer engines fail. A blue pipe cleaner protruding from the engine's hose can serve as water.

Grimm, Jacob. *Hansel and Gretel*. Retold by Rika Lesser; illus. by Paul O. Zelinsky. Putnam, 1984.

The popular fairy tale about a brother and sister who encounter a witch. Incorporate a panel that opens to show the inside of the witch's house. House can be decorated with real candy. A Caldecott Honor book.

Knutson, Barbara. *Sungura and Leopard: A Swahili Trickster Tale*; illus. by the author. Little, 1993.

Sungura, the hare, outwits Leopard when they both build a house on the same spot. The building of the house can be shown by adding layers that have slits cut into the bottom so each addition slips onto the lower level.

Moore, Clement. *The Night before Christmas*; illus. by Arthur Rackham. Doubleday, 1977.

A beautiful picture-book version of this holiday favorite. Indoor and outdoor scenes make it suitable as a panel theater presentation.

Wells, Rosemary. *Benjamin and Tulip*; illus. by the author. Dial, 1973.

Two raccoons resolve their difficulties and develop a friendship by sharing a watermelon.

# Chapter 18 STORIES-IN-THE-ROUND

SOME STORIES ARE best presented in an open space, in which the combination of narrative and space affords the participants maximum freedom to move about in a spontaneous manner. An ideal space consists of a large playing circle, demarcated by the spectators who sit around the perimeter, creating a natural arena for the presentation. Not only does this arrangement leave the center area free for the dramatization, but it also provides a natural "pathway" for characters' walking cycles around the outside circumference. A story such as "Henny Penny," for example, could utilize this feature by having the animal characters move along this pathway in a recurring pattern each time they attempt to visit the King. This patterning gives the movements form and order while depicting passage of time. If space is limited, and a story-in-the-round is not possible, plan seating to face the open area in front of the room. Then any walking segment can take place back and forth in a linear fashion across this space rather than in a circular pattern.

The story selections most conducive to this particular technique are those that include strong action segments or travel sequences. Stories such as "The Old Woman and Her Pig" or "The Travels of a Fox," an English folktale about a fox's visit from house to house and his adventures with a mysterious sack he delivers, are two excellent examples of stories well suited for depiction in the round. Both are cumulative-type stories with repeated actions. Noncumulative stories are also appropriate provided they have a clear traveling sequence.

Certain puppet types seem to enhance this sort of story presentation involving children on a participatory level, the main criterion being that the puppets should be large in scale and compatible with the bold movements of the accompanying actions. Stick puppets, string puppets, and bodi-puppets are forms of puppetry that can be easily maneuvered through space, thus emphasizing the action. While Henny Penny would be well portrayed by any of these puppet types, the Fox in "The Travels of a Fox" is best portrayed by a bodi-puppet because this puppet frees the performer's hands for the tasks described in the story of the Fox delivering the sack.

In setting up the space, the scenery generally can be imagined by the children. However, landmarks for indicating important elements,

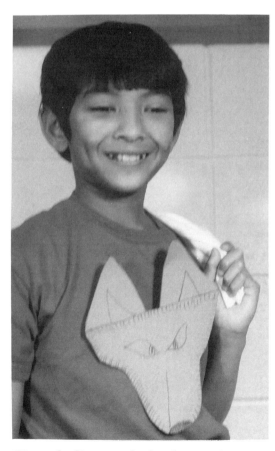

**Picture bodi-puppet for fox character in "The Travels of a Fox" (Photo of David Champlin by Michelle Owen)**

such as a plant for a forest or garden; blue circle of paper for a pond; playhouse for a house, neighborhood, or town; or tabletop for an upstairs level can be quickly mobilized for impromptu play. Props also can be integrated into stories for accentuating ideas. A pillowcase or other sack for "The Travels of a Fox" or an umbrella for Arnold Lobel's "The Baboon's Umbrella" from his book *Fables* are nice additions, as shown in the story examples that follow.

Because of the space requirements of these stories, they are marvelous for use in outdoor presentations. Parks, campsites, and recreational areas are perfect locations for achieving high drama in stories-in-the-round. Consider expanding the space for story dramatization by using an entire city plaza, a wooded or garden area, or park grounds.

While stories-in-the-round require more creative dramatic skills than other story settings, this technique brings to children a total participatory experience that can only enhance the storyteller's repertoire.

## EXAMPLES OF STORIES-IN-THE-ROUND

### "The Travels of a Fox"

A fox tries to take advantage of some people by preying upon their natural sense of curiosity; however, in this folktale he is eventually outwitted by an ordinary house dog.

### Approach

Leader narrates the entire story while children pantomime the actions. Ask a child to play the part of the woman. Only the child who plays the Fox is required to wear a puppet.

## Puppets/Props

| Characters/Props | Types/Materials |
|---|---|
| Fox | Bodi-puppet or picture |
| Bumble Bee | Cardboard cutouts |
| Rooster | |
| Pig | |
| Ox | |
| Boy | |
| Housedog | Hand puppet or stuffed toy |
| Sack | Pillowcase or other type of sack |
| Stump | Chair or grocery box |

## Presentation

### General procedures

Assign a child to play the part of the Fox and attach puppet or picture to child's body. Give child sack to carry.

Assign parts to other children, each representing a household member; children hold their cardboard characters. Arrange them in order of appearance around the playing space.

Put stump (chair or box) to one side of playing space. Place child holding Bee next to stump.

Plan the sequencing of the story with the children and explain the story's actions.

### Introduction

Start by asking, "Does anyone know what the word 'curiosity' means?"

Then ask, "Have you ever been curious about something? What?"

"I know a story about some very curious people. They were told not to peek at something but they did, which caused quite a bit of trouble."

## Story actions

Begin story. Fox digs around stump and finds Bumble Bee. He puts it in sack, which he throws over his shoulder.

Fox walks in a large circle (or other pattern), knocks at imaginary door, and leaves sack with woman who answers the door.

Woman peeks into sack and out flies the Bumble Bee (she pulls it out), which is eaten by Rooster (she handles Rooster as it goes through the motions of eating Bee).

Fox comes back, discovers Bumble Bee is gone, and replaces it by putting Rooster into his sack.

Repeat action with each new character.

Fox sits down to rest. He opens bag and out jumps the Housedog (child in last house pulls out Housedog and operates it).

Housedog chases Fox in large circle pattern.

## Follow-Up Activities

Let children think of other characters to replace in sack. Repeat story with new characters added. An entirely different theme may be substituted, such as sea life, jungle, or zoo. For example, a sea captain with a sack could collect sea life creatures in the same manner.

## "The Baboon's Umbrella"

The Baboon takes some excessively practical advice from his friend the Gibbon and finds himself with an unhappy solution. Moral: Advice from friends is like the weather. Some of it is good; some of it is bad. This fable is taken from Arnold Lobel's book *Fables*.

## Approach

Leader narrates the story while the children pantomime the action with puppets.

## Puppets/Props

| Characters/Props | Types/Materials |
| --- | --- |
| Baboon Gibbon | Bodi-puppets or pictures |
| Umbrella | Old umbrella or large paper circle cut out and attached to stick |
| Scissors | Real (blunt ends) |
| Rain | Christmas tree tinsel or fringed foil on stick |
| Home | Table or chair |

## Presentation

### General procedures

Assign a child to play the Baboon. Put the bodi-puppet or picture on child and place the Baboon to the right. Give child the umbrella prop.

Assign a child to play the Gibbon and put the bodi-puppet or picture on child. Seat the Gibbon to the left.

Place scissors in a space designated as "home" (on a table or chair).

Place rain prop near leader.

### Introduction

Discuss with the group their experiences in giving and asking for advice.

Ask, "Have you ever asked a friend for advice? Was it good advice?" Allow children an opportunity to share their experiences.

Then say, "I know a story about someone who followed a friend's advice and this is what happened."

Paper-bag bodi-puppet of baboon for "The Baboon's Umbrella"
(Photo of Kristen Morgan)

## Story actions

Begin story. Baboon walks in large circle (or other travel pattern) carrying umbrella over head.

Gibbon pops up and faces Baboon to give advice.

Baboon runs around circle to "home." Baboon picks up scissors and cuts large holes in umbrella.

Baboon proudly walks in circle again showing off transformed umbrella.

Leader waves rain prop over Baboon.

## Follow-Up Activities

Try some of the other fables in Arnold Lobel's book, such as "The Hen and the Apple Tree" or "The Bear and the Crow."

Ask the children to write the silliest piece of advice they have ever heard or could imagine. Read the advice out loud to the group and share reactions.

### SUGGESTED TITLES FOR STORIES-IN-THE-ROUND

Arnott, Kathleen. "Tug of War," in *African Myths and Legends* retold by Kathleen Arnott; illus. by Joan Kiddlee-Monroe. Walck, 1962. Pp.153–55.

Hare tricks Elephant and Hippo into having a tug-of-war. Both think they are pulling against Hare, but in reality they are straining against each other. Storyteller plays role of Hare.

Galdone, Paul. *The Old Woman and Her Pig*; illus. by the author. McGraw, 1960.

Cumulative tale of an old woman who buys a pig but can't get it home because the pig refuses to go over a stile in the road. Children pantomime the actions with stick or bodi-puppets.

Gerson, Mary-Joan. *Why the Sky Is Far Away*; illus. by Carla Golembe. Little, 1992.

A Nigerian folktale explaining how the greed of the villagers caused the sky to move out of reach. Children wearing bodi-puppets act out the story. Attach a piece of blue cloth to poles so it can be raised above the heads of the children at the end of the story.

Gonzalez, Lucia. *The Bossy Gallito*; illus. by Lulu Delacre. Scholastic, 1994.

A bossy rooster needs help to clean the mud off his beak so he can attend his uncle's wedding. He is unsuccessful in his attempts until the sun begins a chain reaction, which results in grass finally cleaning rooster's beak. Children can dramatize this humorous Cuban folktale using stick puppets or bodi-puppet. Attach the mud to the rooster's beak with velcro. Each character can supply the appropriate dialogue: "No I will not." And "Pardon me, but I will _____." This edition includes the Spanish version of the story as well.

Hadithi, Mwenye. *Hungry Hyena*; illus. by Adrienne Kennaway. Little, 1994.

Fish Eagle turns the table on Hyena in a tale that explains why hyenas today can no longer run as fast as the wind across the African plain. Children using stick or anything puppets act out the story. A stick-puppet Sausage tree can provide safety for Fish Eagle and Pangolin.

Kalan, Robert. *Stop, Thief!*; illus. by Yossi Abolafia. Greenwillow, 1993.

A cumulative story about a nut that changes hands until it is returned to the squirrel that dug it up. Children wearing bodi-puppets act out the story, passing the nut from character to character until it is returned to its owner.

Kimmel, Eric A. *The Greatest of All*; illus. by Giora Carmi. Holiday, 1991.

Father Mouse searches for the greatest one of all to be the husband of his daughter, Chuko. Representing all characters visited by Father Mouse as large stick puppets and Father Mouse as a small hand puppet will add to the humor of the telling.

Lobel, Arnold. *Fables*; illus. by the author. Harper, 1980.

Amusing and original fables by a popular author. A Caldecott Medal book.

London, Jonathan. *Fire Race*; illus. by Sylvia Long. Chronicle, 1993.

An exciting, action-filled Karuk tale of how coyote brought fire to the People. Children use talking-mouth puppets for the mountain lion, fox, bear, and turtle. Measuring worm can be a long sock puppet and eagle a bodi-puppet. Frog, who swallows fire, should be a swallowing puppet. For coyote, who travels the most, use a bodi-puppet or picture on a child. The yellow jackets can be yellow paper stick puppets. Laminate the yellow jackets so that coyote can use a washable marker to blacken their eyes and add stripes.

Mack, Stan. *10 Bears in My Bed*; illus. by the author. Pantheon, 1974.

Ten bears in one bed is too many. Each bear leaves the bed in a distinct way; e.g., roared, chugged. Children wear bodi-puppets.

Martin, Rafe. *Foolish Rabbit's Big Mistake*; illus. by Ed Young. Putnam, 1985.

A Jataka tale featuring a foolish rabbit who thinks the earth is breaking up when he hears an apple fall. He panics and is joined in his rush toward safety by other rabbits, bears, and an elephant. It is the brave lion who provides the solution. Children dramatize using large stick puppets.

Rockwell, Anne. "The Travels of a Fox," in *The Old Woman and Her Pig*; illus. by the author. Crowell, 1979. Pp. 23–33.

A fox is unsuccessful in his attempts to outwit some curious people.

Ryan, Cheli Duran. *Hildilid's Night*; illus. by Arnold Lobel. Macmillan, 1986.

Hildilid's attempts to chase away the night can be enacted with bodi-puppets as leader tells the story. A Caldecott Honor book.

Zemach, Margot. *It Could Always Be Worse*; illus. by the author. Farrar, 1976.

When a man complains that his house is too small, the rabbi advises him to move the farm animals into the house. After the animals move out, the man is surprised to see how much larger his house seems. Children wearing bodi-puppets or using stick puppets will enjoy acting out this humorous story. A Caldecott Honor book.

Many versions of this story are available. One example is *A Squash and a Squeeze* by Julia Donaldson (McElderry, 1993). In this version a little old lady receives advice from a wiseman instead of a rabbi.

# Chapter 19  STORY APRONS

T HE STORY APRON can graphically signify the beginning of story sessions, especially when a furry tail, curious nose, or mysterious antenna peeks from one or more of the various pockets. A readily available story apron is almost a prerequisite for the earnest storyteller who regularly uses puppets with young children. Many kinds of aprons or similar garments may be utilized. A half-apron, pinafore, hostess skirt, printer's apron, chef's apron, carpenter's apron, or even farmer's overalls are all suitable. The main requirement is that they have large pockets sewn in various locations. The oversized pockets provide ideal hiding places in which to arrange puppets and props; children's curiosity is aroused whenever they see the apron and inevitably they clamor to know what is hidden in the pockets. By arranging puppets and props in the pockets in reverse order of usage, that is, putting in last those items which are to be pulled out first, one can perform stories and poems with relative ease, simply by pulling out the puppet at the appropriate story or poem line.

A quick puppet apron can be improvised by adding pockets to a ready-made apron or hostess skirt. If an all-purpose apron is created from an assortment of colorful calico and cotton prints, the overall effect of the many large and small pockets will be similar to that of a patchwork quilt and will add festivity to the story session. It is especially appropriate to choose fabrics that will fit into particular themes—flower

**A basic story apron**

prints for springtime, gingham or denim for barnyards, and holiday patterns for holidays. Using various sewing notions and trims may also greatly embellish a theme—colorful drapery pom-pom trim for a carnival setting or eyelet lace for stories with a Victorian overtone. A carpenter's apron obtained from a hardware store or a white chef's apron from a restaurant supply shop offer excellent accompaniment for stories. You might wish to decorate the bib sections of these aprons with felt cutout scenery—ocean waves, a moon, a pumpkin, a tepee, a Christmas tree, or other motif. With the addition of Velcro these cutouts can be interchanged for different stories to expand the apron's versatility.

A lapboard is a convenient accessory to use in conjunction with the apron because it provides a stable surface upon which to place props and puppets so that action can occur. Simple set suggestions can easily be arranged on top of this lap "stage," for example, a blue circle for a pond or a picture of a garden patch.

To avoid overwhelming the audience with too many distractions, keep the number of props to a minimum and choose only those that play an important role in emphasizing the action.

A lapboard is easy to construct. Cut out a 12- × 18-inch piece of grocery-carton cardboard; cover top of board with a piece of adhesive-backed shelving paper or glued felt. (Cut material at least 1 inch wider on all sides and wrap around edges of the cardboard.)

Special effects, including sound effects, can greatly augment the impact of the experience. Harmonicas, flutes, cymbals, and other instruments or noisemakers can be stored in pockets for distribution to children for providing sound effects. The storyteller can achieve interesting visual effects by throwing a handful of confetti to evoke a snow storm; blowing soap bubbles to connote a water scene for an underwater or bath activity; or waving a cluster of Christmas tinsel to give the impression of rain falling.

Stories for story apron presentations should fall in the category of those that depend on the element of surprise. Hide props and puppets in pockets and pull them out in sequence with the narrative. P. D. Eastman's *Are You My Mother?* is an ideal example of a stream of puppet characters that can be pulled out and given to children prior to the story presentation. *Something from Nothing* by Phoebe Gilman is an example of a story utilizing a series of interesting props to represent how a young boy's grandfather remakes a worn blanket into other objects including a tie, a button, and finally a story; these items can be extracted from pockets as the story progresses.

The story apron worn by the storyteller comes to symbolize to the children the beginning of a storytelling session with anticipation of hidden surprises and fun in store. It is a tool that not only intrigues the children but also helps the storyteller to get organized!

## EXAMPLES OF STORY APRON PRESENTATIONS

### *Are You My Mother?*

After falling out of his nest, a baby bird sets off in search of his mother in this P. D. Eastman story. Since he does not know what his mother looks like, he encounters a number of characters in his search and through deductive reasoning finally discovers who she is.

### Approach

Storyteller narrates story while wearing story apron. Narrator uses normal voice for narration and high or tiny voice for Baby Bird.

Children participate by playing the remaining characters with puppets and providing sounds.

### Puppets/Props

| Characters/Props | Types/Materials |
|---|---|
| Mother Bird | Hand puppets, envelope or |
| Kitten | paper puppets, or stuffed |
| Hen | toys |
| Dog | |
| Cow | |
| | |
| Baby Bird | Finger puppet |
| | |
| Car | Toys or rod puppets |
| Boat | |
| Plane | |
| | |
| Bulldozer | Child, without puppet |
| | |
| Egg | Toy plastic egg |
| | |
| Nest | Straw, fringed paper, or felt |

### Presentation

#### General procedures

Assign one child to play Mother Bird and to stand close to lapboard.

Assign other children the parts of Kitten, Hen, Dog, Cow, Car, Boat, and Plane. Each child holds a puppet and makes appropriate sounds. Children sit to the left and right of the narrator.

Assign a child to portray Bulldozer. Practice the motions of a mechanical arm with a shovel on the end (cupped hand). Arm goes up and then down. Child says "Snort!" loud and clear.

Place Baby Bird inside a plastic egg and tuck all puppets and props into pockets.

As characters are mentioned during storytelling, pull them from the story apron and hand them to designated children.

### Introduction

Ask the children if they have ever found a bird's egg. Was it broken or whole? What color was it? Did they try to hatch it?

Then continue, "I had a very lucky day today! Guess what? I found a bird's egg!"
(Pull out egg with bird inside.)

"I was doubly lucky because I even found a bird's nest."
(Pull out nest and assemble with egg.)

"Hmmm. . . . I know just the right story to go with this egg and nest."

"Mother Bird, will you help me?"
(Instruct Mother Bird to sit on egg.)

### Story actions

Begin narrating story.

Make egg jump.

Wave "bye-bye" while Mother Bird leaves egg.

Make egg jump again and open egg to show Baby Bird.

Let Baby Bird look around for his mother. Hold Baby Bird at a high position and have it fall down to your knee level. Pull Baby Bird up and begin its journey.

Baby walks by Mother Bird, then onto each character.

Each puppet character responds with appropriate animal sounds to indicate "no" response.

Bulldozer performs mechanical motion and carries Baby Bird up, then down to nest.

Mother Bird arrives home again.

Baby Bird kisses Mother at end.

### Follow-Up Activities

Retell the story with the entire group participating by using several children as a character unit. For example, several kittens may be together in one group, several hens in another, etc.

Help children construct a cup theater (refer to chapter 13) in the shape of a nest. Have them make a Baby Bird and put it inside to pop up and down.

## Where the Sidewalk Ends

This collection of poems by Shel Silverstein has enormous appeal to children. Some favorites that lend themselves to puppet presentations are "Shadow Wash," "Tight Hat," "Recipe for a Hippopotamus Sandwich," and "Boa Constrictor."

## "Shadow Wash"

### Approach

Storyteller narrates poem while using puppets and props on lapboard.

### Puppets/Props

| Characters/Props | Types/Materials |
| --- | --- |
| Person's shadow, large and small | Black felt |
| Small bowl | Plastic |
| Bottle of detergent | Real detergent bottle |

### Presentation

#### General procedures

Put folded large shadow and detergent bottle into pocket of apron.

Secretly place small shadow inside bowl. Place bowl on lapboard.

### Introduction

Talk about the children's shadows. If possible, direct a strong light so children can see their own shadows on a wall.

Then ask, "Have any of you ever washed your shadow?"

Wail for responses. Then say, "Well, maybe it's about time you did!"

### Story actions

Begin poem.

Take out folded large shadow and open it up to show group. Refold shadow and tuck into bowl.

Pretend to add some detergent in bowl and stir with fingers as if washing clothes.

Pick up large shadow and pretend to wring it out; then crumple it up and quickly put it down behind bowl to hide.

Bring up small shadow from bowl.

### Follow-Up Activities

Have children make large or small shadows of themselves from black construction paper. With clothespins hang shadows on a clothesline to decorate the room. Later let children take shadows home.

## "Tight Hat"

### Approach

Leader narrates poem while stretching neck of puppet.

### Puppets/Props

| Characters/Props | Types/Materials |
|---|---|
| Tight-Hat Man | Paper cutout with pleated neck |

Story apron pocket components for "Shadow Wash"

small felt shadow

small soap container

large felt shadow

plastic bowl

SOAP

### Presentation

#### General procedures

Fold up neck, which is attached to head, and place in pocket.

#### Introduction

Wear a funny hat, if you have one, to start the discussion. Say, "Has anyone here ever worn a hat that was too tight? Did it hurt? I know someone who got into a different kind of trouble with a hat that was too tight."

#### Story actions

Begin poem.

Pull out character with neck folded and have it sit on lapboard.

Gradually pull head upward to stretch out entire neck.

### Follow-Up Activities

Ask children to think of other items to wear that could be too tight or too big. Have each child create a paper puppet and make up a poem about such problem apparel to present to the group.

## Construction of Tight-Hat Man Puppet

### Materials

Construction paper

Yarn

### Procedures

Cut out paper head.

Add a long strip of paper to bottom for neck; pleat strip.

Attach paper hat, features, and yarn hair.

### Operation

Start poem with neck in folded position. Open up as poem is read.

## "Recipe for a Hippopotamus Sandwich"

### Approach

Leader recites poem and pulls sandwich ingredients from apron pockets.

### Puppets/Props

| Characters/Props | Types/Materials |
| --- | --- |
| Hippopotamus | Hand puppet |
| Slice of bread Slice of cake | Real or foam rubber |
| Dull kitchen knife | Real tableware knife |
| Onion ring | Circle of white felt with concentric drawn lines |
| Piece of string | Real length of string |
| Pepper shaker | Real pepper shaker |

**Paper puppet with pleated neck for "Tight Hat"**

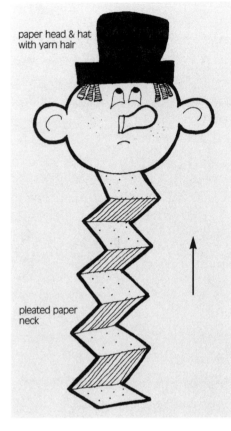

paper head & hat with yarn hair

pleated paper neck

## Presentation

### General procedures

Place all puppets and props in reverse order of appearance in one or two pockets of apron.

### Introduction

Ask the children, "What is your favorite sandwich?" Let the children discuss their favorite sandwiches for a brief period, then break in and say, "I have a favorite sandwich—it's a hippopotamus sandwich! Would you like to have my recipe?"

### Story actions

Begin poem.

Take out slice of bread and cake.

Pretend to spread mayonnaise (with knife).

Hold up each item for children to see (onion ring, string and Hippopotamus) and place on bread as if making a delectable sandwich.

Sprinkle on a dash of pepper (sneeze!)

Hold up finished sandwich and appear to take a big, oversized bite. Make a face and perhaps indicate that you are not as hungry as you thought you were and maybe it would be a wise thing to save the sandwich for a midnight snack—one never knows!

### Follow-Up Activities

Repeat poem with a different character. Then ask children to write a poem or invent a recipe for an unusual sandwich. They could demonstrate to the group with puppets and props.

## "Boa Constrictor"

### Approach

Leader narrates poem. Child uses snake puppet and mimes action.

### Puppets/Props

| Characters/Props | Types/Materials |
|---|---|
| Long snake | Sock or sweater-sleeve puppet or stuffed snake toy |

### Presentation

**General procedures**

Pull snake puppet from pocket and give to a child. Starting with your toes, snake puppet mimes action described in the poem.

**Introduction**

Explain that the snake likes to swallow things whole and digest the food in its stomach. This snake is called a Boa Constrictor, and it can grow to be very long.

**Story actions**

Begin poem.

Snake follows action starting with nibbling on toes, then knees, thighs, middle, and finally head area.

Give a strangled sound when the snake arrives at your head.

### Follow-Up Activities

Let the children make their own snake puppets from colorful knee socks to dramatize the poem.

Select other poems from this collection and present with puppets.

## SUGGESTED TITLES FOR STORY APRONS

de Paola, Tomie. *Charlie Needs a Cloak*; illus. by the author. Prentice-Hall, 1974.

As Charlie, a shepherd, makes himself a new cloak, all the facts of each process are clearly and humorously presented. Pull props such as sheep, yarn, cloth from pockets.

Gilman, Phoebe. *Something from Nothing*; illus. by the author. Scholastic, 1993.

In this Jewish folktale, Joseph's grandfather makes him a wonderful blanket when he is born. As Joseph grows, Grandfather remodels the blanket into smaller and smaller items until nothing is left . . . except a story. Give a child a boy puppet to play the part of Joseph. Storyteller performs the part of Grandfather. Each time the blanket is remade, put the large item into an apron pocket and pull out the smaller item.

Guarino, Deborah. *Is Your Mama a Llama?*; illus. by Steven Kellogg. Scholastic, 1989.

When Lloyd, a baby llama, asks his friends "Is your mama a llama?" they each give him clues to help him figure out the answer. Pull the correct animal puppet out of a story apron pocket as each riddle is answered. Use a llama hand puppet or an anything puppet with a llama face and tail to ask the question and repeat the clues.

Hardendorff, Jeanne B. *The Bed Just So*; illus. by the author. Four Winds, 1975.

A tailor is unable to sleep because a hudgin has come to stay at his house and grumbles all night long. When the tailor finally finds just the right bed for the hudgin, they both get a good night's sleep. Storyteller brings out of the apron pockets beds made from found objects.

Kalan, Robert. *Jump, Frog, Jump!*; illus. by Byron Barton. Greenwillow, 1981.

Frog escapes from one tight spot after another by being able to "Jump, Frog, jump!" Tell the story on a lapboard keeping puppets and props in apron pockets until needed.

Kraus, Robert. *How Spider Saved Halloween*; illus. by the author. Parents, 1980.

Spider saves Halloween for his friends Fly and Ladybug by disguising himself as a jack-o-lantern and frightening two bullies. Hide costume pieces in apron pockets.

Kwon, Holly K. *The Moles and the Mireuk*; illus. by Woodleigh Hubbard. Houghton Mifflin, 1993.

A Korean folktale about a father mole who searches the world to find the most powerful husband for his daughter. He learns that the perfect husband is really very close to home. Pull the characters Papa Mole meets from the apron pockets.

Lewis, J. Patrick. *Two-Legged, Four-Legged, No-Legged Rhymes*; illus. by Pamela Paparone. Knopf, 1991.

Eclectic collection of short animal poems perfect for telling on your lap. Try "Fantasti-Cat," "Padiddle," "Wedding Bears," "Spider," "Bartholo," and "The Hippopot." Pull puppets and props from the apron pockets. Use a lapboard as a platform for the storytelling.

Lionni, Leo. *Fish Is Fish*; illus. by the author. Pantheon Books, 1970.

Fish attempts to view the world from Frog's perspective, but quickly discovers his own view is the most satisfying. Pull scenic elements and puppets from pockets as needed.

McDermott, Gerald. *Zomo the Rabbit*; illus. by the author. Harcourt, 1992.

Zomo is a popular character in West African trickster tales. In this tale, Zomo must perform three impossible tasks before he can gain wisdom. Hide props in apron pockets. Use an anything puppet for all the other characters by taking the face needed for each character from your apron and attaching to the anything puppet as needed.

McDonald, Megan. *Is This a House for Hermit Crab?*; illus. by S. D. Schindler. Orchard, 1990.

A hermit crab searches for a new home along the seashore. Pull found objects from apron pockets for hermit crab to explore: rock, tin can, plastic pail, driftwood, fishing net, shell. Hermit crab and the pricklepine can be finger puppets or paper puppets. The other objects can be paper cutouts.

Mwenye, Hadithi. *Lazy Lion*; illus. by Adrienne Kennaway. Little, 1990.

A lazy lion is not pleased with any of the houses his animal friends build for him. So even today the lion just wanders the African plain without a house to live in. Hide homes from a hand-puppet lion until they are needed.

Silverstein, Shel. *Where the Sidewalk Ends*; illus. by the author. Harper, 1974.

This collection of poems by Shel Silverstein has enormous appeal to children.

# Chapter 20

# STORY TOTES

THE STORY TOTE serves as a suitable "home" in which a puppet dwells, as well as providing an ideal hiding place for carrying the puppet during and after the storytime. Thus it serves appropriately as home base for storing puppets and also props when not in use. This "tote-home" in its simplest form can be a shoe box, grocery sack, handbag, or it may take on a more descriptive shape such as a bird cage for a parrot puppet or a cardboard-box palace for a king.

The story tote can function in either of two ways during storytelling: as a storage unit for puppets and props or as an integral part of the story itself. The tote does not necessarily have to be incorporated into the story, but may serve simply as a storage unit. Or, it can follow a theme fitting the story. A science-fiction character could arrive in a beeping toy spaceship or a genie could reside in a glittering jewelry box. In both instances, the tote becomes a focus and link to the central idea of the story. Young children seem to take great delight in knowing that a puppet has its own special place where paraphernalia, real or imagined, can be stored. A perfect example of this application is Snoopy's doghouse. Snoopy proudly boasts of the many things he keeps inside his house, most of which we have never seen, but still they continue to titillate our imaginations. A squirrel puppet who lives in a grocery box tree may wish to follow Snoopy's example and share with the children his prized collection of stored nuts, flowers, and other find-ings salvaged from the neighborhood. Or a rabbit puppet might hide miniature books from its private library inside a cardboard tube log. Capitalize on such surprises while adding new features each time the children meet the puppet character. For example, to create holiday awareness the squirrel with the nut collection may come out at Halloween with a jack-o-lantern around which to share stories; at Christmas he may produce a supply of ornaments for the children to pin onto his tree; or he could adorn the children's heads with paper bunny ears from his cache during the Easter season.

The tote may also become an integral part of the story itself. The story examples on the following pages demonstrate several ideas incorporating totes into the storytelling. Richard Margolis's *Wish Again, Big Bear* has the fish spend a great deal of time speaking from the inside of a pail. The pail tote remains a strong focal point for almost the entire story. For this tote, utilize a cardboard paint bucket and cut a hole in the bottom in which to comfortably insert the hand for operating the fish character. In this case the pail is held over the leader's lap and interplay occurs between the fish and the leader, who takes on the main character role of the bear.

The tote approach is an obvious choice for Rita Gelman's *Hey Kid!* in which the central action focuses around a mysterious crate containing "the Thing." *The Mitten* by Jan Brett provides the opportunity to use a real mitten as a tote. Other stories may have less defined yet adaptable tote features. Therefore, with a certain amount of

**Pail tote with hole in the bottom to insert fish puppet for *Wish Again, Big Bear***

ingenuity, decorated grocery bag totes may serve as scenes for a variety of stories. A bag adorned with waves, seashells, and dried seaweed makes an ideal ocean; or two grocery bags make a dual set, one a city dwelling and the other a country cottage for "The City Mouse and Country Mouse."

Another good example for using dual bag totes is Rose Gerald's *The Tiger-Skin Rug*, a story about a tiger who disguises himself as a tiger-skin rug so he may live in a palace in India, which can be enhanced with totes used as scenic setting. Two grocery bags decorated as jungle and castle totes serve a double purpose as convenient storage units for props and puppets as well as scenic suggestion when propped up on a tabletop or floor. The two bags can have a cord stretched between them to represent the clothesline for hanging up the tiger skin.

Hand and finger puppets seem to lend themselves best to story totes since they can comfortably be hidden inside the tote and mobilized into action quickly. Small-scale totes with finger puppets make charming match mates for presenting stories. A baby bird inside a plastic egg-shaped container or a Tom Thumb character in a matchbox are fun to try. The variety of totes is unlimited. Let your imagination be your guide as you explore new combinations with puppets, containers, and story adaptations.

## EXAMPLES OF STORY TOTE PRESENTATIONS

 *Crictor*

In Tomi Ungerer's story, an elderly French lady gains a new outlook on life when she receives a boa constrictor from her son in Africa. This newly acquired pet becomes useful in several unique ways for the lady and is notably rewarded.

## Approach

Leader narrates story as the children pantomime the characters' actions in the storytelling area.

## Puppets/Props

| Characters/Props | Types/Materials |
|---|---|
| Crictor | Snake puppet or stuffed knee socks (linked together) |
| Madame Bodot Postman Burglar Policeman Mayor | Played by children without puppets |
| Hatbox tote | Round or other shaped box with lid (not necessarily a hatbox) |
| Lady's hat Baby bib Plastic baby bottle Ruler | Real objects |
| Winter clothes (tube sweater and/or winter hat) | Tube of fabric to fit Crictor |
| Snow | White paper confetti |
| Eye mask | Halloween mask or black fabric to cover eyes |
| Mouth gag | Scarf or fabric square |
| Gun | Pointed finger |
| Medal | Cardboard with ribbon and safety pin to attach to Crictor |

## Presentation

### General procedures

Assign parts to children, giving each his or her appropriate prop; position in storytelling area as designated.

Instruct the children about their actions:

Madame Bodot puts on lady's hat and sits in center of chair. (Madame Bodot also serves as puppeteer, manipulating Crictor.)

Postman holds hatbox with Crictor coiled inside and stands to far left side or out in hallway ready to approach Madame Bodot's door.

Burglar puts on eye mask, holds mouth gag, and stands to far right.

Policeman points finger in shape of gun and stands to far right, behind Burglar.

Mayor holds medal and stands to far left, behind Postman.

Hide baby bottle, bib, ruler, and Crictor's winter clothing in a box, bag, or apron pockets near Madame Bodot.

Arrange snow confetti near the leader.

### Introduction

Let the children share their experiences with unusual pets.

Then ask, "Does anyone know what a boa constrictor is?"

Discuss boa constrictors with the children, particularly where boa constrictors come from and their habits.

Then say, "I know a story about a French lady who had a boa constrictor for a pet."

### Story actions

Begin story. Postman arrives with box and gives it to Madame Bodot. (Text for "O-shaped box" may be changed to describe the box being used.)

Madame Bodot feeds her pet boa constrictor in a scene based on *Crictor*. (Photo of Penny Paraskevas by Michelle Owen)

Madame Bodot opens the box and screams.

Madame Bodot puts bib on Crictor and feeds him with a baby bottle.

Madame Bodot lays Crictor on floor and measures him with the ruler.

Madame Bodot puts winter clothes on Crictor and he wiggles about in snow while leader throws confetti into the air.

Crictor is formed into letters and numbers (children from the group may be asked to help with forming various letters and numbers with Crictor).

Crictor is used as a jumping rope (another child from audience can take other end of Crictor to turn).

Crictor is made into knots.

Burglar arrives and pretends to tie Madame Bodot to chair. He gags her.

Crictor captures the Burglar by coiling around him.

Police arrive and take Burglar away.

Mayor pins medal onto Crictor.

## Follow-Up Activities

Let the children think up stories about other animals that would make unusual pets.

Have children form teams and present their own versions of this story with paper-bag, envelope, or other puppets.

 *Wish Again, Big Bear*

A bear catches a Wish-Fish and has his wishes granted in this story by Richard J. Margolis. However, in the process the two main characters find that what originated as trickery on the part of the fish eventually develops into a new and meaningful friendship.

## Approach

Leader narrates story using Fish puppet in a bucket tote, while wearing paper bear ears and assuming the additional role of Big Bear. Leader uses varied voices: a normal voice for narration, a deep voice for Big Bear, and a high voice for the Fish.

## Puppets/Props

| Characters/Props | Types/Materials |
|---|---|
| Big Bear | Paper bear ears |
| Fish | Envelope or hand puppet |
| Pond | Large grocery bag, decorated |
| Fish net | Fish net or vegetable strainer |
| Pail | Ice cream container or paper paint bucket (available at hardware store) |
| Bush | Real twig in pot |
| Bubbles | Bubble-blowing set |
| Bread crumbs | Real |

## Presentation

### General procedures

Open grocery bag pond, place Fish inside; arrange on floor in front of you.

Put bucket and net to one side.

### Introduction

Have the children share their wishes.

Ask, "Have you ever made a wish that came true?"

"What would you wish for if you could have anything you wanted?"

"I know a story about someone who caught a very unusual fish—it was a Wish-Fish."

### Story actions

Begin story. Pick up net and "catch" Fish in bag pond.

Hold up Fish and vigorously flop it around in net.

Provide coughing and gasping sounds for Fish.

Drop Fish in bucket.

Fish laughs (blow bubbles).

Fish chants poem.

Big Bear dances and falls.

Fish laughs.

Fish chants poem.

Bear appears puzzled over his "smallness."

Cover Fish's eyes with your hand.

Big Bear hides behind imaginary bush, then fans himself with it.

Feed Fish bread crumbs.

Big Bear attempts to swallow Fish, then puts him back in bag pond.

### Follow-Up Activities

Repeat story, asking a child to pantomime actions of Big Bear.

Have children make their own paper envelope Wish-Fish and bag ponds. Ask children to find some-one to "catch" their fish and make three wishes, just as Big Bear did.

### SUGGESTED TITLES FOR STORY TOTES

Bernstein, Margery, and Janet Kobrin. *The First Morning: An African Myth*; illus. by Enid Warner Romanek. Scribner, 1976.

Mouse, Spider, and Fly bring light to the earth in this African myth. Hold a red box tote on your lap when telling the story. At appropriate moment open box and take out rooster puppet. When rooster crows, the sun (rod puppet) rises.

Brett, Jan. *The Mitten*; illus. by the author. Putnam, 1989.

Forest animals crowd into a lost mitten until it finally bursts. Pull finger puppet characters from a mitten tote.

Bruchac, Joseph. *Native American Animal Stories*; illus. by John Kahionhes Fadden and David Kanietakeron Fadden. Fulcrum, 1992.

A large, brightly colored shopping bag makes a perfect tote for the story "How Butterflies Came to Be." Children can draw colored flowers and leaves to place in the tote. Storyteller adds the remaining ingredients. As the butterfly stick puppets "fly" out of the bag, play a tape-recording of flute or harp music.

Florian, Douglas. *Monster Motel*; illus. by the author. Harcourt, 1993.

Poems about the monstrous dwellers of the horrid Monster Motel. Residents include the Slender Slimy Snatch, the Crim, and the Fabled Feerz. Decorate a large bag or box as the Monster Motel. Pull out each inhabitant as you recite the poem.

Harris, Joel Chandler. "The Tar Baby," in *Jump Again!*; adapted by Van Dyke Parks; illus. by Barry Moser. Harcourt, 1987. Pp. 6–13.

Brer Fox uses a tar baby to catch Brer Rabbit. But Brer Rabbit escapes by tricking Brer Fox into throw-ing him into the Briar Patch. A grocery bag or box can be converted into a very convincing briar patch by attaching twigs to it.

Lionni, Leo. *Swimmy*; illus. by the author. Pantheon, 1963.

A decorated paper-bag ocean tote not only pro-vides scenery, it also becomes a storage container for the underwater creatures in this story. A Caldecott Honor book.

MacDonald, Margaret Reed. "The Old Woman in a Pumpkin Shell," in *Celebrate the World*. Wilson, 1994. Pp. 61–67.

A folktale from Iran about a woman who hides in a pumpkin shell from animals that want to eat her. A plastic Halloween pumpkin makes an appropriate tote.

Margolis, Richard. *Wish Again, Big Bear*; illus. by Robert Lopshire. Macmillan, 1972.

A friendship develops between a bear and the Wish-Fish he catches.

Petersham, Maud and Miska. *The Box with Red Wheels*; illus. by the authors. Macmillan, 1949. (Paperback: Collier, 1973.)

Farm animals investigate a strange-looking box with red wheels, which contains a baby.

Rose, Gerald. *The Tiger-Skin Rug*; illus. by the author. Prentice-Hall, 1979.

A hungry tiger imitates a tiger-skin rug to gain entrance to the palace where he saves the family from robbers. Decorate paper-bag totes to represent the jungle and the palace.

Sloat, Teri. *The Hungry Giant of the Tundra*; illus. by Robert and Teri Sloat. Dutton, 1993.

In a Yupik tale from Alaska, Akaguagankak, the giant of the tundra, collects children for his meal and drops them into his trouser bag. With the help of a strong-beaked chickadee and crane-with-the-long-legs, the children escape. A cloth bag makes a fitting tote, into which finger puppet children are dropped.

Takabatake, Jun. *Rub-A-Dub-Dub Who's in the Tub?*; illus. by the author. Chronicle Books, 1991.

At bath time, a little boy creates a variety of soap-suds animals who fill up the tub until finally there's no more room and everyone has to get out of the tub. Give a child a sponge and a bucket filled with white styrofoam packing material. As the child "Rub-a-dub-dubs" pull a puppet or stuffed animal from the bucket and place it in a bathtub box tote.

Ungerer, Tomi. *Crictor*; illus. by the author. Harper, 1958.

An amusing story of an old lady who has a boa constrictor as a pet.

*Chapter 21*

# TABLETOP THEATERS

**S**INCE TABLES HAVE so many functions, we rarely think of them as a tool for puppetry. However, the top of a table can be transformed into an informal theater with minimal preparation and with very satisfactory results. There are two methods of tabletop puppetry: frontal and perimeter styles of presentation.

sentation. Stand-up cardboard panels or cutaway grocery cartons can be cut out and painted to create the detailed frontal sets these and other stories may require. A colorful circus tent, an Italian village, or a cityscape to match a particular story could be fun to try. If you need a custom set built, consider asking an artistic child to create one for you.

## FRONTAL SETS

In the frontal set the scenes, props, and puppets, arranged in linear fashion along the tabletop, are in full view of the audience who sit in front. The storyteller may either stand or sit in back of or to the side of the set. Scenery constructed from boxes or stand-up panels, painted or cut to represent any imaginable scene outdoors or indoors, may be arranged as backdrops.

Arlene Mosel's *Tikki Tikki Tembo*, a story in which a boy's overly long name creates near disaster when his little brother calls for help, is suited to the frontal set for depicting the exciting Chinese landscape featuring the two jutting hilltops and nestling bamboo cottages. The classic "Gunniwolf" is another example for tabletop pre-

Tabletop presentation of "The Gunniwolf" (Photo of Connie Champlin by Michelle Owen)

216

Puppets that serve this method best are stand-up puppets made from milk cartons or from oatmeal, cereal, pudding, cosmetic, or other similar boxes. Simply adding paper feet to the bottoms of puppets allows them to be maneuvered around the set artfully. Another type of puppet appropriate for use with a frontal-type table setting is the free-hanging hand-type puppet in which the hand is placed behind or inside the puppet's head and the body hangs down freely. A puppet constructed with a paper plate, cup, or box head allows the hand to manipulate the head as the paper body hangs securely from the neck area. This puppet is usually held above table level and moved through the set components with relative ease.

## PERIMETER SETS

The perimeter set is one in which the viewers may stand or sit *around* the table, so that the actions may be viewed from all four sides. A unique characteristic of this approach is the addition of a groundscape that establishes an aerial view in three dimensions, as contrasted with the flat elevation view of the frontal set. Perimeter style may include sidewalks, rivers, gardens, and other pathways to give visual interest to the scene and provide a place for puppets to walk and meander along the table's surface.

An important feature of the perimeter set is that puppets can ambulate or travel throughout the set, and stories can be chosen on that basis. "Little Red Riding Hood" and "The Gingerbread Boy" are familiar stories in which characters can experience interesting travel sequences among the set's groundscape, following pathways through the woods. The travel sequence can also occur over an ocean, solar system, or other sets in addition to the typically conceived groundscape. Islands floating in a blue ocean or planets and stars against a black groundscape are all interesting ideas to explore. When appropriate, the characters may travel by boat or spaceship. Sets may also be arranged on the floor for informal story sessions or to serve children with a disability.

The walking finger puppet is ideal to use with the perimeter set. It can be a figure drawn on cardboard, a cutout image from a magazine or greeting card, or some other picture. Stapling a small rubber band across the back or cutting two holes in the puppet allows fingers to serve as walking legs throughout the story's actions. Small-scale stand-up puppets also invite direct audience participation in the perimeter method. Since viewers are close at hand, the storyteller simply asks the audience to join in the story by operating the puppets along the groundscape and providing dialogue.

The details of the sets may be as simple or as elaborate as one chooses. Improvise buildings, trees, planets, ships, etc., from boxes and other throwaways. The addition of plastic bubble or polystyrene-foam packaging materials will give outer space sets an ethereal touch. Cardboard tubes serve well as stand-up trees with cardboard bases and green fringed paper foliage. Search for ready-made items to produce instant sets, such as plants, for a forest or garden; fish bowls, for an aquatic theme; or a variety of toys (cars, trucks, trains, fences, barns, etc.), for appropriate themes, to facilitate set building. Groundscapes can be painted on mural paper and may be cut to fit the entire length of the tabletop or even several tabletops. Painted roads, sidewalks, and other features can be clearly marked off. Dried flowers and grasses, sand, and pebbles will define garden areas or shorelines for beaches. Special paper overlays can be used to create certain effects. Aluminum foil makes a frozen pond; shiny blue paper or sandwich-wrap over a blue painted area makes an ideal lake. Jungles and botanical gardens can be improvised from wallpapers with flowered motifs.

Once a set is built, it may become a backdrop on which to display books when not in use in a puppet presentation. Children will undoubtedly gravitate to the set for spontaneous and creative play during free time. Consequently, the tabletop theater will be used for more than storytelling alone.

Stand-up box puppets for Toby Tinker (left) and for the ghost from *The Bump in the Night*. The ghost is made of assorted boxes that come apart.

## EXAMPLES OF TABLETOP STORIES

### *The Bump in the Night* (frontal style)

A disjointed ghost and previous owner of a castle appears unexpectedly one night down a chimney shaft in this Anne Rockwell story. Toby Tinker helps the ghost reassemble itself and is rewarded with a treasure.

### Approach

Story is narrated by leader while sitting to one side of table. Some children provide sound effect of "bumps" while other children sit in storytelling area.

### Puppets/Props

| Characters/Props | Types/Materials |
| --- | --- |
| Toby Tinker | Box stand-up puppet |
| Ghost | Stand-up puppet made from several boxes or tubes (comes apart in sections— use double-stick tape to assemble) |
| Turnaround castle | Cutaway box, showing inside and outside |
| Olive tree | Tube with green fringe |
| Pot | Real |
| Tools | |
| Spoon | |
| Silver ring | |
| Bag of copper coins | |

### Presentation

#### General procedures

Place castle on table with outside facing audience.

Arrange olive tree and treasures to one end of table.

Hide puppets and props behind castle.

Choose and instruct children to thump their hands on tabletop when cued for "bump" sound.

**Introduction**

Encourage children to share with one another stories about haunted houses they have seen or of which they know. Why do they think these houses are haunted? What things might happen in a haunted house? What sounds might be heard?

**Story actions**

Begin story.

Cue children at appropriate times to make "bump" sound.

Bring Toby Tinker around to front of castle.

Show Toby's tools and have him tinker on a pot with them.

Turn castle around to show inside.

"Bump!" Leg of Ghost falls down fireplace.

Repeat with second leg, body, and arms.

Toby assembles parts of Ghost.

"Bump!" Head of Ghost falls down fireplace.

Place head of Ghost on puppet.

Toby Tinker and Ghost search in garden for the silver ring, spoon, and bag of copper.

Ghost goes away from castle.

**Follow-Up Activities**

Children assemble their own versions of ghosts from a variety of throwaway materials. Find haunted places for ghosts to live, such as castle, house, school, or library.

Display the following books about ghosts and haunted places:

Gage, Wilson. *My Stars, It's Mrs. Gaddy!*; illus. by Marilyn Hafner. Greenwillow, 1991.

Kimmel, Eric. *Hershel and the Hanukkah Goblins*; illus. by Trina Schart Hyman. Holiday, 1989.

San Souci, Robert. *Boy and the Ghost*; illus. by Brian Pinkney. Simon & Schuster, 1989.

Taylor, C. J. *Ghost and Lone Warrior: An Arapaho Legend*; illus. by the author. Childrens Press, 1991.

Yep, Lawrence. *Man Who Tricked a Ghost*; illus. by Isadore Seltzer. BridgeWater, 1993.

Tabletop theater for "Little Red Riding Hood." The walking finger puppets are made from cardboard cutouts; small rubber bands are stapled across the back for fingers. The bridge is made from paper plates; the tree from a tube; and the house from a box.

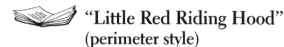 ## "Little Red Riding Hood"
(perimeter style)

The popular story of a young girl who visits her grandmother and finds a wolf instead.

### Approach

Leader narrates story while children pantomime the action with puppets.

### Puppets/Props

| Characters/Props | Types/Materials |
| --- | --- |
| Little Red Riding Hood Granny Wolf Woodsman | Walking finger puppets |
| Groundscape showing river and pathways | Mural paper or felt |
| Granny's house | Large box (cut away roof or back wall to enter house) |
| Bed | Small box |
| Trees | Cardboard tubes with paper fringe |
| Bridge | Paper plates |

### Presentation

#### General procedures

Children stand around perimeter of table and perform actions while leader narrates.

Assign parts to children and explain the general action sequence to them. Let them practice walking their characters along pathways.

Place Granny in bed, wolf behind a tree, woodsman in woods, and Little Red Riding Hood at beginning of pathway.

#### Introduction

Elicit from the children their experiences of being lost.

Ask, "Have you ever been lost?"

"How did you feel when you discovered you were lost?"

"How did you find your way again?"

#### Story actions

Begin story.

Little Red Riding Hood follows the path over the bridge into the woods.

Little Red Riding Hood meets Wolf.

Wolf takes shortcut to Grandmother's house.

Wolf takes Granny's place in bed.

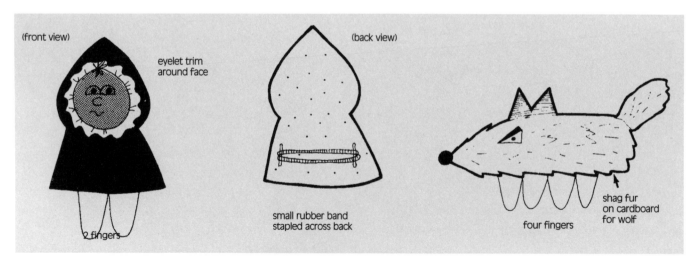

**Walking finger puppet construction for Little Red Riding Hood and a wolf**

Little Red Riding Hood mistakes Wolf for Granny.
Wolf chases Little Red Riding Hood around room.
Woodsman slays Wolf.

### Follow-Up Activities

Give the children large sheets of construction paper on which to draw and color their own groundscapes and pathways for a "Little Red Riding Hood" presentation. Let them construct simple walking finger puppets to follow pathways.

Children delight in a revamped version of this tale with the substitution of other creatures. For example, "Little Red Riding Hood" could be converted into an all mice cast and be called "Little Red Riding Mouse."

## Construction of Walking Finger Puppet

### Materials

Stiff paper, tagboard, or poster board

Scrap materials and trim

Small rubber band

Plastic craft eyes (optional)

### Procedures

Draw and cut out characters from stiff paper. Magazine or reproduced pictures can also be glued to stiff paper to create characters quickly. A wolf and other furry animals can be made by covering paper with a layer of soft fake fur or velour fabric.

Use felt-tip marking pens to color in features. Costumes, lace, and other trim can be used to embellish a character; add eyes.

Then staple rubber band across lower back of puppet for fingers.

### Operation

Slip fingers down under rubber band and "walk" fingers across set.

## SUGGESTED TITLES FOR TABLETOP THEATERS

### Frontal Presentations

Bryan, Ashley. *The Ox of the Wonderful Horns and Other African Folktales*; illus. by the author. Atheneum, 1993.

Five stories from Africa, four are full of fun and the title story is a wonder tale. Create a frontal style tabletop jungle to tell "Frog and His Two Wives" and "Elephant and Frog Go Courting."

Compton, Patricia A. *The Terrible Eek*; illus. by Shelia Hamanaka. Simon & Schuster, 1991.

A humorous Japanese tale about a family saved from a thief and a wolf by a misunderstanding. Boxes can serve as the home and trees. Stand-up puppets will allow the storyteller to manipulate the needed characters easily.

Dunbar, Joyce. *Seven Sillies*; illus. by Chris Downing. Golden Books, 1993.

Six farm animals become entranced by their reflections in a pond until Frog tricks them. But it is Frog who turns out to be the silliest of all. A long piece of blue material or paper spread along the front of a table can serve as the pond.

Harper, Wilhelmina, reteller. *The Gunniwolf*; illus. by William Wiesner. Dutton, 1967.

A little girl meets a gunniwolf one day when she is walking through the jungle gathering flowers.

Kent, Jack. *Little Peep*; illus. by the author. Prentice-Hall, 1981.

All the barnyard animals warn baby chick not to annoy the rooster because he might get angry and refuse to crow and keep the sun from coming up.

How chick and the other animals learn that the rooster crows because the sun comes up and not the reverse makes an amusing story.

Mosel, Arlene. *Tikki Tikki Tembo*; illus. by Blair Lent. Holt, 1968.

> An extremely long name almost proves disastrous for a young Chinese boy.

Polushkin, Maria. *Mother, Mother, I Want Another*; illus. by the author. Crown, 1978.

> Baby Mouse's request for "another, Mother" sets off a misunderstanding that is finally resolved when he gets his wish—another kiss, not another mother.

Rockwell, Anne. *The Bump in the Night*; illus. by the author. Greenwillow, 1979.

> Toby Tinker helps a ghost reassemble itself and is rewarded with a treasure.

"The Tiger, the Brahman, and the Jackal," in *Favorite Stories Told in India* by Virginia Haviland; illus. by Blair Lent. Little, 1973.

> The jackal helps a wise man outwit a tiger.

## Perimeter Presentations

Barrows, Walt, and Bernard Zaretsky. "The Little White Duck," in *Eye Winker, Tom Tinker, Chin Chopper* by Tom Glazer; illus. by Ron Himler. Doubleday, 1973. Pp. 46–47.

> Song about a little white duck who meets a frog, a bug, and a snake while floating in the water.

Grimm, Jacob. *Little Red Riding Hood*; illus. by Trina Schart Hyman. Holiday, 1983.

> Trina Schart Hyman's illustrations add greatly to the enjoyment of this traditional tale. A Caldecott Honor book.

Johnson, Crockett. *Harold's Trip to the Sky*; illus. by the author. Harper, 1957.

> A little boy's trip through the sky is illustrated in an unusual manner with line drawings on black background. The concept could be cleverly presented with a puppet accompanied by or constructing improvised chalk drawings on a skyscape.

Marshall, Edward. *Space Case*; illus. by James Marshall. Dial, 1980.

> A creature from the unknown visits earth and receives an unfriendly reception. It adapts by fitting into a procession of trick-and-treaters on Halloween night and befriends an earthling who tries to make it feel at home. Boxes can designate the various houses linked together by pathways on a groundscape for use by walking finger puppets.

Mwalimu. *Awful Aardvark*; illus. by Adrienne Kennedy. Little, 1989.

> In this original African story, Aardvark keeps all the animals awake with his snoring. With the help of Rhinoceros, the animals solve their problem as well as provide an explanation for why the Aardvark now sleeps all day and searches for termites at night. Use a box for the tree on which a hand puppet aardvark sleeps.

San Souci, Robert D. *The Hobyahs*; illus. by Alexi Natchev. Doubleday, 1994.

> Five loyal dogs protect their mistress from the menacing Hobyahs. Tell the tale with stand-up puppets and a box house.

Taylor, Harriet Peck. *Coyote and the Laughing Butterflies*; illus. by the author. Macmillan, 1995.

> The butterflies play a trick on Coyote in this amusing Tewa Indian legend. A group puppet using a series of wires with a butterfly on the tip of each will effectively convey the fluttering of the butterflies as they carry Coyote from the salty lake to his home. Coyote can be a walking finger puppet, and the animals he meets can be stand-up box puppets.

# Part Six

# AFTER THE STORY

**Troll puppet made from a pudding box**

**O**NCE THE STORY is over, you may wish to try related activities to add a creative, personalizing dimension to what has gone before. Included in this chapter are examples of varying levels of participation by children—from tabletop displays to deeper involvement in problem solving and creative dramatics.

Specific projects for increasing language skills might include designing new dialogue and actions for story characters, writing letters to puppet characters, or presenting a formal puppet-show version of a story. Additionally, children might brainstorm possible answers to "what if" questions about characters or forecast how a character will look or behave in the future. Imagination is stretched and motor skills are developed as children reenact the story through creative dramatics or constructing a puppet version of a character.

These activities may be simple or complex depending on time and objectives—but involvement of the child is what makes them worthwhile. All such exercises elicit from the child thinking skills on a higher level than those required for supplying factual information at the literal comprehension level.

Choosing the appropriate project for specific goals is an important step in wise utilization of these activities. Nothing grandiose is required, however. For example, having just shared *The Tomten*, a story about trolls by Astrid Lindgren, a simple goal of extending the children's repertoire of troll stories might lead to the development of an interest center. Such a center may include a variety of books, videos, and/or other media depicting trolls in the folklore of various cultures. Children might be asked to make a troll puppet, compare trolls in several stories, or locate and display illustrations of trolls by various artists.

# Chapter 22

# THE STORY'S OVER; WHAT'S NEXT?

NY STORY CAN be reinforced and enriched by the addition of a related follow-up puppet activity.

## DISPLAYS

Displaying puppets and books after a story is a traditional but surefire way of making the preceding story memorable, while at the same time opening children's eyes to new avenues of content and expression. Matching a set of puppets with a storybook is an invitation to informal dramatization. Feature a different story weekly to heighten anticipation and sustain interest based on the initial set of puppets. Story poems and folk songs sprinkled among the stories will provide novelty. As children use the puppets to create original dialogue or to portray their own adapted versions of the story, enjoyment of the literature will be extended and language skills increased.

## Tabletop Displays

One simple display technique is that of propping up puppets with pop bottles or weighted plastic bottles in an eye-catching arrangement on a table, desk, or bookcase. Books may be matched to their puppet characters with the purpose of encouraging children to read, dramatize, or tell the stories on their own.

A tabletop may easily serve as a "farm" on which barns, silos, and other farm buildings made from paper boxes are situated. For the story *Ornery Morning* by Patricia Brennan Demuth, one merely needs to add a few barnyard puppets for children to have great fun guiding the puppets through a retelling of the story. This same set may be used for other farm stories with simple rearrangement of scenery. Other themes, such as sea life or outer space, may also be cleverly displayed on the tops of large pieces of furniture.

## Wall Hangings

A more elaborate display area may be created by painting a background appropriate to the story on mural paper and tacking it onto the wall or standing it behind the table. Children can participate by decorating the scene with appropriate elements—flowers and trees for an exterior scene, furniture for an interior scene. Consider incorporating large manila envelopes or paper pockets into the mural scene to hold the puppets.

A single tree or complete forest theme mural background offers a wealth of possible related activities for a

A Halloween cast of characters in manila-envelope pockets occupies a forest mural wall hanging.

**225**

story with a forest setting. Add paper pockets for puppets among the branches of the trees to serve as hideaways. A nest and a knothole would also be delightful places in which to store puppets. Many songs, poems, and stories naturally fit in with the tree and nature theme. The more popular might include: *The Tortoise and the Tree* by Janina Domanska: *Goodnight Owl!* by Pat Hutchins; *Mousekin's Close Call* by Edna Miller; *In the Eyes of the Cat: Japanese Poetry for All Seasons*, selected by Demi; and *Are You My Mother?* by P. D. Eastman.

Puppet characters temporarily living in the tree may be changed to represent a variety of stories, seasons, and holidays. At Halloween, a witch, a bat, a black cat, a vampire, and even a talking pumpkin may suddenly take up residence in the tree. Try any of the poems from *Nightmares or Poems to Trouble Your Sleep* by Jack Prelutsky for a chilling opening to a Halloween story hour.

Later, transform the puppet tree into a winter wonderland with the addition of cotton puffs or paper snowflakes. Storytelling sessions held under the tree might include stories, poems, or songs about the winter season and its holidays.

As a follow-up to stories about animal or human families, you might introduce a host family of animal puppets who have taken up residence in the tree. Sam could be introduced as a special friend of the children and could lead discussions about how squirrels gather food, why they live in trees, and other facts about the life of a squirrel. He may also help emcee story time, introduce holidays and seasons, and give library or classroom tours to mothers and fathers.

Later Sam may want to introduce Sarah Squirrel, his sweetheart, to the children. And shortly after, they would naturally announce their engagement. Would the children want to help in planning the wedding and reception? Of course they would! With Sarah's arrival on the scene there would be two puppets to choose from to serve as host for story time and related activities!

Baby, Stanley Squirrel, is next to make an appearance. The proud parents will want to show off their darling child. Sam and Sarah will need a small box-cradle to hang on the tree. Would the children help build it? Some children may locate or write poems to honor the new arrival. Others may wish to sing lullabies or recite Mother Goose rhymes. This is a perfect opportunity to tell stories about other baby animals, such as *Am I Beautiful?* by Else Holmelund Minarik.

## Clothesline Displays

Suspending a length of clothesline between bookcases or windows, or across a bulletin board, was discussed

Clothesline characters—and real socks—for "The Night Before Christmas"

Various tote displays (top to bottom)—
boot, hatbox, cereal box, and box converted into a skyscraper

earlier as a unique method of displaying puppets. Puppets are easily "hung" on the clothesline with clothespins. Children will relive a story over and over as the puppet characters continue to catch their eye. Thematic clothesline displays are exciting to explore. Imagine the colorful sight made by original puppets of holiday characters for "The Night before Christmas" or of water creatures based on the African folktale *Why the Sun and Moon Live in the Sky*. Likewise, the children could be artistically challenged to design large puppets to accompany the poems about months in *Alligators and Others All Year Long!* by Crescent Dragonwagon.

## Tote Displays

Many of the objects we take for granted every day have the potential to become unique display cases for puppets and props. Here are a few ideas for a start!

*Cloth shoe bag.* This pocketed hideaway is a perfect resting place for a collection of hand puppet characters, such as Mr. Gumpy and his animal friends from John Burningham's story *Mr. Gumpy's Outing.*

*Aquarium.* Fill with aquatic finger puppets, such as the creatures highlighted in David McCord's

poems "Sunfish," "Frog Music," and "The Starfish" in *One at a Time.*

*Flowerpots.* In each of several dirt-filled pots, stand a stick puppet for one of the characters from *The Grouchy Ladybug* by Eric Carle. On the front of each pot, paste a number for the time of day the character appears.

*Laundry baskets or shopping carts.* These are appropriate for any story with a large cast of puppet characters. Rod puppets for use in the story *Too Much Noise* by Ann McGovern will stand comfortably in such large spaces.

*Cowboy hat.* A natural setting that is indeed appropriate for such tall-tale puppet characters as Pecos Bill; his wife, Slue Foot Sue; and his horse, Widow Maker.

*Shoe or boot.* Such footwear can easily accommodate finger or hand puppets of "The Old Woman Who Lived in a Shoe" and her many children, or the characters from the popular Grimm story of "The Elves and the Shoemaker."

*Clothes tree.* The arms become ideal branches for the monkeys and the peddler from *Caps for Sale* by Esphyr Slobodkina.

*Hatbox. Crictor,* the boa constrictor of Tomi Ungerer's popular story, would love to be transported in a spacious hatbox.

*Egg carton.* Egg "cups" are just right for a finger puppet collection of nursery-rhyme characters.

*Boxes.* All kinds of large and small boxes can be adapted to serve as skyscrapers, barns, castles, haystacks, and almost any other backdrop desired. Cereal boxes are suitable choices for displaying the city mouse and the country mouse from the well-known fable.

## THE PUPPET CORNER

A colorful addition to any classroom or library is the "Puppet Corner." Designate a little-used section of the room as a puppet corner, a special area devoted exclusively to puppets and their exploration. When children have the opportunity to experiment with puppets on their own, they discover personal ways of using puppets inventively. Gather the puppets together in interesting containers—baskets, brightly covered cartons, or one of the display ideas described above. Arrange collections of poems, fairy tales, picture books, and songs nearby. The space need not be large but should be out of the main traffic flow.

### Posting Signs

Post signs near your puppet corner display to give it further interest and focus. Illustrated signs with messages like these will encourage exploration!

| Find a Story, Act It Out | Sing a Song with a Puppet Partner! | Poetry Pals Available Here |
|---|---|---|

### Prop Collection

Set up a series of small baskets or boxes containing a variety of props to enhance storytelling and spontaneous puppet play by children. Props will help stimulate children to find new ways to improvise stories with puppets. These need not be elaborate. Children's vivid imaginations will extend the use of even the simplest props. Some props to have on hand to spark creative thinking include:

Toy or rhythm instruments

Plastic bowls and play dishes

Wooden spoons and other utensils

Toy telephone, vehicles, doll furniture, etc.

Tinkertoy and building blocks

Small boxes and other containers

Noisemakers and party hats

Feathers of assorted sizes

Costume jewelry

Ribbons, scarves, pieces of lace

Feather duster, dish mop, sponge.

### Stages

A puppet stage can brighten up the puppet corner as well as encourage informal play by children. Some children will take delight in using puppets on an improvisational level as a follow-up activity after hearing a story. They enjoy retelling stories in their own words. Arrange puppets, props, and sound makers near the stage so children can gravitate to this particular spot during spare time and feel free to interpret the story in an unstructured atmosphere. The focus of this technique should be to promote language skills and foster story comprehension on a spontaneous level, rather than to recite a script for an audience on a more formal level.

## Stage Suppliers

The following is a sample of suppliers of informal stages who offer quality products at reasonable prices:

Brodart, a library products company, offers stages. Write to: P.O. Box 3037, 1609 Memorial Avenue, Williamsport, PA 17705.

Gaylord Bros., Inc. markets a lightweight, plastic corrugated small stage with window opening suitable for informal tabletop performances. Order #L 104. Write to: Gaylord Bros., Inc., Box 61, Syracuse, NY 13201.

The Puppetry Store, a service of the Puppeteers of America, is a good source of information about stages. The store carries a number of books on stage construction. There is a small charge for a catalog. Write to: The Puppetry Store, 1525 - 24th S.E., Auburn, WA 98002-7837.

Nancy Renfro Studios will build custom stages for storytellers and puppeteers. Write to: Nancy Renfro Studios, 3312 Pecan Springs Road, Austin, TX 78723.

## INTEREST CENTERS

Interest centers may help provide focus for children who are just beginning to experiment with puppets. An interest center contains one or more activities which children may choose to do independently or with others. All interest centers have two common objectives for children: (1) to learn to read and follow specific directions independently and (2) to decide how to accomplish the required task. Individual tasks should be designed to accomplish additional specific objectives. Depending on the age and ability of the children, such objectives may include strengthening written communication skills; developing motor coordination; increasing problem-solving ability; using information in an original way.

It is necessary that all materials required for interest center activities be easily accessible to the children. Directions are typed or printed on large cards and must be clear and easy to follow. Most interest center activities are designed to be performed by children without assistance. Projects that require the child's reactions to stories through various media can be incorporated into interest centers. These may include: designing new puppet versions of characters; audiotaping an alternative conclusion for a story; writing letters to puppets; using puppets in combination with a multimedia version of a story.

Print the directions for the following interest center ideas on the outside of large manila envelopes. Puppet-making materials and other related supplies needed to complete the activity may be kept inside the envelope. In this way directions for children to follow and materials necessary for the completion of each project are conveniently packaged as a total unit.

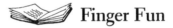 **Finger Fun**

### Materials

Collection of finger puppets. A variety of finger puppets are available from the Mary Meyer Corporation, P.O. Box 275, Townshend, VT 05353-0275.

### Directions

1. Find the puppets for one story and tell the story using the puppets.
    "The Three Bears"
    "The Three Little Pigs"
    "Little Red Riding Hood"
    "The Three Billy Goats Gruff"
2. Make up a new story using at least four of the puppets in the kit.
3. Give your story an exciting title.
4. Share your story with a friend.

 ## Meet Martha and Elmer

### Materials

Two large hand puppets—a yellow bird and a purple dragon. However, any two large hand puppets that are contrasting in appearance can be used.

Letter writing paper and pencils

Drawing paper and crayons

Bulletin board

### Directions

1. Introduce yourself to Martha, who is a yellow bird.
2. Introduce yourself to Elmer, who is a purple dragon.
3. Try them on your hand.
4. Talk to them.
5. Write a letter or draw a picture asking them something about themselves.
6. Put the letter or picture in the envelope.
7. In a few days check the bulletin board for the answer to your question.

Primary children will enjoy writing to Martha and Elmer. The letters might be answered by the characters with the help of fifth and sixth graders. The letters and their answers may then be posted on a bulletin board near the interest center.

## Build a Puppet Show for "Jack and the Beanstalk"

### Materials

An audiotape and book of the story "Jack and the Beanstalk." (Scholastic produces a cassette and book set of this title.)

Drawing paper

Crayons

Felt-tip markers

Popsicle sticks or drinking straws

Tape

Cassette player

Prepare envelope beforehand by marking the outside with check-off boxes indicating characters and scenery components:

**Characters**
- ☐ Jack
- ☐ Jack's mother
- ☐ Man
- ☐ Giant
- ☐ Giant's wife

**Scenery/Props**
- ☐ Jack's house
- ☐ Beanstalk
- ☐ Giant's house
- ☐ Bag of gold
- ☐ Hen
- ☐ Harp

### Directions

1. Listen to the story and read along with the tape.
2. Make a stick puppet of a character from one of the unchecked boxes on the envelope. Put the puppet in the envelope and put a check in the box for that character.
3. If all the boxes are checked, make one piece of scenery that is needed. Put the scenery in the envelope and check the appropriate box.
4. Put everything back in the envelope when done.

The next person using the center will likewise choose and make a character or scenery item from the unchecked boxes. When all the characters and scenery have been completed, they will be used in the follow-up interest center "Listen and Act."

**Listen and Act**

### Materials

Puppets and scenery from Build
and Puppet Show for "Jack and
the Beanstalk" interest center

Tape and book of the story

Cassette player

### Directions

1. Listen to the tape and read along with the book.
2. Rewind the tape.
3. Now listen to the tape again as you act out the story using the puppets.
4. Use the puppets and retell the story in your own words. (Optional enrichment activity)
5. Create a new story about the puppet characters from this story. You may want to do this with a friend. (Optional enrichment activity)

### "What If . . ." Situations

One interest center might be devoted to "what if" questions. Present a situation based on a story which has recently been shared that will challenge children to look at the story from a new perspective. Consider the suggestion that follows. Would a new factor change the story? How? For example:

"What if Rapunzel had short hair?" or "What if Little Miss Muffet liked spiders?" or "What if Cinderella's stepmother were kind and beautiful?"

Children will prove adept at improvising different versions of the story based on the "what if" questions.

Write out the "what if" questions on cards and place them in an envelope. Blank cards should be included for the responses of the children. Provide an opportunity for children to share and discuss their ideas.

An alternative to "what if" questions is to request youngsters to portray story characters as they might look in the future. How does a child perceive Little Red Riding Hood when she is a grandmother; Leo in *Leo, the Late Bloomer* when he is an adult; or Max of *Where the Wild Things Are* should he be transformed into a beast? Simply provide drawing materials and "futuristic" questions to find yourself awed by the children's portrayals.

## STORY KITS

For very popular special stories, rhymes, and poems build a collection of puppet story kits. Examine the plot of the story and decide which characters are essential. Think about the scenery needed to suggest the locale. Only those scenic elements significant to the action line, such as the bridge in "The Three Billy Goats Gruff," need be included. Most other scenery may be imagined. Also consider which props, if any, are crucial to the forward movement of the story. An excellent example is the pebble in *Sylvester and the Magic Pebble*. Refer to chapter 20, Story Totes, for a more detailed examination of this idea.

In a sturdy box with a lid, or some other suitable container, place the following:

Puppets

A copy of the book or story

Simple props and scenery

Related audiovisual materials.

Place the kit in an accessible location so that individual children or small groups can use it to retell a favorite story.

 ### There's a Nightmare in My Closet

A story kit for *There's a Nightmare in My Closet* by Mercer Mayer might include:

Boy and Monster (hand puppets)

Some plastic toys

Toy gun

Helmet (small plastic bowl)

Book: *There's a Nightmare in My Closet.*

### The Amazing Bone

A story kit for *The Amazing Bone* by William Steig might include the following puppets and props:

Pig and Fox (hand puppets)

Mother and Father Pig (stick puppets)

Bone (chicken bone)

Child's purse

Small cooking pot

Robber (mask for Father Pig to wear)

Book: *The Amazing Bone.*

### "Humpty Dumpty"

The story kit for the nursery rhyme "Humpty Dumpty" might consist of:

Humpty Dumpty puppet (a plastic egg)

King's horses and men (a picture)

Wall (toy brick or small decorated box).

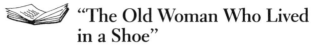 ### "The Old Woman Who Lived in a Shoe"

The story kit for the nursery rhyme "The Old Woman Who Lived in a Shoe" could include:

Old woman (thread-spool puppet)

Shoe or boot

Children (cardboard cutout of many children).

Since the kits will be used repeatedly to bring cherished stories to life, be sure that the puppets included are sturdy and made of washable materials. Also, be sure that all items are safe for children to use as well as childproof. Periodically check the boxes, cleaning puppets and replacing other items as needed. A check-off list of items in the boxes will be helpful in keeping inventory of missing items.

## INSTANT PUPPETS

Children love to make puppets, especially of characters newly met or revisited in a story. Many ordinary objects not usually associated with puppetry can be transformed into instant puppets quickly and inexpensively for "after the story" activities. These puppets can be used immediately to highlight story participation and then taken home as a special friend. Ideas follow for instant puppet making.

*Hand.* A fist becomes a puppet with the addition of features drawn with water soluble felt-tip markers. To operate, hold hand straight with fingers extended. Bend under thumb and move joint up and down as shown for talking mouth. Paper ears, teeth, and eyes can be added to hand with small pieces of double-stick tape. Complete characters with "mouth holes" can also be cut from paper in a variety of shapes:

flower, ghost, tree, person, animal. Secure shapes to hand with double-stick tape and align "mouth hole" over cavity area of moving thumb.

*Penny wrapper.* Available at any bank, tubular penny wrappers make quick finger puppets and form a solid base onto which features can be drawn or glued. Open penny wrapper and slip over finger. Add yarn legs for a caterpillar; a paper hat and cotton beard for Santa; long, pointed paper ears and whiskers for a rabbit. It is also fun to glue cutouts from coloring books, magazines, greeting cards, catalogs, and family photos to the wrapper. These finger puppets are capable of portraying creatures that walk, crawl, and fly.

*Tongue depressor or popsicle stick.* With a paper head glued to it, either makes a quick stick puppet. Two characters, or one character with two different expressions, may be represented by making two different faces, one for each side. When the puppet is turned, the character or expression changes. Tongue depressors and ice-cream spoons are also ideally shaped surfaces on which to draw or attach features.

*Egg-carton sections.* The individual "cups" in an egg carton trans-

**Some instant puppets**

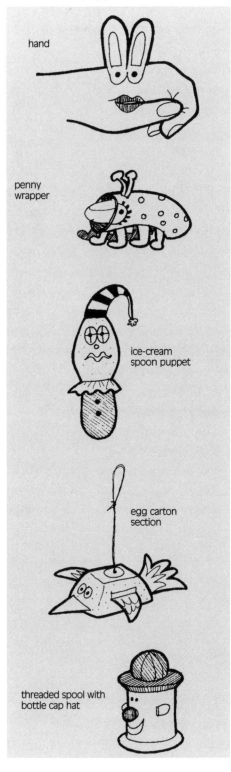

hand

penny wrapper

ice-cream spoon puppet

egg carton section

threaded spool with bottle cap hat

form easily into a set of string puppets. Thread a length of string through the top center of the cup section and make a knot inside so it will not pull out. Tie a loop at the opposite end of the string for a finger control. Decorate the "cup" with paper eyes, ears, and nose—small pom-poms make excellent tails or noses. Attach yarn for a tail, legs, and whiskers. Wiggly spiders and flying creatures are especially effective done in this style.

*Empty thread spools.* Sparsely decorated thread spools turn into convincing tabletop puppets or pocket companions. Add just enough detail with felt-tip markers to suggest the character. A dab of cotton to indicate a beard; a piece of lace for a dress; two felt triangles for pointed ears will complete the character.

Other simple puppets for children to make from easily available materials such as boxes, clothespins, envelopes, paper cups, and bags have been suggested throughout the book.

## Using Instant Puppets

Two examples using instant puppets in follow-up activities are included here.

## The Knee-High Man

Children can make their own versions (empty thread spool, penny wrapper, or egg-carton section puppets) of the Knee-High Man, for *The Knee-High Man and Other Tales* by Julius Lester. When the puppets are finished, ask children to select partners. Using the Knee-High Man puppets, children share with their partners the problems and advantages of being only knee-high—problems encountered might include climbing stairs, trying to reach ice cream in the freezer, watching a parade. Encourage children to suggest other difficulties.

## "Mr. Gaffe"

The poem "Mr. Gaffe" by Jack Prelutsky introduces a character who says everything backwards. Recite this poem using a puppet to speak Mr. Gaffe's lines. Then ask children to construct an instant puppet that has its own peculiarity. While Mr. Gaffe's idiosyncrasy is speaking backwards, the students can ponder other unusual traits for their characters. You might suggest that the puppet's expression or the feature—eyes, eyebrows, nose, etc.—associated with the unusual trait be exaggerated. These unique puppet characters might be interviewed during a mock or live student-produced videotape production.

## Tuesday

Using the Caldecott Medal book *Tuesday* by David Wiesner as a model, invite children to create a series of adventures for another character such as a rabbit or a hummingbird. Then each child can make an instant puppet of the character and act out the new adventures.

## SUGGESTED TITLES FOR THE STORY'S OVER; WHAT'S NEXT?

Burningham, John. *Mr. Gumpy's Outing:* illus. by the author. Holt, 1971.

Mr. Gumpy's guests forget their promise to behave on the boat ride—with disastrous results.

Carle, Eric. *The Grouchy Ladybug;* illus. by the author. Crowell, 1977.

An angry ladybug searches all day for someone to argue with, only to return to her starting place and a peaceable solution.

Dayrell, Elphinstone. *Why the Sun and Moon Live in the Sky;* illus. by Blair Lent. Houghton, 1990.

This African folktale explains how the water creatures forced the sun and moon into the sky. A Caldecott Honor book.

Demuth, Patricia Brennan. *Ornery Morning;* illus. by Craig McFarland Brown. Dutton, 1991.

Farm animals reverse their decision not to work when they learn they won't be fed until they work.

Domanska, Janina. *The Tortoise and the Tree;* illus. by the author. Morrow, 1978.

A Bantu folktale explains how the tortoise got his patchwork shell.

Dragonwagon, Crescent. *Alligators and Others All Year Long;* illus. by Jose Aruego and Ariane Dewey. Macmillan, 1993.

Amusing poems for all seasons featuring alligators and other animals.

Eastman, P. D. *Are You My Mother?;* illus. by the author. Random, 1960.

A baby bird falls from the nest and searches for his mother.

Howe, James. *There's a Monster Under My Bed*; illus. by David Rose. Atheneum, 1986.

Simon's fear of a monster under his bed grows until he's sure there are many monsters ready to pounce on him. Host puppet can share something he is afraid of before this story is read. After the story children can share their fears and talk about ways of dealing with them. Make a puppet of what the creatures under the bed might look like.

Hutchins, Pat. *Goodnight Owl*; illus. by the author. Macmillan, 1972.

During the day when Owl tries to sleep, all the other creatures that live in the tree make their usual sounds. While they try to sleep at night, Owl takes a turn at noisemaking.

*Jack and the Beanstalk*. Scholastic Book and Cassette, Scholastic.

A read-along version of this popular fairy tale provides an interesting alternative for the child and the educator.

Kellogg, Steven, reteller. *Pecos Bill*; illus. by the author. Morrow, 1986.

Adventures of that all-American tall-tale cowboy, Pecos Bill, are retold here.

Lester, Julius. *The Knee-High Man and Other Tales*; illus. by Ralph Pinto. Dial, 1972.

Collection of six stories from African-American folklore features animals.

Lindgren, Astrid. *The Tomten*; illus. by Harald Wiberg. Putnam, 1965.

Only animals in the barn understand the gentle Tomten.

Mayer, Mercer. *There's Nightmare in My Closet*; illus. by the author. Dial, 1968.

A humorous fantasy about a boy who befriends the Nightmare in his closet will provide some relief and laughter for children's popular fears.

McCord, David. *One at a Time*; illus. by Henry B. Kane. Little Brown, 1986.

A collection of poems by this popular poet contains refreshing and novel sounds in its verses.

McGovern, Ann. *Too Much Noise*; illus. by Simms Taback. Houghton, 1967.

The unusual advice a wise man gives a farmer who finds his house too noisy helps solve the problem.

Miller, Edna. *Mousekin's Close Call*; illus. by the author. Prentice-Hall, 1978.

Mousekin plays dead to protect himself from enemies in the forest.

Minarik, Else Holmelund. *Am I Beautiful?*; illus. by Yossi Abolafia. Greenwillow, 1992.

A young hippo on a walk sees mothers telling their children how beautiful they are. She asks each "Am I beautiful?" but doesn't receive the right answer until she returns to her own mother.

Prelutsky, Jack. *Nightmares: Poems to Trouble Your Sleep*; illus. by Arnold Lobel. Greenwillow, 1976.

Poems about horrible creatures are guaranteed to trouble your sleep.

Prelutsky, Jack. *The Queen of Eene*; illus. by Victoria Chess. Greenwillow, 1978.

Collection of poems about silly characters, such as "Mister Gaffe" who says everything backwards, is sure to make your listeners laugh.

Slobodkina, Esphyr. *Caps for Sale*; illus. by the author. Addison Wesley, 1947.

Humorous tale of how a peddler outwits monkeys who have taken his caps makes for fun listening and original dramatizing.

Steig, William. *The Amazing Bone*; illus. by the author. Farrar, 1976.

A magic bone saves Pearl, a young pig, from a cruel fate at the hands of a villainous fox. A Caldecott Honor book.

Wiesner, David. *Tuesday*; illus. by the author. Clarion, 1991.

On a Tuesday evening flying frogs float above a small town on a series of novel adventures. A Caldecott Medal book.

# PUPPETRY AND STORYTELLING ORGANIZATIONS

British Puppet Centre, Battersea Town Hall, Lavender Hill, London S.W. 11, England

This British organization offers various services.

Center for Puppetry Arts Museum, Vincent Anthony, Director, 1404 Spring Street NW, Atlanta, GA 30309-2820.

"Puppets: The Power of Wonder," is a permanent exhibit of over 200 puppets including Indonesian shadow puppets, Muppets, and puppets made from "junk." Kids can operate puppets using joysticks and find puppets in unexpected places. A theater offers shows for children and adults.

National Storytelling Association (NAS), Box 112, Jonesboro, TN 37659.

The oldest and largest storytelling organization in the United States. Sponsors the National Story-telling Festival, held yearly on the first weekend in October in Jonesboro. Also sponsors a National Storytelling Conference, held in a different city each summer. Publishes the bi-monthly *Storytelling Magazine*, which contains articles on trends and happenings in the storytelling world. *Story Net*, available on the Internet, is an online resource for storytelling materials and provides an opportunity for storytellers to network.

*National Storytelling Directory* (Canada)

Lists major Canadian storytelling circles and orga-nizations. For information write to the Vancouver Society of Storytelling, 14-2414 Main Street, Vancouver, BC V5T 3E3, Canada.

Ontario Puppetry Association, Kenneth McKay, Executive Secretary, 10 Skyview Crescent, Willowdale, Ontario M2J 1B8, Canada.

This Canadian puppetry organization offers vari-ous activities and services.

Puppeteers of America, Gayle G. Schluter, Member-ship Office, #5 Cricklewood Path, Pasadena, CA 91107-1002.

The "Puppeteers of America" is a worldwide organization that supports the betterment of pup-petry: semi-annual national festival; regional work-shops; a Puppetry Store for purchasing books and puppet items; a bimonthly magazine; consultant services to individuals and affiliated guilds. A small membership fee is required. Write for information concerning your local puppet guild.

The Union Internationale de la Marionnette (UNIMA), Allelu Kurten, General Secretary, Browning Road, Hyde Park, NY 12538.

Dedicated to uniting puppetry on an interna-tional level, this organization publishes a journal and sponsors yearly conventions.

UNIMA-USA, Inc., 1404 Spring Street NW, Atlanta GA 30309-2820.

Promotes international understanding and friend-ship through the art of puppetry. The group focuses on encouraging and providing contacts to North American puppeteers traveling throughout the world as well as extending hospitality to international pup-peteers traveling in North America.

# BIBLIOGRAPHY OF PUPPETRY

Barr, Marilynn. *Story Hour Patterns*; illus. by the author. Good Apple, 1990.

Simple finger and stick puppets for a pig, monkey, mouse, monster, frog, elephant, bunny, bear, and alligator.

Champlin, Connie. *Puppetry and Creative Dramatics in Storytelling*; illus. by Nancy Renfro. Nancy Renfro Studios, 1980.

A novel approach is presented that combines puppetry and movement in storytelling. Geared for teachers and librarians, this book is built upon a series of "how-to" projects incorporating new ways to combine traditional and modern children's stories with simple puppetry and creative dramatics. Includes such aspects as participation, dialogue, sound effects, action, and pantomime.

Condon, Camy. *Try on My Shoe — Step into Another Culture*; illus. by Lynne Jennings. Condon, 1981.

How to use puppetry to increase cultural awareness is the goal of this booklet. Presents a unique approach involving the audience in the storytelling. Folktales from four cultures offered: East Africa, Mexico, Vietnam, and Native American. Available from The Puppetry Store, Puppeteers of America.

Engler, Larry, and Carol Fijan. *Making Puppets Come Alive*; illus. by David Attie. Taplinger, 1973.

Puppeteers seeking puppet manipulation skills with hand puppets will find this a "must." Aspects covered include: puppet technique, voice use, improvisation, role characterization, and other fundamental elements.

Frazier, Nancy, and Nancy Renfro. *Imagination*; illus. by Nancy Renfro. Nancy Renfro Studios, 1987.

Very original ideas for involving children in puppetry and creative drama activities.

Freericks, Mary, and Joyce Segal. *Creative Puppetry in the Classroom*; illus. by Katherine McCabe. New Play Books, 1979.

Educators will find within the covers a basic introduction to creating and using puppets effectively. Ideas discussed include: using a puppet to introduce yourself to a group; ways of using a mascot puppet; integrating puppets in reading and the curriculum. Available from The Puppetry Store.

Hunt, Tamara, and Nancy Renfro. *Puppetry in Early Childhood Education*; illus. by Nancy Renfro. Nancy Renfro Studios, 1982.

An excellent resource brimming with ideas for using, making, "puppetteaching," and collecting puppets. Includes many ideas for storytelling with puppets.

Keefe, Betty. *Fingerpuppet Tales*; illus. by the author. Special Literature Press, 1986.

Contains clear directions for telling the story, patterns for making the puppets, the story, and follow-up activities for a variety of folk and fairytales. Also by the same author, *Fingerpuppets, Fingerplays and Holidays*. Available from The Puppetry Store.

Pocketful of Puppets series. Nancy Renfro Studios, 1983– .

Titles in this expanding series explore puppet activities based on Mother Goose rhymes, animal stories, and poems. Many puppet patterns are also included.

Robson, Denny, and Vanessa Bailey. *Shadow Theater.* Glouster Press, 1990.

Wonderful ideas for creating a shadow theater, simple shadow puppets, jointed puppets, and colored puppets. Ideas can be adapted for overhead storytelling.

Schmidt, Hans J., and Karl J. Schmidt. *Learning with Puppets*; illus. by the authors. Puppet Masters, 1977.

This title serves as a guide to making and using puppets in the classroom. Stresses ways to enhance individual artistic expression and the acquisition of social and academic skills. Available from The Puppetry Store.

Schramm, Toni A. *Puppet Plays from Workshop to Performance*; illus. by Leann Mullineaux. Teachers Ideas Press, 1993.

Contains construction and manipulation information for stick, felt, and styrofoam hand puppets. A chapter on stages, scenery, and props offers practical suggestions.

Sierra, Judy. *Fantastic Theater.* Wilson, 1991.

Clear discussion of shadow and rod puppets including screens, puppets, stages, lighting, props, scenery, and rehearsal and performance tips. Thirty plays adapted from nursery rhymes, folk songs, myths, folklore, and poetry. Follow-up activities are provided for each play.

Wright, Denise Anton. *One-Person Puppet Plays*; illus. by John Wright. Libraries Unlimited, 1990.

Original easy-to-produce plays adapted from folklore, plays with a holiday theme, plays with an emphasis on reading and libraries, and plays suitable for any occasions. Many of these one-person plays can easily be adapted to a storytelling format. Contains patterns for simple bag, stick, and mouth puppets.

# BIBLIOGRAPHY OF STORYTELLING

Many excellent books are available on the subject of storytelling. The following recommended titles are concerned mainly with technique. Each contains bibliographies of story sources.

Bauer, Caroline. *New Handbook for Storytellers.* American Library Association, 1993.

All facets of storytelling are covered: planning, promotion, story sources, multimedia storytelling, and programs. A must for all storytellers.

Cullum, Carolyn N. *The Storytime Sourcebook.* Neal-Schuman, 1990.

A subject guide to story hours, this book presents ideas and activities for hundreds of books and stories. The aim of this book is to provide a reference to help the storyteller locate appropriate ideas for programs or lessons for preschoolers based on books available in public libraries.

Greene, Ellin. *Storytelling: Art and Technique,* 3rd ed. Bowker, 1996.

A valuable book for the novice storyteller. Contains a history of storytelling in libraries.

MacDonald, Margaret Read. *The Storyteller's Start-Up Book.* August House, 1993.

An excellent resource for both the beginning and experienced storyteller. The author covers finding, learning, and performing folktales. Includes twelve tellable tales and excellent lists of resources for storytellers. Other titles by this author: *Celebrate the World: Twenty Tellable Folktales for Multicultural Festivals* (Wilson, 1994); *Twenty Tellable Tales: Audience Participation Folktales for the Beginning Storyteller* (Wilson, 1986) and *Storyteller's Sourcebook* (Gale, 1982).

Marsh, Valerie. *Paper-Cutting Stories for Holidays and Special Events;* illus. by Patrick K. Luzadder. Alleyside, 1994.

Explains the unique technique of telling stories while cutting out a story-related shape. Both the story and directions for the paper cutting are included. Children are fascinated by this approach. Other books in this series include: *Paper Cutting Stories from A to Z* and *Mystery-Fold.*

Mellon, Nancy. *Storytelling and the Art of Imagination.* Element, 1992.

The author encourages storytellers to create their own stories using visualization and imagination. Presents a unique perspective.

Painter, William. *Musical Story Hours: Using Music with Storytelling and Puppetry.* Shoe String Press, 1989.

The subtitle of this book sums up the content very well. The main focus is on how to incorporate classical music into the telling, but other forms of music are suggested as well, including Dixieland, Western, and folk melodies. Another title by the same author, *Storytelling with Music, Puppets, and Arts for Libraries and Classrooms* (Shoe String Press, 1994), includes additional ideas.

Pellowski, Anne. *The World of Storytelling.* Rev. ed., Wilson, 1990.

For those interested in stories from near and far, this volume compares storytelling in different cultures and contains a section devoted to the art of listening. The author has also written a book designed for young people who tell stories, *The Storytelling Handbook* (Simon & Schuster, 1995), and a book for parents and beginning storytellers, *Family Storytelling Handbook* (Collier Macmillan, 1987).

Schimmel, Nancy. *Just Enough to Make a Story.* Sisters' Choice Press. 3rd ed., 1992.

A small book filled with advice for storytellers written in a refreshing, personal style. Samples of story types include a fingerplay, cante fable (story with a song in it), and a story accompanied by paperfolding.

Sierra, Judy, and Robert Kaminski. *Multicultural Folktales: Stories to Tell Young Children.* Oryx, 1991.

Collection of twenty-five tales from around the world that are easy to tell. Includes patterns for puppets and flannelboard characters.

# INDEX

## A

Action/response activities. *See* Warm-up activities
Action stories, 14–15, 97–99, 140–51
  example, 142–44
  suggested titles, 151–53
  types, 140–42
Adventure storis, 11
*African Animal Tales*, 186–87
Age groups, 10–12, 19
  *see also* specific age groups
Aggression, 10–11
*Albert's Toothache*, 8
*Aliens Ate My Homework*, 11
*Alligators and Others All Year Long!*, 227
*The Amazing Bone*, 84, 232
Ambulatory movements, 72–73
*Amos and Boris*, 9, 23, 25, 178
Analyzing the story, 16–20
Anansi tales, 186
"Androcles and the Lion," 100
*Andy and the Lion*, 100
Anger, 73
Animal puppets, 26, 43–44, 52–54, 80, 125–26, 131–35, 141, 142, 147
  costumes, 54–55
  features, 31–32
  totes, 210–11
  zoo, 169
  *see also* Barnyard puppets; names of specific animals
Animal sounds, 20, 69, 128–29
Animal stories, 10, 11, 53
*Another Celebrated Dancing Bear*, 45
Answer-back songs, 129–30
"The Ants and the Grasshopper," 186–87
Anything puppets, 115–26, 133, 141
  action/response activities, 117–18
  flat, 116
  interpretative activities, 118–19
  manipulation and construction, 115–19
  pantomime, 119–20
  story dramatization, 123–27
  story involvement, 119–22
  warm-up activities, 117–19

Aquarium displays, 227
*Arabian Nights*, 193
*Are You My Mother?*, 204–5, 226
*Arrow to the Sun*, 14, 141–42
Art projects, 7, 225–28
*Arthur's Nose*, 104
Ask Mr. Bear, 52
Attention, focus of, 89–90
  suggested titles, 89–90
Attention span, 9–12, 19, 95, 111
Audience size, 156
Audience participation. *See* Participatory storytelling
Audiovisual aids, 4, 128

## B

Babar series, 15, 25
"The Baboon's Umbrella," 198, 199–200
"Backward Bell," 168
Bag puppets. *See* Bodi-puppets
*Bah! Humbug*, 99
Balloon string puppets, 10, 43–44, 147–49
  construction, 148–49
Barnyard puppets, 19, 32, 131–33, 141, 147, 168, 225
"The Bear and the Crow," 200
Bear puppets, 52, 97–98, 213
*The Bear's Toothache*, 97–98
*Bearymore*, 6
*The Beast of Monsieur Racine*, 103
"Beauty and the Beast," 53, 186
Bedtime stories, 8
*Benjamin and Tulip*, 192–93
"The Big, Big Turnip," 178–82
Birthday crown, 82
Birthday parties, 6, 9
"Boa Constrictor," 208
Bodi-puppets, 7, 9, 16, 20, 25, 26, 45–46, 53, 104, 141, 142, 146, 155, 156, 164, 197, 198, 199–200
  construction, 45–46
  paper-bag, 200
  paper-plate, 142–44
  picture, 197

Book fairs, 8
Book in storytelling, 7
Book talks, 8, 90
Book theater puppets, 158–60
Book theaters, 156, 157–60
  example, 158–60
  suggested titles, 160–61
Bookworm, 75
Box puppets, 105–8, 223
  construction, 108
Box stand-up puppets. *See* Stand-up puppets
Box theaters. *See* Open-box theaters
Box totes, 228
"The Boy Who Cried Wolf," 141
*Bread and Jam for Frances*, 49–50
Bread-making, 16, 19
"The Bremen Town Musicians," 125–26
  *see also* "The Musicians of Bremen"
*Bringing the Rain to Kapiti Plain*, 49
*The Bump in the Night*, 218–19
*Busy Day*, 120
Butterfly puppets, 92, 125

## C

*Caleb and Kate*, 157
*Caps for Sale*, 227
*The Carrot Seed*, 163
*Cat Goes Fiddle-I-Fee*, 131–33
*Cat in the Hat*, 15
Caterpillar puppet, 92
Character development, 61–74, 91–93
  chart, 66
  specific traits, 61–65
  suggested titles, 74
  through movements, 70–74
  through sounds, 129
  through voice and communication, 67–70
Character sketches, 118–19
Character transformation, 53, 54, 57, 92, 93–95, 125
  "quick-change," 186
  suggested titles, 95–97

*Charlotte's Web,* 46
Cheeks, puppet, 57
"The Chick and the Duckling," 119
Child storyteller, 11
Children as props, 20
*Chin Chiang and the Dragon's Dance,* 9
Christmas, 80
"Cinderella," 14, 86
"The City Mouse and Country Mouse," 211
Classroom puppets, 8–9
*The Clay Pot Boy,* 106–8
   construction, 108
*Clementine's Winter Wardrobe,* 95
Cloth shoe-bag totes, 227
Clothes-tree displays, 227
Clothesline displays, 226–27
Clothesline puppets, 131–33, 226–27
   construction, 133
Clothespin puppets, 135–36, 179, 182–84
   construction, 136
Collection development, puppet, 31, 52–60
   suggested titles, 60
Comic. *See* humor
Communication, 67, 69–70, 77–78
   nonverbal, 77–78
Community resources, 58–59
Concepts interpreted by puppets, 120
   suggested titles, 120–21
Construction, puppet, 55–58
   fabrics, 58
   features, 57
   materials, 56–57
   resources, 55–56
   tools and supplies, 57–58
   trims, 58
   *see also* specific types of puppets
"The Contest," 122
Contrasts
   in movement, 64
   in personality, 61–63, 97
   in shape, 63–64
Costumes, 31, 32, 53, 54
   changes, 31, 53–55, 93–95
   contests, 104
*Count and See,* 89
Cowboy-hat totes, 227
Craft items, 58
*Crictor,* 211–13, 227–28
*Crow Boy,* 57
Cultural traditions, 3–4
Cumulative songs, 131–33, 168

Cumulative stories, 14–15, 46–47, 128, 168, 186, 197
Cup and container theaters, 155–56, 162–66, 205
   suggested titles, 167
Cup puppets, 140, 162–66
Curiosity, 11, 203
*Cut from the Same Cloth,* 157
Cutaway views. *See* See-through views
Cutouts. *See* Paper cutouts
*Cyrus the Unsinkable Sea Serpent,* 178

**D**

Dancing puppets, 141–42
*Dandelion,* 93–94
Deaf children, 9
Dealers, puppet. *See* Manufacturers and dealers, puppet
Dialogue, 19–20, 97–98, 121–22, 129
   suggested titles, 98–99, 122–23
Diminutive theaters. *See* Open-box theaters
Disguises, 94–95
Displays, post-story, 225–28
Distance. *See* Time and distance
"Drakestail," 105
Dramatization, story, 7, 9, 12, 123–27, 155
   suggested titles, 126–27
Drawing. *See* Picture puppets
"Drinking Gourd" song, 47
*Drummer Hoff,* 129
Drums, 146

**E**

Ears, puppet, 32, 36, 57
Educational elements, 20, 156
"Eeyore's Birthday Party," 6
Egg-carton string puppets, 233
Egg-carton totes, 228
*Elephant in a Well,* 142
Elmer (purple dragon character), 230
"The Elves and the Shoemaker," 227
Emberly, Ed, drawing books, 46
Emotions and feelings, 6, 10–11, 27, 67, 70, 73, 77, 147
Engine cardboard puppet, 151
*The Enormous Crocodile,* 26
"The Enormous Turnip," 163
Envelope puppets, 133–35, 204, 213
   construction, 135

*Esteban and the Ghost,* 11
Ethics. *See* Moral issues
Exaggeration, 19, 25, 49, 53, 64
Exterior-interior sets, 193
Eyes, puppet, 57

**F**

*Fables,* 198, 199, 200
Fabrics, 58, 103
Faces, puppet, 37
   *see also* specific features
Facial expressions, 27
Fairy tales, 186, 228
Family themes, 8
Fantasy, 53, 140–41
Farm animals. *See* Barnyard puppets
"The Farmer in the Dell," 168
*Farmer Palmer's Wagon Ride,* 178
Features, puppet, 57
   *see also* specific features
Feelings and emotions. *See* Emotions and feelings
Felt mitt puppets, 133
*Fin M'Coul,* 9
Finger puppets, 6, 7, 9, 20, 25, 26, 52, 70–71, 92, 130–31, 133, 156, 168–76
   book theater performance, 157
   collection, 229
   construction, 28–30, 221
   hospital performance, 9
   instant puppets, 168, 232–34
   paper, 169–74
   paper-tissue, 146, 175
   story tote performance, 211
   walking, 20, 217, 220–21
Finger stories, 155–56, 168–76
   examples, 169–76
   suggested titles, 176–77
*The Fireside Book of Fun and Game Songs,* 129–30
*The First Dog,* 9
Fish puppets, 210, 213
"Five Little _____," 168
"Five Little Monkeys," 28
Flat hand puppets, 52
Flexibility, 156, 179
Flexible-body hand puppets. *See* Hand puppets
Flowerpot totes, 227
Folk songs, 47–48, 225

Folktales, 11, 25, 125–26, 129, 186
"Follow the Leader," 117–18
Follow-up activities, 113
    *see also* follow-up activities for specific
        types of presentations
Formats. *See* Presentation formats
*Fourteen Rats and a Rat-Catcher*, 193
"The Fox and the Grapes," 92
Fox puppets
    balloon string, 148
    bodi-puppets, 197
Franklin, Ben, 45
*Frederick*, 157
Free-hanging hand-type puppets, 217
Freedom of expression, 131
*Frog and Toad*, 14, 62, 141, 168
"Frog Music," 227
"The Frog Prince," 32, 186
Frog puppets, 140
*Froggy Gets Dressed*, 95
*Frog Went a-Courtin'*, 47
*The Funny Little Woman*, 26, 130–31
Futuristic themes, 11

**G**

*Garbage Delight*, 100–101
*George and Martha*, 62, 141, 168
*Georgie's Halloween*, 146–47, 169, 175–76
Gestures, puppet, 5, 71–73
    *see also* Movements, puppet
Ghost puppets, 94, 175–76, 218–20
    construction, 176
*The Ghost with the Halloween Hiccups*, 146
Giggles (sound effect), 130–31
"The Gingerbread Boy," 129, 186, 217
*The Giving Tree*, 14
Glove and finger puppets, 91, 168–69
    construction of basic glove, 173–74
Goat puppet, 108
"Goldilocks and the Three Bears," 54, 129,
    169, 178
    see also "The Three Bears"
*Goodnight Owl!*, 226
Greeting card pictures. *See* Picture puppets
*Gregory, the Terrible Eater*, 106, 108–9
    construction of Gregory Goat, 108–9
"The Grobbles," 130, 131, 135–36
Grocery bag puppets. *See* Bodi-puppets
*The Grouchy Ladybug*, 227
Group puppets, 186

"Guess What?," 117–18
"The Gunniwolf," 32, 216
*Gus Was a Gorgeous Ghost*, 93–94

**H**

Hair, puppet, 32, 53
Halloween, 79, 80, 94, 104, 142–44, 146–47,
    175–76, 225
Hand as puppet, 232–33
Hand-constructed puppets. *See*
    Construction, puppet
*Hand, Hand, Finger, Thumb*, 146
Hand puppets, 5, 25, 26, 30–42, 49, 52, 53,
    70, 71–74, 95, 133, 141, 146–47,
    155–56, 157, 204, 211, 230
    construction, 31–42
    flexible-body, 16, 20, 30–32, 92
    free-hanging, 217
    nonspeaking, 78
    story tote performance, 211
    talking-mouth, 25, 32–40, 53, 68, 77, 99
Handicapped children, 9
"Hansel and Gretel," 46, 193
Happiness, 67, 73
*Happy Birthday, Sam*, 9
Happy Lion (as lead puppet), 91
Harry (as lead puppet), 91
"The Hare and the Tortoise," 75
*Harlequin and the Gift of Many Colors*,
    103–4
Hatbox totes, 227–28
Hats, puppet, 31, 32, 38, 54, 104
*Hattie the Backstage Bat*, 92–93
Heads, puppet, 5, 102
Hedgehog puppet, 78
"The Hen and the Apple Tree," 200
Hen puppets, 16, 20, 147–49
"Henny Penny," 43, 128, 130, 156, 197
*Henry Finds a Home*, 163
Heracles, 45
"Hey Diddle Diddle," 26
*Hey, Kid!*, 210
"Hickory, Dickory, Dock," 124, 168–69
*Hildilid's Night*, 30
Historical fiction, 53
"A Hole in the Bucket," 129–30
Holiday parties, 9
Holidays, 79–80, 210
Hopping, 73
Horizontal panel theater. *See* Panel theaters

*Horton Hatches the Egg*, 20
Hospital puppet shows, 9
Host puppets, 75, 77–90, 91
    development, 78–80
    nonspeaking, 78, 80–83
    speaking, 83–90
    suggested titles, 83–84
"The House That Jack Built," 46, 186
*How Spider Saved Halloween*, 104
*Howdy Doody*, 4
*Humbug! Witch*, 102–03
Humor, 5, 19, 26, 50, 64, 66, 78, 100–101,
    168
"Humpty Dumpty," 124–25, 162, 166, 232

**I**

"I Eat Kids Yum Yum," 100–101
"I Know an Old Woman Who Swallowed a
    Fly," 14
Identification, 15
Idiosyncrasies, 5, 15, 62, 65
Imagination, 5, 11, 15, 115, 142–44, 147–48,
    158, 197, 223
Improvisation, 121–22, 123–26, 140, 228
*In the Eyes of the Cat: Japanese Poetry for All
    Seasons*, 226
*Inch by Inch*, 168
Informal puppetry, 9
Instant puppets, 168, 232–34
Integration, puppet-story, 52–54
Interest centers, 229–31
Interest stimulation, 84–85, 95
    suggested titles, 85–87
Intermediate-age children, 11–12, 53–54
Interpretative activities. *See* Warm-up
    activities
Introductions, storytelling, 83–84, 113
Involvement, story, 119–23

**J**

"Jack and Jill," 124
"Jack and the Beanstalk," 7, 25, 193, 230–31
"Jack and the Robbers," 131, 133–35
"Jack Be Nimble," 168–69
"Jack-O-Lantern," 162, 166
*Jennie's Hat*, 104
John Henry, 45
*Juba This and Juba That*, 5, 102
*Jump, Frog, Jump!*, 140

## K

*Katy No-Pocket*, 128
Key actions, 19
"King of the Cats," 91–92
*The Knee-High Man and Other Tales*, 234
Kukla, Fran, and Ollie, 4

## L

Lambchop, 4
Lapboards, 52, 74, 93, 203
  construction, 203
Laundry-basket totes, 227
Laziness, 19
"Lazy Jack," 5
"Lazy Mary," 129–30
Lead puppets, 15, 75, 91–108, 146
  nonspeaking, 91–93
  single lead puppet, 93–97, 146
  speaking, 91–93
  two lead puppets, 97–99, 141
*Leo, the Late Bloomer*, 93, 95, 231
Library story hour. *See* Story hour
*A Light in the Attic*, 168
Literature appreciation, 117
Little Bo Peep, 43–44
*The Little Engine That Could*, 147, 149–51
Little Miss Muffet, 45
"The Little Red Hen," 14, 16, 19–20, 27, 129
"Little Red Riding Hood," 14, 26, 53, 61–66, 217, 220–21, 229, 231
"The Little Turtle," 162
Location. *See* Space for storytelling

## M

*Madeline*, 179, 182–84
Magazine pictures. *See* Picture puppets
Main characters. *See* Lead puppets
*Making Puppets Come Alive*, 73
Mannerisms, puppet, 5
Manufacturers and dealers, puppet, 59–60
Map props, 53
Marionettes. *See* String puppets
Martha (yellow bird character), 230
"Mary, Mary, Quite Contrary," 162, 166
Materials for puppets, 49, 56–58
*May I Bring a Friend?*, 168
*Millions of Cats*, 26, 61–66, 192, 193–95

Mime. *See* Pantomime
Mimicry, puppet, 8
Miniature theaters. *See* Book theaters; Cup and container theaters
Miniaturization, 25
"Mirror, Mirror" activity, 117–18
*Miss Nelson Is Missing*, 93–95
Miss Piggy and Kermit, 4
*The Missing Piece*, 14
Mitt puppets. *See* Felt mitt puppets; Flat hand puppets
*The Mitten*, 210
"The Monkey and the Crocodile," 54, 97
Monster puppets, 100–101, 142–44
Moral issues, 10
*More More More Said the Baby*, 8
*Morris and Boris*, 141
Mother Goose rhymes, 52, 90, 124–25, 163
  *see also* Nursery rhymes
*Mother, Mother I Feel Sick*, 187
*Mousekin's Close Call*, 226
Mouth movements. *See* Open and closed mouth movements
*Mouth Sounds*, 129
Mouths, puppet, 57
Movements, puppet, 25–26, 45, 63, 64, 67–68, 70–74, 141, 142, 178, 197
  ambulatory, 72–73
  practicing, 73
  *see also* Gestures, puppet; Mannerisms, puppet
"Mr. Gaffe," 234
*Mr. Gumpy's Outing*, 142, 227
*Mr. Rabbit and the Lovely Present*, 5
Multicast presentations, 178–79
Muppets, 4
*Mushroom in the Rain*, 125, 142
Music, 140–41
Musical instrument sound effects, 130, 204
"The Musicians of Bremen," 133
  *see also* "The Bremen Town Musicians"
Mythology, 53

## N

Negative movements, 73
*The Night before Christmas*, 192, 226–27
*Nightmares or Poems to Trouble Your Sleep*, 226
*No Roses for Harry*, 93–94
*Noah's Ark*, 26

*Noisy Nora*, 92–93
Nonparticipatory stories, 12, 111
Nonspeaking puppets, 69–70, 77–78, 80–83, 91–93
  *see also* Pantomime
Nonverbal communication. *See* Communication
*Norman the Doorman*, 186–87
Noses, puppet, 5, 32, 37, 57
Novelty puppets, 53
Nursery rhyme presentations, 162–66, 168
Nursery stories, 54

## O

"Old King Cole," 69
Old lady puppet, 106–7
"The Old Lady Who Swallowed a Fly," 105–7, 186–87
  construction, 107
"Old MacDonald," 26
"Old Mother Hubbard," 162–65
"Old Stormalong," 9
Old Tom (lead puppet), 92
"The Old Woman and Her Pig," 129, 197
Old Woman and Old Man personalities, 62–65
"The Old Woman Who Lived in a Shoe," 227, 232
"The Old Woman Who Lived in a Vinegar Bottle," 25
*One at a Time*, 227
Open-box theaters, 23, 156, 178–84
  construction, 180–81
  examples, 179–84
  suggested titles, 184–85
*Opposites*, 120
Opposites and opposing views, 99, 120
  suggested titles, 99–100
*Ornery Morning*, 225
*Our Veronica Goes to Petunia's Farm*, 87
Outdoor presentations, 198
Outer space, 225
Overhead shadow puppets, 5, 7, 11, 46–48, 53, 70, 186–90
  construction, 47–48, 189
Overhead shadow stories, 186–90
  examples, 188–90
  suggested titles, 190–91
Owl host puppet, 79

# P

Paddington Bear (as lead puppet), 91
Paddy Bear (as host puppet), 81–83
*The Pancake*, 129
"Pandora's Box," 85
Panel theaters, 192–95
    construction, 195
    examples, 193–95
    horizontal, 192, 195
    open-out, 195
    suggested titles, 195–96
    vertical, 193
Pantomime, 9, 53, 91, 92, 112, 119, 140,
    141, 147–48, 198, 208
    suggested titles, 119–20
    *see also* Nonspeaking puppets
Paper-bag puppets, 7, 20, 94, 103–4, 105–7,
    133, 140, 213
    construction, 107
    swallowing, 106–7
Paper cutout puppets, 131–33, 157, 194, 206
Paper-plate puppets, 5, 94, 140–41, 142–44
    two-sided turnaround, 95, 104
Paper shadow puppets. *See* Overhead
    shadow puppets
Paper stick puppets. *See* Stick puppets
Participatory stories, 10, 11, 12, 19–20,
    26–27
Participatory storytelling, 7, 8, 9–10, 55,
    102–04, 111–26, 128–51, 157, 186–90,
    197–98
    suggested titles, 104–05
Parties. *See* Birthday parties; Holiday parties
Paul Bunyan, 53
Pecos Bill, 227
Peek-through panels, 169, 175
Penny wrapper puppets, 233–34
Personality, puppet, 48, 53, 61–67, 78–79,
    93–95
Peter Rabbit, 5
Petunia, 84
Physical movements. *See* Movements,
    puppet
Physical shapes. *See* Shapes, puppet
Picture puppets, 168–69, 178–79, 198, 199
    bodi-puppets, 197
    pin-on, 147, 149–51
*Pierre*, 25
Pin-on puppets. *See* Picture puppets
Pinocchio, 5

Plush toys. *See* Stuffed-toy puppets
*A Pocket for Corduroy*, 84
"Poem," William Carlos Williams, 47
Poems, 168, 225, 228
Poetry presentations, 47, 135–36, 205–8
"Pooh Goes Visiting," 169
*Poor Richard's Almanac*, 45
Popsicle sticks. *See* Tongue depressors
Post-story activities, 225–34
    suggested titles, 234–36
Posture, puppet, 71–72, 116–17
Practice corner, 74
Practice exercise, storytelling, 73–74
Preschool children, 10–11, 52
Presentation formats, 16–20, 155–56
    *see also* Space for storytelling; specific
      formats
Primary-age children, 11, 52–53
*The Princess and the Pea*, 126
Props, 12, 15, 16, 20, 31, 45, 53, 81, 93–95,
    100, 102–3, 156, 228
    cardboard, 99, 100
    collection of, 228
    for stories-in-the-round, 198
    full-scale, 20, 45
    "quick-change," 178–79
    small, 169
    suggested titles, 85–87
    to stimulate interest, 84–87
    with lapboards, 203
Puppet construction. *See* Construction,
    puppet
Puppet corner, 228–29
Puppet-making projects, 7, 10, 103–4
    *see also* Construction, puppet
Puppet stages. *See* Stages, puppet
Puppet-story integration. *See* Integration,
    puppet-story
Puppet tree, 225–26

# Q

Questioning, 87, 102, 231
    suggested titles, 87–88

# R

Rabbit puppet, 75
*A Rainbow of My Own*, 140
Rainbow stick puppets, 140–41
Rapport, puppet-child, 77

Rapunzel, 53
*Raven: A Trickster Tale from the Pacific
    Northwest*, 25
Reading the story, 88
    suggested titles, 88–89
Realistic stories, 53
*Rechenka's Eggs*, 9
"Recipe for a Hippopotamus Sandwich," 207
Recreational centers, 9, 198
Red Hen bodi-puppet, 155
Religious themes, 9
Repertory, puppet, 54–59
Repetition, 10, 11, 47–48, 102, 128, 197
Rhymes, 26, 52, 69, 90
    *see also* Mother Goose rhymes; Nursery
      rhyme presentations
Robin Hood, 55
Robot puppet, 78
Rod puppets, 7, 25, 26–28, 53, 70, 95, 104,
    147, 157, 227
    construction, 27–28
Role reversal, 100–101
    suggested titles, 101–2
Roles, puppet, 75
    *see also* Host puppets; Lead puppets
Roscoe Wolf (host puppet), 79
*Rosie's Walk*, 146–49
"Row, Row, Row Your Boat," 118
"Rudolph the Red-Nosed Reindeer," 169,
    172–74
"Rumpelstiltskin," 7
*The Runaway Bunny*, 157–60
Running, 73

# S

Sadness, 73
*Sam Who Never Forgets*, 169
Santa Claus, 54, 99, 169
Scenery, 156, 170
    for book theaters, 157
    for cup and container theaters, 162–63
    for open-box theaters, 178–79
    for overhead shadow puppets, 186–87
    for panel theaters, 192
    for stories-in-the-round, 197–98
    for story kits, 231
    for string puppets, 45
    for table-top theaters, 216–17
    for time and distance, 25
    group members as, 20

Scenery *continued*
 on sticks and rods, 157
 "quick-change," 178–79
Science fiction, 11, 53
See-through views, 186–87, 193
Selection of format. *See* Presentation formats
Selection of puppets, 7–12, 14–15, 25–27, 28, 30–31, 32, 43–44, 45, 46–47, 48–50
Selection of story, 14–18
Sensory perception, 6
*Sesame Street*, 4
Set. *See* Scenery
Setting, 19
 *see also* Presentation formats; Space for storytelling
*Seven Chinese Brothers*, 178
*17 Kings and 42 Elephants*, 11
Shadow puppets. *See* Overhead shadow puppets
"Shadow Wash," 205–6
Shapes, puppet, 63–64
*Sheep Take a Hike*, 146
"She'll Be Coming Round the Mountain," 47
Shoe or boot totes, 227
Shopping-cart totes, 227
Sign language, 9
Simplification in puppetry, 14–16, 19, 156
Singing puppets, 8, 20, 26, 46–47, 98, 118
Sluefoot Sue, 45, 227
Snake puppets, 208, 211–12
Snoopy's doghouse, 210
"The Snopp on the Sidewalk," 91
*A Snowy Day*, 46, 119
Sock puppets, 53, 92, 208, 211–13
 tennis-sock, 105–6, 108–9
"Soldier, Soldier," 129–30
*Something from Nothing*, 204
Songs. *See* Folk songs; Singing puppets
Sound and action stories, 146–51
 examples, 147–51
 suggested titles, 151–53
Sound stories, 128–36
 examples, 131–36
 suggested titles, 137–39
 warm-up activities, 130–31
Sounds and sound effects, 92–93, 112, 128–36, 146–51, 188–89, 204
 types of, 129–30
Space for storytelling, 8–9, 19, 25–26, 156, 197–98

Speaking host puppets. *See* Host puppets
Speaking lead puppets. *See* Lead puppets
Speech impediments, 7
Squirrel puppets, 226
Stages, puppet, 228–29
 suppliers, 229
*Stand Back, Said the Elephant, I'm Going to Sneeze*, 54
Stand-up puppets, 20, 217, 218
Standing panel theater. *See* Panel theater
"The Starfish," 227
Stick puppets, 9, 12, 15, 20, 23, 25, 26–28, 49, 70, 131, 140, 141, 142, 147, 156, 157, 163, 179–82, 197
 construction, 27–28
 instant, 233
 paper, 158, 163, 179–82
 *see also* Rod puppets
*Stone Soup*, 85
*The Stonecutter*, 186, 188–90
Stories-in-the-round, 197–200
 examples, 198–200
 suggested titles, 200–2
*A Story, A Story*, 84
Story adaptation, 14–20
 suggested titles, 21
Story analysis chart, 17–18
Story aprons, 155–56, 203–8
 examples, 204–8
 suggested titles, 208–9
Story hour, 8, 77–90
 end of, 90
 preparing children for, 83
Story-hour host puppets. *See* Host puppets
Story kits, 231–32
Story totes. *See* Totes
Storytelling activities. *See* Story adaptation
Storytelling preparation, 3–12
 suggested titles, 12–13
*Strega Nona*, 49, 98
String and rod puppets, 12, 53
String puppets, 25, 26, 43–45, 49, 53, 71, 147–49, 197
 construction, 44–45
 *see also* Balloon string puppets; Egg-carton string puppets
Stuffed-toy puppets, 48–49
Style, puppet, 49–50
 suggested titles, 50–51
"Sunfish," 227
Supplies, 57–58

Surprise in puppetry, 5, 102, 113, 163, 204, 210
Swallowing puppets, 6, 105–8
 suggested titles, 109–10
*Swimmy*, 7, 14, 26, 46
*Sylvester and the Magic Pebble*, 231

**T**

Tabletop displays, 223
Tabletop puppets, 233
Tabletop theaters, 20, 216–21
 examples, 218–21
 frontal sets, 216–17
 perimeter sets, 217–18
 suggested titles, 221–22
Tails, animal puppets, 32
*The Tale of Peter Rabbit*, 28, 75
Talking-mouth movements, 68
Tall-tale puppet characters, 45, 53, 157, 227
Teamwork in storytelling, 11–12, 186
*Teddy Bears 1 to 10*, 52
*The Teeny Tiny Woman*, 25, 168–71
Television puppets, 4
Tennis-sock puppets. *See* Sock puppets
Thanksgiving, 79
Theater-in-the-round, 179
*There's a Nightmare in My Closet*, 163, 232
"This Is the Way," 118
Thread-spool puppets, 232–34
"The Three Bears," 50, 52, 54, 229
 *see also* "Goldilocks and the Three Bears"
"The Three Billy Goats Gruff," 14, 54, 87, 192, 229, 231
"The Three Little Pigs," 52, 54, 168, 229
*The Tiger-Skin Rug*, 211
"Tight Hat," 205–7
*Tiki Tiki Tembo*, 216
Time allotted to story, 9–10
Time and distance, 9–10, 25
"Toads and Diamonds," 99
Toby Tinker, 218
"Tom Thumb," 168
Tom Thumb character, 211
*The Tomten*, 223
Tongue depressors, 233
*Too Much Noise*, 147, 227
Tools and supplies, 57–58
*Tops and Bottoms*, 75, 100
"Tortoise and the Leopard," 186–87

*The Tortoise and the Tree*, 226
Tote displays, 227–28
Totes, 80, 81, 210–214, 227–28
    bag tree totes, 135–36
    barn tote bags, 132
    examples, 211–14
    suggested titles, 214–15
Toys, 179, 204, 208
    *see also* Stuffed-toy puppets
Travel sequences, 26, 178–79, 192–93, 197, 217
"The Travels of a Fox," 197, 198–99
Tree bag totes. *See* Totes
Troll puppet, 223
*Tuesday*, 234
Turnaround puppets. *See* Paper-plate puppets
2095, 11
*Two Good Friends*, 83
"Two Little Blackbirds," 163, 166
"Two of Everything," 187
Types, puppet, 25–49, 70–74
    suggested titles, 50–51
    *see also* specific types

**U**

*The Ugly Duckling*, 11

**V**

Valentine's Day, 80
Ventriloquism, 69
Versatility, 179
Verses. *See* Rhymes
Vertical standing panel theater. *See* Panel theaters
*The Very Hungry Caterpillar*, 14, 92
Visually impaired children, 9
Visuals, 15–16, 20
Vocalization, 7, 129
Voice, puppet, 5, 7–8, 64–65, 67, 79, 91, 97–98, 100–101
    development, 67–70, 83, 97–98

**W**

Walking, 73, 187, 197
Walking finger puppets. *See* Finger puppets
Wall hangings, 225–26
Warm-up activities, 117–19, 130–31
    action/response, 117–18
    interpretative activities, 118–19
"What if" questions, 87, 223, 231
    interest center, 231
Wheat growing and threshing, 19, 20

"Where Are You Going, My Pretty Maid?," 129–30
*Where the Sidewalk Ends*, 14, 205–6
*Where the Wild Things Are*, 231
Whispering, 80
"Why the Bear Is Stumpy-tailed," 98
*Why the Sun and Moon Live in the Sky*, 227
*The Wind and the Sun*, 48, 122
*Winnie the Pooh*, 6, 14, 15, 169
Winter wonderland puppet tree, 226
*Wish Again, Big Bear*, 210, 213–14
Witch/monster paper-plate bodi-puppet, 143–44
Witch puppets, 70, 78, 102, 142–44
*Wizard of Oz*, 14
*A Woggle of Witches*, 142–44
"The Wolf and the Seven Kids," 105
The Worst Person in the World, 54

**Y**

"The Yellow Ribbon," 5, 102
*You Look Ridiculous Said the Rhinoceros to the Hippopotamus*, 104
*Yours Till Niagara Falls, Abby*, 121–22

**C**ONNIE CHAMPLIN combines her experience in the elementary classroom and library with her graduate degrees in children's drama and library science to explore the creative uses of the arts in all curriculums. Her areas of creative emphasis are storytelling, creative dramatics, and educational puppetry. Currently Director of Media Technology for the Metropolitan School District of Pike Township, Indianapolis, Indiana, she has written several other books including *Puppetry and Creative Dramatics in Storytelling, Books in Bloom: Developing Creativity Through Children's Literature* and *Storytelling with the Computer.*

**N**ANCY RENFRO, co-author of the first edition, was a talented architect, artist, and puppeteer and a recognized authority on puppetry, creative dramatics, and the special child. Nancy had written more than a dozen books before her death in 1993, including *A Puppet Corner in Every Library, Puppetry in Early Childhood Education,* and *Puppet Shows Made Easy* as well as the *Pocketful of Puppets* series. The company she established, Nancy Renfro Studios, offers educational books along with an extensive line of original puppet characters and scripts.

Both authors have had extensive experience as storytellers and puppeteers, working in classrooms and libraries with children as well as conducting national and international workshops for teachers, child care workers, and librarians.